Bilingualism in the Commur

Code-switching and Grammars in Contact

Does the use of two languages by bilinguals inevitably bring about grammatical change? Does switching between languages serve as a catalyst in such change? It is widely held that linguistic code-switching inherently promotes grammatical convergence – languages becoming more similar to each other through contact; evidence for this, however, remains elusive. A model of how to study language contact scientifically, *Bilingualism in the Community* highlights variation patterns in speech, using a new bilingual corpus of English and Spanish spontaneously produced by the same speakers. Putting forward quantitative diagnostics of grammatical similarity, it shows how bilinguals' two languages differ from each other, aligning with their respective monolingual benchmarks. The authors argue that grammatical change through contact is far from a foregone conclusion in bilingual communities, where speakers are adept at keeping their languages together, yet separate.

RENA TORRES CACOULLOS is Professor of Spanish and Linguistics at the Pennsylvania State University and editor of *Language Variation and Change*.

CATHERINE E. TRAVIS is Professor of Modern European Languages at the Australian National University, and a Chief Investigator in the Centre of Excellence for the Dynamics of Language.

Bilingualism in the Community

Code-switching and Grammars in Contact

Rena Torres Cacoullos
Pennsylvania State University

Catherine E. Travis
Australian National University

CAMBRIDGE
UNIVERSITY PRESS

CAMBRIDGE
UNIVERSITY PRESS

University Printing House, Cambridge CB2 8BS, United Kingdom

One Liberty Plaza, 20th Floor, New York, NY 10006, USA

477 Williamstown Road, Port Melbourne, VIC 3207, Australia

314-321, 3rd Floor, Plot 3, Splendor Forum, Jasola District Centre, New Delhi - 110025, India

79 Anson Road, #06-04/06, Singapore 079906

Cambridge University Press is part of the University of Cambridge.

It furthers the University's mission by disseminating knowledge in the pursuit of education, learning and research at the highest international levels of excellence.

www.cambridge.org
Information on this title: www.cambridge.org/9781108402415
DOI: 10.1017/9781108235259

First published 2018
First paperback edition 2020

A catalogue record for this publication is available from the British Library

Library of Congress Cataloging in Publication data
Names: Torres Cacoullos, Rena, author. | Travis, Catherine E., author.
Title: Bilingualism in the community: code-switching and grammars in contact / Rena Torres Cacoullos, Pennsylvania State University; Catherine E. Travis, Australian National University.
Description: Cambridge ; New York : Cambridge University Press, 2018. | Includes bibliographical references.
Identifiers: LCCN 2017025021 | ISBN 9781108415828
Subjects: LCSH: Code switching (Linguistics) | Grammar, Comparative and general. | Bilingualism.
Classification: LCC P115.3 .T67 2017 | DDC 306.44/6–dc23
LC record available at https://lccn.loc.gov/2017025021

ISBN 978-1-108-41582-8 Hardback
ISBN 978-1-108-40241-5 Paperback

For Anna
RTC
For Natalie
CT

Contents

Figures

Tables

Acknowledgments

New Mexico, USA, the Land of Enchantment, is home to the bilinguals whose speech permeates this book. Constitution of the spontaneous speech corpus was generously supported by a joint grant to both authors from the National Science Foundation (BCS-1019112/1019122). Recordings for the New Mexico Spanish-English Bilingual (NMSEB) corpus were made by eager interviewers Daniel Abeyta, Rubel Aguilar, Raúl Aragón, Cheryl Conway, Jason Gonzales, Amanda Ortiz, Lillian Sánchez, and Kamie Ulibarrí. Jenny Dumont at the University of New Mexico and Colleen Balukas at the Pennsylvania State University were masterful project managers. Research assistants who took part in the massive effort of transcription, as well as data management, extraction, and coding, are Aubrey Healey, Leah Houle, Rebeca Martínez, Ana Medina Murillo, Andrés Sábogal, Lizeth Trevizo, and Víctor Valdivia Ruíz at UNM; Nicole Benevento, Grant Berry, Yolanda Gordillo, Miguel Ramos, Jonathan Steuck, and Everardo Tapia at Penn State; and Katrina Hayes, Cale Johnstone, and Matthew Callaghan at the Australian National University. Colleagues who have contributed to the project over the years in various capacities include Jessi Aaron, Sonia Balasch, Danielle Barth, Esther Brown, Evan Kidd, Chris Koops, Enrique Lamadrid, and Damian Vergara Wilson. We are grateful to Garland Bills and Neddy Vigil for providing access to the New Mexico-Colorado Spanish Survey (NMCOSS) materials and for their inspiring work on New Mexican Spanish. The College of the Liberal Arts and Center for Language Science (Penn State) and the ARC Centre of Excellence for the Dynamics of Language (ANU) provided invaluable support. The book has benefitted from the external reviews and astute comments by Shana Poplack, Dora LaCasse, and James Walker, who read the full manuscript. We especially thank our editor at Cambridge University Press, Andrew Winnard, for reminding us to keep you, the reader, in mind.

We dedicate this book to bilinguals in New Mexico and elsewhere, in the hope that it contributes to the appreciation of their incredible language skills, as they keep their languages together yet separate, *juntos pero no revueltos*.

1 Language Contact Through the Lens of Variation

Bilingualism has been thrust to the spotlight, with the massive migrations of our times and inexorable contact between speakers of different languages now reaching all corners of the world. This has not only social, but also linguistic consequences. We are all familiar with words that originally came from another language, some more recently than others. For example, for English speakers *latte* is probably more recognizable than *coffee* as a borrowing, or loanword (though neither is likely to be returned to the original language!). Bilingualism can also affect sound systems. With extensive contact, new phonemes may enter the language via loanwords, such as the English consonant /ʒ/ from words such as *rouge*, originally French 'red'.

But whether bilingualism brings about change in grammatical systems is poorly understood and controversial. Many believe that some kind of grammatical change in at least one of the languages is an inevitable outcome of bilingualism. It is also commonly assumed that the propensity for change is heightened when speakers engage in *code-switching* – going back and forth between languages, illustrated in (1). (In the examples, the original appears on the left; in the translation on the right, italics indicate speech produced in English and roman type corresponds to Spanish in the original.[1])

(1)
Miguel: ... *y en inglés,*   '... and in English,
  when I'm speaking,   *when I'm speaking,*
  ... *hay veces que quiero poner*   ... there are times when I want to put
    una .. Spanish word in there.   a .. *Spanish word in there.*'
               (04 Piedras y Gallinas, 1:11:19–1:11:24)

This book is about grammars in contact. Does bilinguals' use of two languages inevitably bring about grammatical change? Is code-switching a catalyst for such change? The scientific answers to these questions have

---

[1] Transcription protocols are presented in Appendix 1. Within parentheses following examples from the New Mexico Spanish-English Bilingual (NMSEB) corpus is the recording number and name, and the beginning-ending time stamps of the lines reproduced. Speaker names are pseudonyms.

social implications, especially in minority-language situations: Should schools conduct classes in only one of the languages spoken by bilingual children or promote use of both? Do blended labels such as *Spanglish* (or *Chinglish, Singlish, Portuñol, Türkendeutsch*) encapsulate changes in a language due to contact or do they disparage groups of bilingual speakers?

Contributors to the discussion on contact-induced change mainly agree that contact is most likely to affect words and sounds, and less likely to impact grammar. The balance sheet from the literature on structural borrowing has been that:

> Though most language contact situations lead to unidirectional, rather than bidirectional linguistic results, conditioned by the social circumstances, it is also the case that linguistic structure overwhelmingly conditions the linguistic outcomes. Morphology and syntax are clearly the domains of linguistic structure least susceptible to the influence of contact, and this statistical generalization is not vitiated by a few exceptional cases. (Sankoff 2002: 658)

Consensus that there are structural limitations on contact-induced change still leaves room for indirect routes to change, however. What is generally ruled out is direct importation of grammatical structures into one language from another language. Contact-induced change in bilingual or minority-language communities may nevertheless be attributed to "loss of semantic-pragmatic constraints" on the choice of one morphosyntactic alternative over another (Silva-Corvalán 1994: 135). An example is postverbal placement of the subject, as in *vino mi papá*, literally 'arrived my father', in Spanish presentative constructions. The decline of postverbal subjects among bilinguals in Los Angeles is consistent with the fairly rigid preverbal positioning of subjects in English, though it "does not constitute a radical change in the system of Spanish" (Silva-Corvalán 1994: 144). Contact-induced change may also come about via "grammatical replication," which again does not involve outright borrowing of structures but occurs when an existing form takes on a grammatical meaning on the model of another language (Heine and Kuteva 2005: 2). Replication occurs in "contact-induced grammaticalization," as with the development of articles from demonstratives (Heine and Kuteva 2011: 293). For example, in the Western Oceanic language Takia spoken on Karkar Island off the coast of Papua New Guinea, a postnominal determiner acting like a definite article has developed from a deictic morpheme in combination with a pronominal suffix, replicating the syntax of the genetically unrelated Papuan language, Waskia (Ross 2001: 142).

Perhaps the kind of change that has attracted the most attention takes the form of increased frequency of a pre-existing option. A famous case is the overextension of subject pronouns (and the corresponding shrinking of unexpressed subjects) in languages such as Spanish, Serbian, and Turkish, in contact with a language like English, in which subject pronouns predominate. This would be grammatical *convergence*, or magnified structural similarity (e.g., Aikhenvald 2002: 2; Bullock and Toribio 2004: 91; Myers-Scotton 2002: 19).

Contact linguistics is rich with competing accounts, frameworks, even terminologies. Any contact proposal, though, will first have to cope with the social requirement that a change must become a regular pattern in a speech community and the linguistic requirement that external influence must be disentangled from cross-linguistic tendencies. The questions to ask right away, then, are: Is there really change? And, is it really due to contact?

Convergence has often been hastily diagnosed on the basis of perceived departures from an idealized monolingual norm. Yet bilingual speech, just like monolingual speech, is characterized by internal variation, which is not coterminous with change. All change implies the existence of variability; however, the converse is not true: "not all variability and heterogeneity in language structure involves change" (Weinreich, Labov, and Herzog 1968: 188). In fact, variation can be stable for quite a long time. Proscribed double negation in English, for example, is not a change. Grammarians began to censure sentences such as *I can not eat none* in the seventeenth century, with increasing ardor in the eighteenth century, itself a corroboration of its persisting use in informal speech (Labov 2001: 85–92; Tieken-Boon van Ostade 1982).

An example of a widely assumed contact-induced change that turns out not to be so is preposition stranding in Québec French, as in *J'avais pas personne à parler avec* 'I had no one to talk with' (Poplack, Zentz, and Dion 2012a). Such phrase-final preposition placement in relative clauses seems similar to English and is proscribed in Standard French (which requires the complement to follow the preposition, as in *avec qui je parle* 'with whom I talk'). Large-scale study of preposition placement patterns in the speech community shows, first of all, that despite the censure it evokes, stranding accounts for approximately just one-tenth of the data. The major statistically significant contributor to choice of stranding over the competing alternatives is the identity of the preposition itself, with "weak" prepositions (*de* 'of', *en* 'in') virtually never stranded. Such a constraint does not apply to the stranded prepositions omnipresent in the putative model, English. It does apply, though, to a pre-existing French construction with bare prepositions, illustrated in *elle le pogne puis elle s'en va dans la forêt avec* 'she grabs it and she goes into the forest with'. Since the probabilistic constraints are parallel to French and distinct from English patterns, the mechanism that gives rise to preposition stranding is analogy, an instance of internally motivated, rather than contact-induced, change.

This case cautions us that contact-induced change cannot be declared on the basis of casual observation of apparently similar forms and/or functions; rather, it must be demonstrated, on the basis of data that contextualize the phenomenon of interest socially and linguistically – with respect to the community of speakers and the grammatical system(s) in which it is embedded.

1.1   Benchmarks and Comparisons

Integral to asserting contact-induced change are comparisons of bilingual varieties with benchmarks. The reference points and lines of comparison are represented in Figure 1.1, at the heart of which are the varieties of each language spoken in the bilingual community (depicted in the center oval of the figure).

The most thorough tests of grammatical change will begin with a pre-contact variety, or an earlier stage of the same variety, to ascertain whether change has occurred (top rectangle). Whether any such change is due to contact is ascertained by comparisons with non-contact varieties of *both* of the languages (left rectangle). The comparisons of bilingual varieties with monolingual benchmarks are premised on comparison *between* the benchmarks. The reason to compare the languages making up the contact pair with each other is to identify

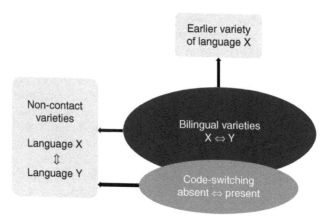

- *Tracking change* – bilinguals' variety of X with earlier variety of X
- *Determining direction of change* – bilinguals' variety of X with non-contact varieties of X and Y
- *Probing convergence* – bilinguals' variety of X with their variety of Y, also compared with non-contact variety of Y
- *Real-time effect of code-switching* – use of X in proximate presence of Y vs. absence of Y

Figure 1.1 Comparisons to evaluate contact-induced change and role of code-switching

diagnostic differences, or "conflict sites," loci of structural divergence at which a determination of the direction of change can be made (Poplack and Meechan 1998: 132).

Cross-language differences may be qualitative, where the difference between languages is the presence vs. absence of a feature, such as between English and Tamil in case inflections (Sankoff, Poplack, and Vanniarajan 1990). For structures that are variable in discourse, the challenge is to develop quantitative measures. An example is the quantitative preference for the definite article in Spanish with nouns designating institutions (*entramos a la escuela* 'we started (the) school') or nouns with generic reference (*la gente no quiere pagar por tu tiempo* '(the) people don't want to pay for your time') in contrast to the preference for bare nouns in English. A comparison pivoted on such diagnostic differences specific to the language pair allows us to rule out cross-linguistic tendencies. Following a widely documented grammaticalization path, the definite article evolved from a demonstrative in both languages, and in both it tends to accompany nouns with identifiable referents, but it has generalized to more contexts in Spanish than in English (Torres Cacoullos and Aaron 2003).

The hypothesis of contact-induced change will be substantiated if the bilingual variety is dissimilar to its non-contact counterpart – that is, its own monolingual benchmark – *and* similar to the monolingual benchmark of the other language making up the contact pair. If, contrariwise, the bilingual variety is similar to its non-contact counterpart and dissimilar to the non-contact variety of the other language, we have evidence for linguistic continuity. Returning to our example of definite articles in Spanish and English, we would look to the fine detail of the differences between Spanish and English to see whether patterns of determiner use in bilinguals' Spanish are similar to non-contact Spanish or whether they are similar to English.

A further comparison, this one between the varieties of each language spoken by the same bilinguals (depicted in the center oval), will provide the most direct and strongest kind of evidence for or against structural convergence. If, from comparisons with monolingual benchmarks, we can eliminate convergence of the contact variety of a minority language toward a majority or official language, there could still be the possibility of contact-induced change. This would be the influence of the minority on the majority language as used by the bilingual speakers, reflecting some kind of "imperfect learning" or "shift-induced interference" (Thomason 2009). For this reason, both contact varieties are compared with their non-contact counterparts. Comparison of the bilingual varieties *with each other* is the most revealing of grammars in contact: Do bilinguals – the instantiation of contact – ultimately mix their two grammars, or do they keep them separate?

If there is evidence of a change and, in addition, evidence that it is contact-induced, whether code-switching promotes that change must be independently verified. Code-switching has been prominently implicated as a mechanism of contact-induced change at least since Gumperz and Wilson's (1971) article showcasing converging language structures in a multilingual village in Maharashtra (India). This has given rise to the more general convergence via code-switching hypothesis: that structural similarity is most enhanced when speakers use one language in proximity to the other. The notion that code-switching encourages a bilingual preference for structures that are shared by the languages is certainly plausible. Also widely entertained is the proposal that the "activation" of both languages during code-switching promotes similarity. Yet, the mechanism by which code-switching would give rise to convergence has not been precisely articulated. An effect that deserves more consideration is *priming*, which is the tendency to repeat the same structure. Example (2) provides an illustration, where, in switching from English to Spanish, the speaker uses a parallel structure of a preverbal subject pronoun across adjacent clauses (*I* in English and *yo* in Spanish, instead of an unexpressed subject).

(2)
Miguel: ...(1.5) <u>I was</u> like nineteen.   '...(1.5) <u>I was</u> like nineteen.
                 ... years old.   ... years old.
                 .. pero <u>yo</u> me acordaba.   .. but <u>I</u> remembered.'
                                        (04 Piedras y Gallinas, 20:08–20:13)

A final set of comparisons will establish whether code-switching heightens the interaction between bilingual speakers' grammars: comparison of linguistic patterns in the context of presence and absence of code-switching by the same speaker in the same conversation (in the bottom oval), as well as comparisons in each context with the monolingual benchmarks (left rectangle). Fulfilling the gamut of comparisons will tell us *whether and how* contact-induced change is occurring.

1.2   Grammatical (dis)Similarity

How do we measure grammatical similarity or difference, and thereby track changes to grammars in contact? Sophisticated models of bilingual grammars have been elaborated, proposing underlying structures or processes in accordance with syntactic or psycholinguistic theories. Convincing reports of language change must nevertheless include a quantitative component, because change in progress is by nature quantitative, as alternative forms increase, or decrease, in frequency, or a new form is introduced and expands in use. Even among contact studies with sufficient data, commonly interpreted as contact-induced change is a difference in overall rate of use, such that the frequency of

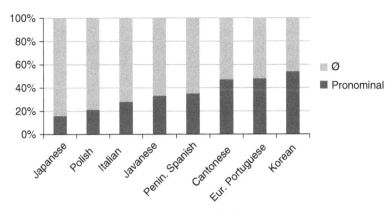

Figure 1.2 Rates of 1sg pronominal subject expression across different languages

a variant form with a counterpart in the contact language rises at the expense of the variant without such a counterpart. A difference in overall rates alone, however, is a spurious test of grammatical (dis)similarity.

Consider the typology of languages according to the expression of pronominal subjects. A major class is "null-subject" languages (Roberts and Holmberg 2010), in which the "normal expression" of subjects is by an affix on the verb (Dryer 2013). Such a label and description suggest low rates of subject pronouns. The a priori problem is determining what qualifies as a "low" rate. The empirical problem is that rates of subject pronouns in null-subject languages vary. Figure 1.2 lists eight languages by increasing rate of subject pronouns vs. unexpressed subjects (Ø), shorthand for the absence of any subject noun phrase. Polish and European Portuguese, both considered null-subject languages, are closer to Japanese and Korean, respectively, than to each other. And Japanese and Korean, classed as "discourse pro-drop" languages (Roberts and Holmberg 2010) with "optional pronouns in subject position" (Dryer 2013), are at opposite ends of the spectrum.[2] The divergence in rates of subject expression between languages supposedly of the same type gives reason to question the validity of the typology. Overall rates of use are not a dependable diagnostic measure of language type, however.

---

[2] The comparison is restricted to first-person singular, to control for grammatical person differences. Japanese 16 percent (Lee and Yonezawa 2008: 738, N=1,571), Polish 21 percent (Chociej 2011: 52, N=536), Italian 28 percent (Nagy p.c.; cf. Nagy, Aghdasi, Denis, and Motut 2011, N=224), Javanese 33 percent (Ewing 2014: 51, N=289), Peninsular Spanish 35 percent (Posio 2013: 269, N=787), Cantonese 47 percent (Nagy p.c.; cf. Nagy et al. 2011, N=362), European Portuguese 48 percent (Posio 2013: 269, N=704), Korean 54 percent (Oh 2007: 466, N=433).

Inferences of change have been based on differences of five to ten percentage points, invoking statistical significance (usually, $p < 0.05$). But overall rate differences, even if statistically significant, are an equivocal gauge of linguistic difference. The American Statistical Association (ASA) insists that:

Statistical significance is not equivalent to scientific, human, or economic significance. ... Any effect, no matter how tiny, can produce a small p-value if the sample size or measurement precision is high enough. (ASA Statement on Statistical Significance and P-values, Wasserstein and Lazar 2016)

Besides the general susceptibility of statistical significance to sample size, it is also the case for speech data that overall rates fluctuate due to factors extraneous to the grammar, including data collection procedures bearing on interviewer, topic, or genre (Bailey and Tillery 2004; Hernández 2009). Given the notable fluctuation according to extra-grammatical factors, it is far from obvious how much of a rate difference would be linguistically significant. Moreover, within the very same corpus, when comparing individual speakers or groups of speakers, aggregate rate differences may arise because of the fortuitous preponderance or dearth of some very propitious context (Poplack 1997). And the more sensitive the distribution of variant forms is to features of the discourse context, as we will see is the case with subject pronoun realization, the less revealing it is to "simply count ... the total number of overt subjects or preverbal subjects produced" (Sorace 2004: 144). Above all, aggregate rate differences cannot speak to the *direction* of change. Indeed, the outcome of contact-induced change is ambiguous as concerns overall rates. Higher pronoun rates would fit a scenario of overextension, but lower rates would be in line with loss of pragmatic functions of subject pronouns.

To confront this problem, the variationist comparative method incorporates systematic variation into the traditional comparative method of historical linguistics, by examining co-occurrence patterns. The idea is that integral to grammatical principles and language users' knowledge is the covariation between elements of language that is probabilistic (Cedergren and Sankoff 1974; Labov 1969; Poplack and Meechan 1998). The structure of variation – the way linguistic forms are *used* – becomes the tool for measuring grammatical similarity or difference. This structure lies in the configuration of probabilistic constraints on speakers' choices among variants. The *linguistic conditioning* is seen in the direction and magnitude of effect of language-internal factors favoring the occurrence of one variant over another.

The linguistic conditioning holds across extralinguistic circumstances of genre, style, or topic, where overall rates can be fickle. Just as divergence in overall rates may mask grammatical similarity, close rates may misrepresent dissimilarity. This is the case with the superficially similar bare nouns in English and Spanish, which occur at approximately the same rate (30 percent of all noun tokens). The difference between the languages is exposed in the disparity of the linguistic conditioning of bare nouns, located in the factors of the syntactic role and semantic class of the noun and the specificity of its referent in the discourse context. For example, while predicate nominals tend to have no determiner in Spanish, they tend to have an indefinite determiner in English (Torres Cacoullos and Aaron 2003). As the linguistic conditioning serves to gauge grammatical (dis)similarity, the existence and nature of *change* is evinced in alteration in the conditioning of variation.

1.3   This Book

This book responds to the proliferation of claims of contact-induced change in the growing number of articles, books, and conferences on bilingualism, despite which scholarly consensus remains elusive. Discord in contact linguistics has been exacerbated by the problems of meager data and disparate standards of proof. Unresolved debates have been fueled by reliance on poor data, such as elicited judgments, which may display random error, or amalgams of assorted individuals, which are uninformative of systematic community patterns. We would like here to contribute to cumulative progress in the field by offering bilingual speech data, evaluation metrics, and analyses that can serve as the basis for cross-fertilization.

Languages are in contact through the people who speak them. At the heart of the research we report is "variation as it exists in unedited performance, minimally influenced by the observer-linguist" (Cedergren and Sankoff 1974: 354). We capitalize on contact between Spanish and English in a long-standing community in New Mexico, in the southwest of the United States. The linguistic variable of interest is subject pronoun expression, a viable candidate for convergence because subject pronouns are obviously similar but variably expressed in Spanish (as a null-subject language) and overwhelmingly expressed in English. Since Silva-Corvalán's pioneering *Language contact and change: Spanish in Los Angeles* (1994), the variable use of Spanish subject pronouns in the USA has become a poster child for contact-induced change. The overwhelming preference for subject pronouns in English is widely predicted to boost the rate of pronouns in contact-Spanish varieties, an idea put forward as early as Granda (1972) and as recently as Otheguy and Zentella (2012). The implications of this abundant research for long-term change in the grammar are still unclear, however, because of a focus on immigrant groups, data from speakers whose bilingualism and linguistic experiences are unknown, or study participants who are poorly balanced for testing other-language influence.

Here, we showcase accountable quantitative analysis of more than 10,000 instances of first- and third-person singular subjects: nearly 6,000 from

Table 1.1 *Data: Bilingual corpus and benchmark corpora*

	Bilingual Corpus	Benchmark Corpora		
	NMSEB New Mexico Spanish-English Bilingual corpus	NMCOSS New Mexico-Colorado Spanish Survey	CCCS Corpus of Conversational Colombian Spanish	SBCSAE Santa Barbara Corpus of Spoken American English
Variety	Spanish–English bilingual; northern NM	Spanish-dominant; northern NM	Monolingual Spanish; Cali, Colombia	Monolingual English; USA (various)
Speakers	40	11	37	207
Socially Stratified	Yes	Yes	No	No
Recordings	31	11	30	60
Hours Transcribed	29	5	9	23
Words	300,000	45,000	96,000	249,000
Intonation Units	98,000	15,000	33,000	70,000
Tokens*	5,571 (Spanish) 294 (English)	1,694	2,802	987
Genre	Sociolinguistic interviews, with in-group members	Interviews interspersed between linguistic elicitation	Face-to-face conversation between close family and friends	Varied, primarily face-to-face conversation between friends
Year Recorded	2010–2011	1992–1995	1997, 2004	1988–1996
Reference		(cf. Bills and Vigil 2008: 21–27)**	(cf. Travis 2005: 9–25)	(Du Bois, Chafe, Myer, Thompson, Englebretson, and Martey 2000–2005)

* Number of tokens of 1sg and 3sg Ø and pronominal subjects within the variable context for subject expression; on the protocol for sampling of English pronouns, see Chapter 6, Section 6.5.1.

** The entire NMCOSS corpus consists of interviews with 357 participants; here, we use a sample of older, Spanish-dominant participants. See Chapter 7, Section 7.4.

a community-based bilingual speech corpus and over 5,000 from three corpora serving as baselines for an earlier variety, monolingual Spanish and monolingual English. These comparable corpora of spontaneous speech, transcribed prosodically in the same way, are depicted in Table 1.1. The unprecedented NMSEB corpus records juxtaposed stretches of both languages produced by the same speakers. This allows us to offer, for the first time, comparison of the bilingual varieties with each other – the null-subject and non-null-subject language as spoken by the very same language users. By considering both bilingual varieties together with monolingual benchmarks of both languages, we can truly address this question: Are grammars in contact different from grammars not in contact?

The research questions are built into compiling the corpus from the outset. In Chapter 2, we discuss apposite language contact settings and characterize this study's speaker sample. Representation of a range of demographic backgrounds allows testing of social indices of language change. For testing the widely invoked role of *contact* in change, the speaker sample is ideal: bilinguals who regularly use both languages together. The topic of Chapter 3 is bilingual corpus constitution, guided by a focus on unelicited code-switching in spontaneous speech and thorough transcription. Such a corpus allows elaboration of internal measures of degree of contact based on the production data, which provide an initial test of contact-induced change, discussed in Chapter 4. Here, we devise community-appropriate measures of degree of contact, eschewing dichotomies in second language acquisition research such as first vs. second language (L1 vs. L2). These chapters contextualize the linguistic analyses that follow.

Chapter 5 characterizes the grammar of subject pronoun expression in Spanish, challenging cherished beliefs about the function of subject pronouns and reconsidering the constraints in cross-linguistic perspective. Lacking from the literature on null-subject languages in contact with English has been consideration of the conditioning of the variability that does exist in English. This is tackled in Chapter 6, which reveals commonalities across languages in cognitive and discourse factors, evidenced in similarities in the probabilistic constraints. These indicate candidate cross-linguistic tendencies in subject pronoun expression that cut across traditional classifications of language types. At the same time, quantitative analysis locates diagnostic differences in the language-specific variable contexts, strength of effects, and lexically particular constructions.

With the knowledge of how speakers treat subject expression in each of the languages in contact, in Chapter 7 bilingual behavior is compared with earlier-stage and monolingual Spanish benchmarks and, in Chapter 8, across both language varieties spoken in the bilingual community and with English, delivering the promised comparisons. Chapter 9 provides the first direct test of the role of code-switching in language change, and Chapter 10 weighs cross-language structural priming as a window into the associations between bilinguals' grammars. By the linguistic conditioning of variation, code-switching leaves no mark on the contact varieties. Rather, its impact is to be found in the distribution of contextual features relevant to variation.

Does code-switching and language contact lead to grammatical changes? Systematic quantitative analysis of bilingual speech situated in its social context holds the answers.

2   The Community Basis of Bilingual Phenomena

Contact-induced change has been asserted or disputed based on data deriving from often disparate sources, from introspection and elicitation in laboratory settings to systematic recordings of regular interactions in the speech community. And though all kinds of data have their place in bilingualism research (e.g., Gullberg, Indefrey and Muysken 2009), the ultimate yardstick must be the sociolinguistically constructed corpus: spontaneous speech from a principled sample of members of a well-defined bilingual speech community (Poplack 1989, 1993). The New Mexico Spanish-English Bilingual (NMSEB) corpus is such a resource, and is unparalleled in both the amount of code-switching and the even amounts of both of the bilinguals' languages it records. The compilation of NMSEB is the topic of the following chapter; here we situate the speakers in the contact setting.

Linguistic patterns are community specific, and this is no less so for bilingual phenomena. Poplack's (1998) comparison of Spanish/English Puerto Ricans in New York and French/English Canadians in Ottawa-Hull revealed differences in how these bilingual groups combine their two languages, despite typological similarity between the language pairs. While the former alternate between Spanish and English seamlessly as a discourse mode, the latter switch from French to English to fulfill certain rhetorical functions, such as deploying the appropriate lexical item or making metalinguistic commentary.

Bilingual speech practices may differ across communities even within the same language pair. Consider, for example, the light verb or bilingual compound verb strategy (Muysken 2016). An English-origin verb can be integrated into Spanish using [*hacer* 'do' + Verb$_{Eng}$], as in *y todos hacen meet* 'and they all meet' (18, 1:06:02) and *lo hicieron hire pa' eso* 'they hired him for that' (04, 53:28).[1] This device is absent from reports on Puerto Rican bilinguals, but is used productively by New Mexicans (Wilson and Dumont 2015). The first step in obtaining good data, then, is to delimit a speech community,

---

[1] In-text examples are referenced with the NMSEB transcript number and the time stamp of the start of the speech given.

which has "well-defined limits, a common structural base, and a unified set of sociolinguistic norms" (Labov 2007: 347).

First we delineate the contact setting (Section 2.1) and the contact variety of the minority language (2.2). New Mexico is an ideal site to probe contact-induced change because of the length and intensity of Spanish–English contact (2.3). The speaker sample is distributed across a range of demographics (2.4), allowing us to draw on social factors in assessing change (2.5).

2.1   The Contact Site: Spanish and English in New Mexico

Studies of immigrant communities in the United States and Western Europe prominently report changes in the immigrant language, occurring as abruptly as within a single generation. For example, in Los Angeles (Silva-Corvalán 1994) and New York (Otheguy and Zentella 2012), differences are observed between the Spanish spoken by first-generation immigrants and their children or grand-children. But to the extent that the second or third generation is shifting to the majority language, the "changes" would be transitory if the language itself fails to be transmitted. A *lack* of intergenerational differences may also be incon-clusive if the contact situation is construed as being "too young" to have induced changes – for example, with Turkish in the Netherlands (Doğruöz and Backus 2007: 218). Recent immigrant settings, then, may not be instructive as to convergence.

An apposite site for testing contact-induced grammatical change is a long-term, bilingual community. Such a community is found in northern New Mexico, where English has been spoken for over 150 years and Spanish for over 400, rendering it the oldest Spanish-speaking area in what is now the United States. Given that length of contact is considered a predictor of convergence (e.g., Thomason 2001: 66), this contact situation allows for a particularly compelling assessment of its outcomes.

After explorations, expeditions, and colonization endeavors in the 1500s, Santa Fe was established as Spanish provincial headquarters of what today is northern New Mexico in 1610. Permanent settlement by Spanish speakers dates to the 1693 reconquest of Santa Fe following the Pueblo Revolt. At 1,500 miles (2,400 km) from Mexico City, northern New Mexico was one of the most isolated areas of the Spanish-speaking world, first as a remote colony of New Spain, then on the periphery of newly independent Mexico in the early nineteenth century, and subsequently as part of the United States with the 1848 Treaty of Guadalupe Hidalgo (Bills and Vigil 1999a: 43).

Today, New Mexico (NM) has a higher proportion of Hispanics than any other US state: 48 percent – close to one million people – compared with the national average of 17 percent (United States Census Bureau 2014). NM also has the highest proportion of Hispanic-owned businesses in the US (24 percent

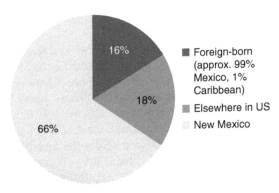

Figure 2.1 Place of birth of Hispanics in New Mexico
(United States Census Bureau 2014)

in the 2010 census), Hispanics are appointed at all levels of government, and a Hispanic cultural presence is readily felt – anyone in NM knows that the question *red or green?* at a restaurant refers to *chile*.

Unlike the rest of the US, the Hispanic population in NM is overwhelmingly native to the region. As depicted in Figure 2.1, first-generation immigrants across the state, mostly Mexican-born, account for just 16 percent of New Mexican Hispanics, while nearly two-thirds were born in New Mexico. In northern New Mexico, this is even more pronounced – in the counties of Mora, Rio Arriba, San Miguel, and Taos, between 92 percent and 96 percent of Hispanics are US-born. Most of the immigration from Mexico has been to the south of the state and to Albuquerque, the largest city (e.g., García-Acevedo 2000: 226–229; Gonzales-Berry and Maciel 2000: 3–4). These demographics make northern NM all the more valuable for testing contact-induced change since, unlike the immigrant settings that have been the site of many studies, contact with monolingual speakers of the minority language is limited at best.

2.2 The Contact Variety

Northern New Mexico remains today the heart of the variety spoken by the descendants of the original Spanish-speaking settlers, what we will call here *New Mexican Spanish*, also referred to as Traditional Spanish (cf. Bills and Vigil 2008: 7; Lope Blanch 1987: 202). The difference vis-à-vis immigrant varieties has been demonstrated for the lexicon in the monumental linguistic atlas compiled by Garland Bills and Neddy Vigil (2008) from the New Mexico-Colorado Spanish Survey (NMCOSS). The geographical distribution of the words for 'apricot' and 'dress' serve to illustrate. Traditional New Mexican terms *albarcoque* or *albercoque* and *túnico* dominate in the north of the state, while participants in the south give forms that reflect contact with Mexico, *chabacan* and *vestido* (Bills and Vigil 2008: 57, 63).

New Mexican Spanish is commonly held to exhibit archaic features, and is sometimes (erroneously) described as "the Spanish of 16th Century Spain" (cf. Bills and Vigil 2008: 14–17). Examples listed in the pioneering studies of New Mexican linguist Aurelio M. Espinosa are irregular Preterit forms for 'see' (*vide* 'I saw' vs. *vi*) and 'bring' (with the root *truj*-, e.g., *trujo* 'he brought', vs. *traj*-, e.g., *trajo*) (Espinosa 1911: 9). Such forms were robust in literary texts until the seventeenth century, but are retained across the Spanish-speaking world today only in "non-standard, chiefly rural, use" (Penny 2000: 220). Some of these retentions are heard in New Mexican Spanish, and appear in the NMSEB corpus (cf. Bills and Vigil 2008: 68–69). For example, the Preterit forms of these two verbs occur in the recordings both in the archaic variant, *vide* or *truj*- (N = 34) and the standard variant, *vi* or *traj*- (N = 23). Nine NMSEB speakers make use of the archaic form and not the standard form, seven use the standard form only, and a further five make use of both forms. In (3), a young New Mexican reports being ridiculed by her (Spanish-speaking, non-New Mexican) coworkers for use of archaic *truje*. (Note that this meta-linguistic use is not included in the counts above.)

(3)
Clara: *I always used to say=,*
　　　.. yo= truje algo=,
　　　a la fiesta, ('I brought something to the party')
　　　or whatever.
((14 intervening lines))
　　　and they're like,
　　　no no,
　　　it's .. trajiste or=, ('you brought')
　　　traje or, ('I brought')
　　　whatever.
　　　I was like,
　　　... well okay,
　　　whatever.
　　　.. and they'd make fun of me,

(22 Farolitos, 42:02–42:20)[2]

New Mexican Spanish, though, "*really is* Mexican Spanish" (Bills and Vigil 2008: 192), as part of the same macro- (Lozano 1977) or super-dialect (Cárdenas 1975). As Bills and Vigil (1999a: 43) remind us, many settlers of "La Nueva

---

[2] See Appendix 1 for the transcription conventions. In this and following examples, each line is a distinct Intonation Unit (Chapter 3, Section 3.4); dots represent pauses, and the equal sign lengthening. Omitted IUs not relevant to the point being made are indicated by the number of lines omitted in parentheses.

México" had been born in the New World and brought with them a language already evolving from Peninsular Spanish varieties. In terms of morphosyntax, New Mexican Spanish follows Mexican rather than Castillian norms in using, for example, the Preterit (*canté* 'I sang') and not the Present Perfect (*he cantado* 'I have sung') as the default past perfective; *lo* not *le* ('him') for the direct object pronoun for human masculine referents; and *qué tanto* instead of *cuánto* 'how much/many' as in *qué tantos años llevamos de casados* 'how many years have we been married' (28, 48:05) (Bills and Vigil 2008: 15). As for the sound system, the voiceless interdental fricative heard in Spain is absent (such that orthographic 'z', 'c', and 's' are pronounced the same way, as in Latin American varieties), and there are commonalities in pronunciation and intonation with northern Mexican varieties (e.g., Brown 2005a; Brown 2005b; Brown and Torres Cacoullos 2002). Comparison of linguistic atlas data from New Mexico and Mexico confirms shared lexical variants such as *cuates* 'twins', *borrega* 'ewe', and *chuparrosa* 'hummingbird' rather than *gemelos, oveja*, and *colibrí*, the terms listed in the Spanish Royal Academy dictionary (Bills and Vigil 2008: 192–193). New Mexican Spanish speakers are aware of these similarities; a NMSEB participant tells of being taken for a Mexican during travels in Bogotá, Colombia (4), and another notes a general linguistic similarity when he visited northern Mexico as a hunting guide (5).

(4)

Pedro: ...*(0.8) y entré en,*   '...(0.8) I went to,
     en un centro de,   to a center,
     ...*(1.4) un centro de uh,*   ...(1.4) a center uh,
     .. *turismo.*   .. tourist center.
     ...*(0.8) dijeron,*   ...(0.8) they said,
     oye mexicano,   listen Mexican,
     si no sales hoy,   if you don't leave today,
     ...*(0.9) no vas a salir hasta después de* ...(0.9) you're not going to leave until
       las navidades.   after Christmas.
     You know it will be booked solid.   *You know it will be booked solid.*'

               (10 El Timbre Portátil, 38:30–38:55)

(5)

Manuel: *I met a lot of different,*
     .. *people over there.*
     ... *Mexicans that uh,*
     ... *they --*
     .. *they talk uh,*
     .. *pretty much like we do here.*

              (16 Trip to Africa Pt1, 36:02–36:09)

While generally a Mexican variety, New Mexican Spanish has some "independently developed" words and phonetic features (Bills and Vigil

2008: 15). Bills and Vigil document lexical innovations such as *muchitos* and *plebe* 'children', *arrear* 'drive a car', and *ratón volador* 'bat', literally, 'flying mouse' (2008: 123–151). Phonetic features include variable aspiration of syllable-initial /s/ (e.g., *la señora* vs. *la* [h]*eñora* 'the woman'), deletion of intervocalic [j] corresponding to <ll> (e.g., *ella* vs. *eØa* 'she') and addition (paragoge) of /e/ phrase finally following an alveolar consonant (/r, l, n, s/) in a stressed syllable (e.g., *trabajar*[e] 'to work') (Bills and Vigil 2008: 148–151; Brown 2005a, 2005b; Espinosa 1911; Lipski 2008: 204–208; Torres Cacoullos and Berry 2018). One homegrown morphological feature may be the first-person present perfect form *ha* 'I have' vs. standard *he*, for example, *yo no me ha subido en una de esas* 'I haven't gotten on one of those' (31, 51:07) (Bills and Vigil 1999b: 53–54; 2008: 145–151). Of the first-person present perfect occurrences in NMSEB (N = 62), *ha* is used about one-half of the time, and by half the participants, most of whom use one or the other variant, rather than varying between them.

2.3   Intense Contact: Stigmatization and Endangerment

What makes New Mexican Spanish ideal for assessing linguistic repercussions of contact is its long-standing coexistence with English. Spanish and English have been the main competing languages in New Mexico for over 150 years. In 1850, some 250 years after settlement by Spanish speakers, New Mexico was pronounced a Territory of the United States, and in 1878 the railroad arrived. The proportion of Anglo-Americans grew from under 10 percent in 1880 to about 50 percent by the 1940s (Bills and Vigil 1999b: 48–49, and references therein). In 1890, the US Census recorded that 70 percent of the New Mexican population could not speak English, a figure that dropped to 51 percent in 1900 and to 33 percent in 1910 (Fernández-Gibert 2010: 48).

Following statehood in 1912, English increasingly supplanted Spanish in the school system, and even in northern rural communities by the mid-1940s (Gonzales 1999: 20; Lipski 2008: 203). Early on, Espinosa (1911: 1–2) called for Spanish to be taught in the public schools, "for the benefit of the Spanish speaking children of these regions, who have no opportunity to learn to read their native tongue. To learn English no one has to forget Spanish or any other language." But policy makers heeded linguists as little then as they do now.

Through the first half of the twentieth century, public schools were an instrument for the imposition of English through suppression of Spanish (Gonzales-Berry 2000). Of the nine NMSEB participants who had the occasion to talk about their experiences at school in the recording, none had anything good to say. For example, Sandra (born 1943) was brought to tears on her first day of primary school because her teacher told her she lacked English, as recounted in example (6). In (7), Anita (b. 1941) talks of punishment for speaking Spanish and of being denied the bilingual "back and forth" between languages she had enjoyed at home and in the community. In (8), Trinidad (b. 1938) recalls students being given demerits if they spoke Spanish, which, when added up, resulted in suspension. In the most benign scenario, teachers ignored Spanish-speaking children, remembers Rocío (b. 1945) in (9).

(6)

Sandra:	*cuando salimos del clase,*	'when we got out of class,
	que ya nos íbanos para la casa,	and we were going to go home,
	nomás lo vi,	as soon as I saw him,
	y me solté llorando.	I burst into tears.
	... qué te pasa,	... what's wrong,
	dijo,	he said,
	que te pegó la maestra?	did the teacher hit you?
	no,	no,
	le dije,	I told him,
	... pero me dijo la maestra,	... but the teacher told me,
	que yo no podía venir a la escuela,	that I couldn't come to school,
	porque yo no sé hablar inglés.	because I don't know how to speak English.'

(03 Dos Comadres, 57:41–57:53)

(7)

Anita: *... even if I had to use the bathroom I couldn't ask in Spanish.*
... a=nd,
if you did,
you got punished.
((7 intervening lines))
going back and forth,
... was not there anymore.
.. and so you really had to discipline yourself.
I cried a lot.

(14 Proper Spanish, 02:35–03:01)

(8)

Trinidad:	*te daban lo que le decían*	'they gave you what they called
	demerits,	demerits,
	si hablabas en español.	if you spoke in Spanish.
	Durante las horas de la escuela.	During school hours.
	... te comenzaban .. con cien= merits,	... they started you .. with a hundred merits,
	... y si hacías cosas buenas= te daban merits,	... and if you did good things they gave you merits,
	... si te bajabas hasta setenta=,	... if you got down to seventy,
	... merits,	... merits,
	... salías de la escuela,	... you left school,
	y- .. you were suspended.	*y- .. you were suspended.*'

(21 Demerits, 05:21–05:39)

(9)

Rocío:	... *me acuerdo que cuando comencé la escuela,*	'... I remember that when I started school,
	.. *siempre .. yo,*	.. all the time .. I,
	.. *y= um,*	.. and um,
	...*(1.9) como,*	...(1.9) like,
	cuatro otros niños hablábanos puro español.	four other kids spoke only Spanish.
	... *y los sentaban detrás de la class,*	... and they would sit us in the back of the class,
	porque --	because --
	... *porque la maestra no se quería estar.. molestada con nosotros.*	... because the teacher didn't want to be .. bothered by us.'

(05 Las Tortillas, 50:26–50:44)

Even as these repressive practices were phased out, and Spanish came to be taught in public schools, it has been taught primarily as a foreign or second language and to the detriment of the local variety (cf. Gonzales-Berry 2000). For example, as Diana describes in (10), her daughter (who we can estimate would have attended primary school in the 1960s or 1970s) refused to speak Spanish once she started primary school but then took a course in high school; tellingly, Diana believes that having learned (standard) Spanish at school, her daughter now speaks it and writes it "better" than Diana herself. In (11) Inmaculada tells the story of helping her granddaughter with Spanish homework (in what we can estimate would have been the 2000s), which was marked wrong by the teacher.

(10)

Diana:	...*(1.4) la Evelyn hablaba bien español.*	'...(1.4) Evelyn spoke Spanish well.'
Ricardo:	.. *sí?*	'.. yes?'
Diana:	... *bien bien,*	'... really well,
	cuando estaba más mediana?	when she was little?'
Ricardo:	.. *uh huh.*	'.. uh huh.'
Marco:	... *no más fue a la escuela y ya no.*	'... not any more as soon as she went to school.'
Diana:	*no más fue a la escuela y ya no quiso.*	'as soon as she went to school she refused to.
	...*(0.7) y luego ya después,*	...(0.7) and then,
	cuando entró a high school,	when she went to high school,
	...*(1.0) she started taking clases de es=pañol.*	...(1.0) *she started taking Spanish classes.*'
Ricardo:	.. *yeah=.*	'.. yeah.'
Diana:	...*(0.7) sí lo habla.*	'...(0.7) she does speak it.'
Ricardo:	.. *[yeah].*	'.. [yeah].'
Diana:	*[y lo es]cribe.*	'[and] writes it.
	...*(1.1) m=ejor que,*	...(1.1) better than,
	... *mejor que yo.*	... better than me.'

(24 La Floresta, 46:39–47:01)

(11)

Inmaculada:	*so me senté áhi yo,*	'so I sat there,
	yo y mi suegra=,	me and my mother-in-law,
	los sentamos y c- --	we sat and --
	y y=,	and and,
	y= le ayudamos.	and we helped her.
	pues agarró todo mal.	well she got everything wrong.'
((21 intervening lines))		
	.. they c- called it proper Spanish.	'.. they called it proper Spanish.'
Lucy:	*mhm.*	'mhm.'
Inmaculada:	*o=r,*	'or,
	whatever,	whatever,
	it was called,	it was called,
	but it wasn't our Spanish.	but it wasn't our Spanish.'
Lucy:	*hm.*	'hm.'
Inmaculada:	*so she got everything wrong.*	'so she got everything wrong.
	so I went to the school,	so I went to the school,
	and I complained.	and I complained.
	and I said wait you can't,	and I said wait you can't,
	.. mark her wrong,	.. mark her wrong,
	because that's how .. the community,	because that's how .. the community,
	communicates.	communicates.'

(14 Proper Spanish, 25:55–26:32)

Unsurprisingly, then, the numbers of New Mexican Spanish speakers have diminished over the years, and with them the unique Spanish variety they speak. Shift to English is underway across the Southwest (e.g., Bills, Hernández Chávez, and Hudson 1995). In New Mexico, Spanish is spoken in the home by over a quarter of the population (29 percent), double the national average of 13 percent, as seen in Figure 2.2. However, gross percentages of

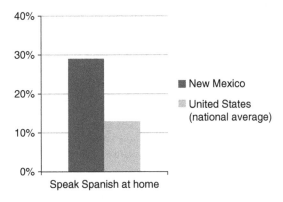

Figure 2.2 Proportion of US general population speaking Spanish in the home (United States Census Bureau 2014)

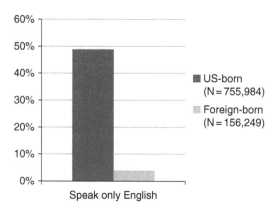

Figure 2.3 Measure of language shift in New Mexico: Proportion of NM Hispanic population who speak only English, US- vs. foreign-born (United States Census Bureau 2014)

Spanish speakers tell us nothing about the transmission of the language to younger generations. When we consider just those who identify themselves as Hispanic (or Latino), evidence of language loss can be seen in the fact that 41 percent report speaking no Spanish. Even this percentage, however, understates the loss among US-born Hispanics. As shown in Figure 2.3, while just 6 percent of the Mexican-born Hispanic population "speak only English," this is the case for as many as 49 percent of the US-born.

NMSEB speakers remark on the shift to English in various ways. There is more and more English, reflects Susan (b. 1934) in (12), as grandchildren simply do not speak Spanish, in the experience of Eduardo (b. 1935) (13). That language preference has changed may be gleaned from Diana's (b. 1941) comparison of then and now in (14).

(12)

Susan:	... and even .. though my grandpa was a teacher,	'... and even .. though my grandpa was a teacher,
	...(0.9) and taught .. his --	...(0.9) and taught .. his --
	eh his students to speak English,	eh his students to speak English,
	my grandma d- didn't speak English.	my grandma d- didn't speak English.'
Gabriel:	uh huh huh,	'uh huh huh.'
Susan:	.. unh-unh.	'.. unh-unh.
	... and uh --	... and uh --
	.. and so we --	.. and so we --
	uh,	uh,
	you know,	you know,
	we just spoke .. Spanish.	we just spoke .. Spanish.
	.. [at the house].	.. [at the house].'

Gabriel:	*[yeah].*	'*[yeah].*'
Susan:	*yeah.*	'*yeah.*'
Gabriel:	*...(1.0) pero fuera de la casa=,*	'*...(1.0) but outside the house,*
	en inglés?	*in English?*'
Susan:	*.. yeah.*	'*.. yeah.*
	.. y luego ya d- --	*.. and then af- --*
	ya después,	*then afterwards,*
	ya=,	*then,*
	a- --	*a- --*
	after --	*after --*
	...(1.0) you know,	*...(1.0) you know,*
	había más inglés,	*there was more English,*
	y más,	*and more,*
	y .. poquito más,	*and .. a little more,*
	y poquito más.	*and a little more.*'

(01 El Abuelo, 44:15–44:45)

(13)

Eduardo:	*.. comprenden,*	'*.. they understand,*
	uh,	*uh,*
	le --	*th- --*
	la idomia,	*the language,*
	... y todo,	*... and everything,*
	pero no sé por qué no lo usan.	*but I don't know why they don't use it.*'

(27 Climate Change, 17:10–17:14)

(14)

Ricardo:	*.. decían esto?*	'*.. they would say that?*
	@@	*@@*'
Diana:	*.. <Q vamos pa'l*	'*.. <Q we're going to*
	Alburque Q>.	*Alburque Q>.*'
Ricardo:	*.. yeah.*	'*.. yeah.*
	...(1.7) sheesh.	*...(1.7) sheesh.*'
Diana:	*... y ahora no=,*	'*... and nowadays no,*
	ahora dicen,	*now they say,*
	... <Q we're going to	*... <Q we're going to*
	Albuquerque Q>.	*Albuquerque Q>.*'
Ricardo:	*... mhm.*	'*... mhm.*'
Diana:	*... que ya cambiaron de voz.*	'*... they have changed tune.*'

(24 La Floresta, 24:25–24:39)

The disparagement of the local variety feeds linguistic insecurity (Labov 1972b: 117). Linguistic insecurity is discernable among NMSEB participants who regard New Mexican Spanish as not "real Spanish" (15). The language Carmela acquired was the local "slang" (16), in contrast to Trinidad's daughter who learned to speak nicely, "like the Mexicans," because she didn't learn Spanish at home but with her Mexican friends at the university (17). Thus, New

Mexican Spanish is undervalued in comparison with English *and* monolingual Spanish, both that of the Mexican immigrant population and the textbook variety taught in schools, a stigmatization that has propelled it toward highly endangered status (Bills and Vigil 2008: 313).

(15)

Eduardo: *my f- family were Spanish Americans but,*
              eh,
              ... really,
              ... we do not know the real Spanish,
              ... from Spain.

(27 Climate Change, 26:38–26:47)

(16)

Alfredo:	*y la Carmela también lo agarró,*	'and Carmela also got it,'
Benita:	*really.*	'really.'
Aurora:	*también.*	'also.'
Alfredo:	*agarró el slang de nosotros.*	'she got our slang.'

(31 Speed Limit, 35:08–35:11)

(17)

Trinidad:	*lo hablaba muy bonito,*	'she spoke it very nicely,
	como los de México.	like people from Mexico.
	... porque .. aprendió más por ella,	... because .. she learned it more on her own,
	que por nosotros.	than from us.'

(21 Demerits, 03:33–03:39)

Resisting the shift to English, there remain a large number of Hispanic New Mexicans who still speak Spanish, approximately one-half (see Figure 2.3). The proportion is even higher in the northern counties of Mora, Rio Arriba, and San Miguel, where approximately two-thirds of the Hispanic population report speaking Spanish in the home (percentages of native Hispanics who "speak only English" are as low as 29–36 percent, United States Census Bureau 2014). Furthermore, a large proportion of these Spanish speakers are registered on the census as bilingual. Figure 2.4 depicts proportions of Hispanics in NM (US- and foreign-born) who report speaking both another language and English "very well": 45 percent of the US-born Hispanic population. It is precisely this bilingual population that the NMSEB corpus samples.

2.4   A Principled Speaker Sample

Once we have identified an apposite contact site, the next step is to assemble a sample of speakers. How do we select a bilingual speaker sample? Studies pooling assorted participants of unknown demographic characteristics, including heterogeneous groups of university students, fail to yield interpretable results

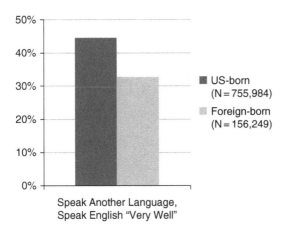

Figure 2.4 Bilingualism among Hispanics in New Mexico, US- vs. foreign-born (United States Census Bureau 2014)

(Labov 1972a: 287). Addressing this issue is not a matter of screening participants for proficiency, cognitive skills, or other individual traits as assessed by different tests, nor is it one of classifying participants according to self-reports of code-switching or domains of language use. For bilinguals just as for monolinguals, "the behavior of an individual can be understood only through the study of the social groups of which he or she is a member" (Labov 2010: 7).

The speakers of the NMSEB corpus are members of a well-defined bilingual *speech community*, sharing a specified geographical location, a uniform structural base, and common sociolinguistic experiences. As an established *bilingual* speech community, they also share ethnicity, the same variety of each of their languages, and unified conventions for combining them. The 40 speakers are all at least third-generation *Nuevomexicanos* 'Hispanic New Mexicans' from counties with a high proportion of Hispanics in northern New Mexico. Figure 2.5 shows the major birthplaces of the NMSEB participants, with darker shades in the map indicating counties with higher proportions of Hispanics, of 66–80 percent in Río Arriba and San Miguel, and 47–61 percent in Taos and Valencia. NMSEB participants come from these counties, in particular Rio Arriba (19/40 participants) and Taos (10/40). They reside primarily in rural areas (29/40), including, for example, Llano de la Yegua, Ojo Sarco, Embudo, Chamisal, and Los Brazos, with fewer living in cities with 10,000 or more residents – Albuquerque, Santa Fe, Los Lunas, Las Vegas, and Española.

Table 2.1 lists demographics of the individual NMSEB participants, namely sex, date of birth, occupation, level of formal instruction, birthplace, and current residence.

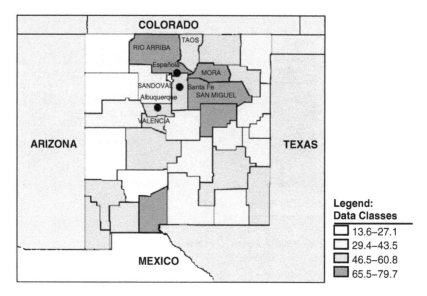

Figure 2.5 Counties of New Mexico according to Hispanic population and major birthplaces of NMSEB participants (COUNTIES and Cities) (United States Census Bureau 2011)

The corpus comprises 23 women and 17 men, aged between 18 and 89 at the time of the recording in 2010–2011 (with years of birth ranging from 1922 to 1993). Consistent with the loss of intergenerational transmission of New Mexican Spanish noted above, the sample is skewed toward older speakers, and 60 percent (25/40) were over 60 at the time of recording. Occupations of the participants include miner, rancher, and schoolteacher. Formal education levels also vary, as is summarized in Figure 2.6, which shows that NMSEB participants (the left bar) have a similar distribution to the Hispanic population in New Mexico (the right bar).

2.5   Using Social Factors to Diagnose Change in Progress

The distribution of linguistic *variants* – different ways of saying essentially the same thing – is "correlated with features of the internal environment" and may also pattern "with external characteristics of the speaker and the situation" (Labov 1982: 18). Analysis of social factors can serve to diagnose language change in progress. While gender and age are often included, a social factor that has been overlooked in most contact studies is social class. The assumption is that linguistic patterns in minority communities, as with Spanish in the United States, will not correlate with speakers' occupation or education since

Table 2.1 *NMSEB corpus constitution*

Recording no.*	Pseudonym	Sex	Date of birth	Occupation	Formal instruction	Birthplace**	Current residence**
01	Susan	F	1934	stay-at-home mom	high school	Albuquerque	Albuquerque
02	Bartolomé	M	1928	firefighter	10th grade	Sthn Colorado	Albuquerque
03	Sandra	F	1943	administration	some college	Española	Española
04	Miguel	M	1944	laborer	8th grade	Valencia	Los Lunas
05	Rocío	F	1945	teacher aid	high school	Santa Fe	Santa Fe
06	Ivette	F	1946	factory worker	GED	Valencia	Albuquerque
07	Samuel	M	1922	school coach	MA	Taos	Taos
08 (14)	Inmaculada	F	1952	social worker	college degree	Las Vegas	Albuquerque
09	Fabiola	F	1954	secretary	some college	Taos	Taos
09	Molly	F	1939	school cook	middle school	Taos	Taos
10 (07)	Pedro	M	1953	school administrator	MA	Rio Arriba	Taos
11	Mónica	F	1941	factory worker, school custodian	high school	Taos	Albuquerque
12	Victoria	F	1959	school teacher	MA	Española	Rio Arriba
12	Marta	F	1964	guest services manager	some college	Albuquerque	Rio Arriba
13	Betty	F	1925	(unknown)	high school	Rio Arriba	Sandoval
14	Anita	F	1941	executive director	high school	San Miguel	Albuquerque
15 (31)	Aurora	F	1962	teacher	college	Española	Sandoval
16 (12)	Manuel	M	1954	electrician, rancher	trade school	Rio Arriba	Rio Arriba
17	Javier	M	1936	rancher, janitor	high school	Taos	Taos
18	Francisco	M	1963	miner	high school	Rio Arriba	Rio Arriba
19	Mariana	F	1944	mom/volunteer	high school	Taos	Taos
20	Dora	F	1953	housewife	(unknown)	Rio Arriba	Rio Arriba
20	Tomás	M	1989	unemployed	high school	Rio Arriba	Rio Arriba

Table 2.1 (*cont.*)

Recording no.	Pseudonym	Sex	Date of birth	Occupation	Formal instruction	Birthplace	Current residence
21	Trinidad	F	1938	substitute teacher	high school	Española	Taos
22	Dolores	F	1963	school secretary	some college	Española	Rio Arriba
22	Clara	F	1985	TV editor	college degree	Española	Rio Arriba
23	Enrique	M	1933	miner, forest service, veteran	middle school	Taos	Taos
24	Diana	F	1941	dry cleaner manager	high school	Taos	Taos
24	Marco	M	1941	miner, construction	middle school	Taos	Taos
25	Leandro	M	1931	miner	middle school	Taos	Rio Arriba
26	Carlos	M	1993	rancher, auctioneer	high school	Española	Rio Arriba
27	Eduardo	M	1935	general contractor, store owner	trade school	Rio Arriba	Rio Arriba
28	Norma	F	1940	bank clerk, B&B owner	high school	Rio Arriba	Rio Arriba
29	Victor	M	1928	rancher	high school	Rio Arriba	Valencia
29	Rubén	M	1925	financial administrator	college	Rio Arriba	Valencia
30	Neddy	M	1968	car salesman	some college	Mora	Las Vegas
30	Cristina	F	1973	self-employed	two-year college	San Miguel	Las Vegas
31	Alfredo	M	1941	highway maintenance	high school	Sandoval	Sandoval
31	Benita	F	1941	homemaker	high school	Rio Arriba	Sandoval
31	Carmela	F	1978	teacher	college degree	Española	Sandoval

* Numbers within parentheses indicate a second recording in which the speaker participated.

** Cities (urban locales) are named only for those with a population of 10,000 or more; otherwise, county names are given.

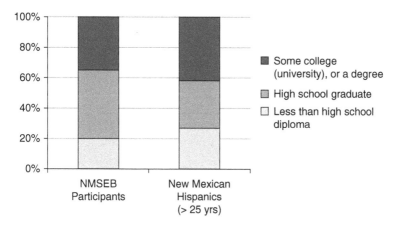

Figure 2.6 Level of formal instruction for NMSEB participants compared
with New Mexican Hispanics
(United States Census Bureau 2014)

the minority language is not instrumental in the employment market (e.g., García and Tallon 2000: 358, n. 351). This is an empirical question, but what has also contributed to the neglect of social factors in bilingualism research is the problem that social categories are generally less well-defined than linguistic categories. In addition, social factors often correlate with one another.

A solution to the problem of demarcating social categories is to use the linguistic data to group speakers, through a data optimization method such as Principal Component Analysis (PCA) (Horvath and Sankoff 1987; Poplack 1979: 190–223). PCA is a way to condense a large number of variables. It "projects a multidimensional data configuration down to a subspace of low dimensionality, yet one which conserves as much of the variance in the data as possible" (Poplack and Sankoff 1984: 118).

Here we use PCA as a heuristic for grouping NMSEB speakers strictly on the basis of their linguistic behavior, with the groups thus defined then interpreted according to social characteristics.

2.5.1 Social Stratification of New Mexican Spanish

The distribution of the NMSEB speaker sample, representing a range of demographic backgrounds, allows extralinguistic constraints on language variation to be assessed. Hints of the social conditioning of variable usage can already be found in early descriptions. Over a century ago, Espinosa (1911: 10), in *The Spanish language in New Mexico and Southern Colorado*, suggested the social evaluation of the aspirated variant of /s/, qualifying it as "widespread among the rural uneducated classes." In 1990s data for the New Mexico-Colorado Spanish Survey (Bills and Vigil 2008), Brown found that aspiration rates of onset (syllable-initial) /s/ – for example, *ahina* (*asina*) 'so' or *la heñora* (*señora*) 'the woman' – tended to be higher in rural than in urban areas and greater for men than for women (2005b: 25–27).

To identify social factors that may condition variation in NM bilinguals' Spanish, PCA was applied to counts of familiar phonetic variables: lenition of onset and coda /s/, intervocalic /d/, and intervocalic [j] (<ll>) (Torres Cacoullos and Berry 2018). For intervocalic /d/, for example, counts were taken of approximants against the number of deleted tokens (in which there was no perceptible frication as well as audible vowel coarticulation, e.g., *casado* [kasau], *casada* [kasaː] 'married'). The PCA resulted in clusterings of speakers with similar linguistic behavior on the phonetic variables. These clusterings were then interpreted based on our extralinguistic knowledge of the speakers (Table 2.1) to identify social characteristics that the individuals within those clusters have in common.

The social factors derived from the PCA of the linguistic data are sex, demographic locale, and socioeconomic status. Occupation and formal instruction provide a composite socioeconomic index. Participants working in production had been to middle or high school (e.g., mineworker, laborer, rancher), those in service or trades had attended high school, technical schools, or university (e.g., dry-cleaning manager, electrician, secretary), and those employed in professional occupations nearly all had university degrees (e.g., teacher, financial administrator, executive director). The social factors thus suggested were tested via regression analysis for the phonetic variables. Returning to intervocalic /d/, social-class and sex effects were confirmed: speakers from production occupations delete more often than those from service and professional occupations, and men delete more often than women. This sociolinguistic pattern replicates that found across the Spanish-speaking world, for example, in Panama (Cedergren 1973) and Venezuela (D'Introno and Sosa 1986). As in other varieties, however, the primary factors conditioning intervocalic /d/ elision are linguistic (phonetic context and participle status work together, such that the highest deletion rates are seen with participles from the first conjugation, -*ado*).

In sum, there *is* social stratification in bilinguals' Spanish, at least for these phonetic variables. We can now test whether the social factors identified condition a morphosyntactic variable such as subject pronoun expression.

2.5.2   Testing Social Factors in Bilinguals' Subject Expression

Our target linguistic variable is subject pronoun expression, focusing on first- and third-person singular human specific referents, where the competing variants are pronominal and unexpressed subjects (see Chapter 5). A long-term trend of increased rates of expression might be expected from the historical development of subject pronouns in Romance languages. Variable subject expression in Spanish (as in Italian and Portuguese) could be said to sit somewhere between Latin, which had no personal pronouns of the third person (Greenough, Kittredge, Howard and D'ooge 1903: 176, §295c), and French, in which subject pronouns are no longer optional (Lamiroy and De Mulder 2011: 303–304). But there is no evidence of a general change in progress toward increased subject pronoun use across Spanish varieties. Dialect differences in overall expression rates – for instance, elevated rates of subject pronouns in Caribbean varieties – have been interpreted as a reflex of change in progress (e.g., Toribio 2000). However, as Silva-Corvalán and Enrique-Arias (2017: 176) caution, cross-study comparisons are not always meaningful due to disparate procedures. And even when the same method is followed, an overall rate difference alone, as Cameron sagely advises, "does not permit us to say if speakers from San Juan are changing in the direction of a greater frequency of pronominal expression or if the speakers from Madrid are so doing in the direction of lesser frequency of pronominal expression" (1995: 24, n. 26).

Changes in progress can be detected synchronically in apparent time, through comparison of the distribution of variant forms across age cohorts (Labov 1994: 43–72). Gender can also be revealing, as we know that women adopt innovative forms earlier than men, both for prestige variants and for linguistic changes from below (i.e., language-internal changes below the level of conscious awareness, as indicated by lack of style shifting) (Labov 2001: 261–293). Gender interacts with a third factor, social class, after the initial stages of linguistic change and as the level of social awareness rises (Labov 2001: 294–322). Finally, most changes are initiated in large cities (Labov 2001: 437).

Congruent with the absence of change in progress for Spanish subject expression is the fact that, where they have been examined, social factors are found to be non-significant, weak, incoherent, or inconsistent (Silva-Corvalán and Enrique-Arias 2017: 174–175). Social effects of speaker occu-pation, education, or sex have failed to emerge from studies in Barranquilla (Orozco and Guy 2008: 78), Caracas (Bentivoglio 1987: 57–58), and Mexico City (Lastra and Butragueño 2015: 49). And where social factors appear to play a role, they are not always the same or do not have the same direction of effect.

Among studies that report an effect for speaker age, for example, while some show higher subject expression rates among younger than older cohorts (Ávila Jiménez 1995: 30; Flores-Ferrán 2010: 75; Morales 1986: 78), more show the opposite tendency (Alfaraz 2015: 11; Carvalho and Child 2011: 22;

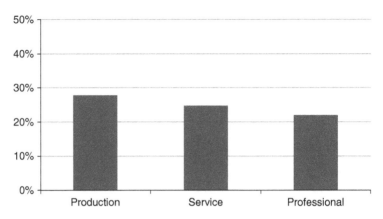

Figure 2.7 Rate of subject pronouns according to social class
13 production speakers (N = 2,604; M = 28%, SD = 12.8),
15 service (N = 1,662; M = 25%, SD = 11.8),
12 professional (N = 1,305; M = 22%, SD = 14), F = 0.64, p = .53.

Lastra and Butragueño 2015: 49; Orozco 2015: 30). Similarly discrepant are statements for speaker gender: some conclude that women favor subject pronouns (Alfaraz 2015: 11; Carvalho and Child 2011: 22; Orozco 2015: 30; Shin and Otheguy 2013: 439), others that men do (Enríquez 1984: 350). Claims for socioeconomic status are also inconsistent, with higher-education speakers reported both to favor pronouns (Ávila Jiménez 1995: 35) and not to (Alfaraz 2015: 11). The lack of trends for socioeconomic status indicates that subject pronouns do not especially carry prestige (cf. Claes 2011: 207–208).

In the absence of accountable diachronic studies and consistent apparent time trends or social conditioning, we must conclude that subject expression is, in the short term at least, a case of stable variation. But does it remain so in language contact situations?

Subject pronoun expression rates range from 9 percent to 62 percent across individual NMSEB speakers. However, the rates do not correlate systematically with any social grouping studied, as shown in the following figures. Comparisons of the means of the groups within each social category indicate no statistically significant difference for social class (Figure 2.7) nor for rural vs. urban groups (Figure 2.8)[3]. An apparent difference between men and women (Figure 2.9, left panel) disappears when only speakers with 100 or

---

[3] Statistics done in R (R Core Team 2015) using the base package or the package {Hmisc} (Harrell 2015). All t-tests are Unequal Variance (Welch) t-test; the number in the parentheses gives the adjusted df.

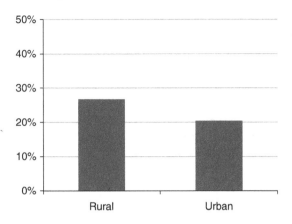

Figure 2.8 Rate of subject pronouns according to demographic locale
29 rural speakers (N = 3,286; M = 27%, SD = 13.8),
11 urban speakers (N = 2,285; M = 20%, SD = 8.9), $t(27.97)$ = 1.70, p = .10.

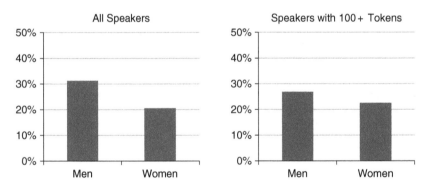

Figure 2.9 Rate of subject pronouns according to speaker sex
All speakers: 17 men (N = 2,050; M = 31%, SD = 14.0), 23 women
(N = 3,521; M = 21%, SD = 9.9), $t(27.15)$ = 2.69, $p < .05$.
Speakers with 100+ tokens: 7 men (N = 1,477; M = 27%, SD = 11.3),
13 women (N = 3,118; M = 23%, SD = 11.5), $t(12.60)$ = 0.83, p = .42.

more tokens are considered (right panel) (on false conclusions based on
insufficient data per individual, see Bayley, Cárdenas, Treviño Schouten and
Vélez Salas 2012: 57; Guy 1980: 15–26). Thus, in accordance with the general
lack of social effects in other varieties, subject expression is not socially
conditioned in NMSEB bilinguals' Spanish.

2.6   Conclusion

Spanish and English have co-existed as the main competing languages for over 150 years in northern New Mexico. This allows for a compelling assessment of the linguistic outcomes of contact, not afforded by studies of immigrant communities or studies without a community footing, such as those based on assorted university students. New Mexican Spanish today is an endangered variety, under threat from the shift to English but also from non-local Spanish varieties considered to be of greater prestige (both immigrant Mexican Spanish, and the "proper" Spanish taught in schools).

In *Languages in Contact*, the enduring foundation for empirical studies of multilingual communities, Weinreich reminds us that "two or more languages [are] *in contact* if they are used alternately by the same persons" (1953/1968: 1). Because "the language-using individuals are thus the locus of the contact" (Weinreich 1953/1968: 1), the remaining speakers of New Mexican Spanish and English – bilinguals who habitually alternate between languages – provide a precious test of contact-induced grammatical change.

The speaker sample is comprised of participants who are all at least third-generation *Nuevomexicanos* 'Hispanic New Mexicans' from a range of demographic backgrounds, allowing extralinguistic constraints on language variation to be assessed. As in other varieties of Spanish, subject pronoun expression rates are not sensitive to the social factors of speaker occupation, education level, sex, and locale. In Chapter 4, we will take on the problem of how to assess degree of contact for bilingual speakers, and ask whether subject pronoun rates are influenced by language preference or self-rating, measures of degree of contact that should have an effect per a hypothesis of contact-induced change. First, though, we have to collect appropriate data, which is the topic of the following chapter.

3   Good Data: Capturing Language Use

The credibility of any assertion of contact-induced change is only as good as the data source. Specifying a linguistic data source includes both the speaker sample and the observation method: who are the bilinguals, and how were the data obtained?

We adopt a community-based data collection method, because "the aim of linguistic analysis is to describe the regular patterns of the speech community, rather than the eccentricities of any given individual" (Labov 1969: 738). The precedence of community norms for bilingual phenomena is borne out by the remarkable findings in Poplack, Sankoff, and Miller's (1988) mammoth study of lexical borrowing from English into French, based on 20,000 tokens of English-origin single words extracted from conversations with 120 francophones in the national capital region of Canada. English proficiency is not the major predictor, neither for overall borrowing *rates* (the proportion of borrowed tokens and types in the interview) nor for borrowing *patterns* (the proportion of these that are nonce vs. widespread). For overall borrowing rate, a better predictor than individual English proficiency was social class membership – working-class speakers led in borrowings as a percentage of the total number of words. As to borrowing pattern, the major predictor was neighborhood of residence – the proportion of instances of active borrowing (nonce words directly drawn from English) to established borrowings was higher in neighborhoods with greater proportions of anglophones (Poplack et al. 1988: 75–84). The inescapable conclusion is that "an individual's personal ability is operative but is mediated by the norms of his speech community" (Poplack et al. 1988: 98).

The previous chapter set out the contact setting and situated the bilingual speakers in their social context. This chapter takes on corpus constitution. We begin with the primacy of community conventions, which are thrown into relief by the preferred semantic domains of borrowed nouns (Section 3.1). Community-based corpus constitution involves recordings of spontaneous speech (3.2). A collection of recordings becomes most useful with thorough transcription and responsible handling of the resulting corpus (3.3). The transcription is prosodically based, utilizing the Intonation

Unit, following standardized protocols for replicable transcription of running speech (3.4). Prosody turns out to be pivotal for delineating code-switching boundaries (3.5), and prosodically based transcription facilitates demarcation of syntactic structures (3.6).

3.1   Bilingual Community Norms of Lexical Borrowability

The priority of community norms is verified in the NMSEB corpus, taking lexical borrowability as a starkly clear case. Commonly asserted are borrowability scales whereby, for example, loanwords from the basic vocabulary are less likely than "cultural borrowings" (Myers-Scotton 2002: 239; cf. Hock and Joseph 1996: 257; Thomason 2001: 71–72). We may ask, then, whether English-origin nouns that are incorporated in the Spanish of bilinguals in New Mexico, as in (18), are associated with particular semantic domains.

(18)

| Ivette: | ... *yo agarro la key.* | '... I get the key. |
| | ... *para abrirlas.* | ... to open them.' |

(06 El Túnico, 38:46–38:47)

Figure 3.1 depicts the distribution of English-origin nouns across different semantic domains: kin terms, technology items and vehicles (such as *treadmill* and *troca* 'pick-up truck'), designations of people (such as *friend* or *firefighter*), everyday items (such as *key* in (18)), events and places (such as *birthday*), years and numbers, and other minor classes. From such a distribution we might surmise that kin terms, such as *dad* or *grandma*, are the single most frequent class. The high frequency of kin terms would be contrary to the assertion that cultural items are more readily borrowed than basic items. In agreement with this assertion, however, it appears that technology and vehicle terms are among the relatively frequent categories, more so than borrowed nouns referring to years and numbers.

But before making pronouncements on semantic domains of lexical borrowings, we must first apply the variationist principle of accountability (Labov 1972b: 72):

any variable form (a member of a set of alternative ways of "saying the same thing") *should be reported with the proportion of cases in which the form did occur in the relevant environment, compared to the total number of cases in which it might have occurred.* Unless this principle is followed, it is possible to prove any theoretical preconception by citing isolated instances of what individuals have been heard saying. Speech is perceived categorically, and linguists who are searching for an invariant, homogeneous dialect will perceive even more categorically than most. The problem is most severe in the study of non-standard dialects. (Labov 1969: 738, n. 720) (Emphasis in original)

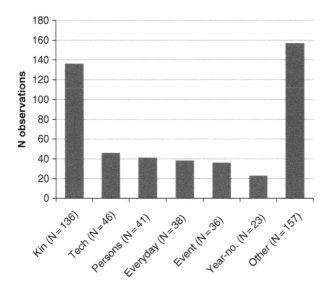

Figure 3.1 Semantic domains of borrowings I: Distribution of English-origin nouns in NM Spanish discourse across semantic domains
(from Aaron 2015: Table 1)
Other includes, for example, *mountain, homework, eyedrops, weekend, bird*

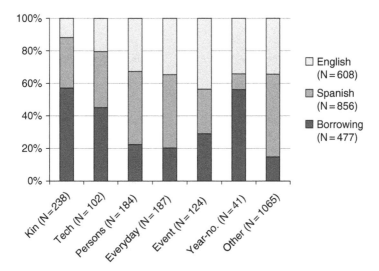

Figure 3.2 Semantic domains of borrowings II: Proportions per semantic domain of English-origin nouns in NM Spanish discourse, and Spanish and English benchmark data (from Aaron 2015: Table 1)
Benchmark data are extracted from a portion of the corpus (N = 1,464). Thus, valid is the comparison of proportions across semantic domains, not the absolute values of the proportions.

To answer the question of borrowability of nouns according to semantic domain, Aaron (2015) applies the principle of accountability by looking at monolingual benchmark counterparts, drawn from the speech of the same speakers. Figure 3.2, unlike Figure 3.1, counts both cases where borrowed nouns "did occur" and those where they "might have occurred." That is, in Figure 3.2 the proportions of borrowed nouns are tabulated against samples of native Spanish-origin nouns in Spanish discourse and English-origin nouns in English discourse, in each semantic domain. Here we see that the two semantic domains most propitious to borrowing (comparing the heights of the darker portion in each column) are indeed kinship terms, but also years and numbers. Technology-vehicle terms now come in third. This category is not only less favorable to borrowings in the aggregate, but also less productive. One-third (15/46) of the borrowed technology-vehicle cases are tokens of the same word, the established and phonologically adapted loanword *troca* 'pick-up truck'.

General borrowability scales, such as those positing the greater borrowability of cultural vs. core items, cannot explain the community norms observed here. Example (19) illustrates use of the English-origin kinship term *grandma* in Spanish discourse. An indication of its loanword status is its embedding in the possessive duplication (literally, 'his grandma of this young man'), a structure of Mexican varieties since Spanish colonial times (Company Company 1995). Examples (20) and (21) exemplify English-origin numbers in Spanish, used for dates and age respectively.

(19)
Mariana: *su grandma de este jovencito,*   'the grandma of this young man,'
                                                                    (20 School Bus 19:38–19:39)

(20)
Aurora: *nacieron en fifty-two.*   'they were born in fifty-two.'
                                                            (31 Speed Limit, 28:15–28:16)

(21)
Francisco: *la viejita esa ya tiene ninety-seven.*   'that old lady is already ninety-seven.'
                                                                (18 Las Minas, 53:47–53:49)

The primacy of bilingual community patterns is further corroborated by the choices for individual kin terms by New Mexican bilinguals. As Table 3.1 reveals, the lexical patterns are asymmetrical. The borrowed *dad(dy)* is by far the preferred term for 'father', but native *mamá* is favored for 'mother'. And while grandparents of both sexes tend to be referred to with loanwords, sons, daughters, and siblings are not. This is "evidence that the conventionalization

Table 3.1 *English-origin vs. native kinship terms in Spanish discourse*

Borrowing	N	Native Spanish	N
dad, daddy	76	*papá*	4
mom, mama	8	*mamá*	15
grandpa	20	*abuelo*	3
grandma	30	*abuela*	1
son/daughter	0	*hijo/hija*	18
brother/sister	0	*hermano/hermana*	11

(from Aaron 2015: 467)

of English-origin nouns occurs at both the lexical and semantic levels" (Aaron 2015: 467).

Such community-particular bilingual patterns cannot be detected with speaker samples consisting of university students at hand nor with corpora amalgamating texts culled from a range of dialects or contact sites. Nor could the patterns have been deduced from speech productions of community members elicited in the lab, where data distribution is typically controlled. In addition, test situations and lab-based activities are associated with schools – institutions where the speakers and their local varieties have been denigrated. Experimental procedures are thus particularly uninformative about non-standard usage (D. Sankoff 1988b: 145–146). More generally, the uniformity of the speech community fails to appear in "word lists and formal elicitations [which] are the primary sources of confusion in our descriptions of language" (Labov 1989: 2). What kind of data, then, offer insights on patterns of language use within the speech community?

3.2 A Premium on Spontaneous Speech

Analysts naturally draw on intuitions to come up with hypotheses, but analyst intuitions and speaker judgments about variable phenomena, especially ones involving stigmatized variants, are unreliable as a data source on which to *test* hypotheses. This has been amply documented in the study of African American Vernacular English (AAVE) (Labov 1996: 86–90). When speakers of subordinate varieties are asked direct questions about their language, as is the case with acceptability judgments, their answers shift toward (or away from) the prestige variety in unsystematic and unpredictable ways (Labov 1972c: 111).

In the study of bilingualism, the unreliability of data obtained from elicited evaluations of examples combining elements from two languages was already exposed in the 1970s – for example, in reports that bilinguals judged utterances that they themselves had produced as incorrect (Huerta 1978; Poplack 1983: 115, and references therein). Even language processing, as registered by eye tracking during reading, is distorted if bilinguals are asked for acceptability judgments of code-switched sentences (Guzzardo Tamargo, Valdés Kroff, and Dussias 2016). Also unsound are generalizations based on "overheard" speech, due to the problem of categorical perception by the analyst, which inflates a few unsystematically collected examples into an overall tendency. For production data, a sine qua non for discovering bilingual norms is the socio-linguistically constructed corpus – recordings of large amounts of spontaneous everyday speech.

3.2.1   The Sociolinguistic Interview

The "most systematic data for linguistic analysis" comes from the *vernacular*, the mode of everyday speech, in which variation has been demonstrated to be more patterned than in less informal, superposed styles (Labov 1984: 29). It might seem expedient to simply leave a recording device running in the course of daily conversations with friends, but this would limit participants to the researcher's social circles or those of their students. The *sociolinguistic interview* by trained fieldworkers mitigates the effects of observation and records large amounts of speech least affected by self-monitoring. Moreover, often arising naturally in the recording are linguistic experiences that illumi-nate the nature of bilingualism in the community and the sociolinguistic profile of the speaker (as described in the following chapter), topics less likely in daily conversations.

A successful technique is the "narrative of personal experience," in which the participant, not the university-affiliated interviewer, is the indisputable authority (Labov 1984: 32–42). Topics may be of general interest, such as childhood games or past jobs, or may be specific to the community. In New Mexico, for example, such "insider topics" are pole vaulting in the *acequia* 'irrigation ditch', working in the uranium mines, moving cattle, and making medicine with sage. In Southern Papua New Guinea, where coconut trees are planted to mark important events (a fight with a neighbor, the birth of a child, the coming of a new year), such "coconut stories" can serve as linguistic data (Evans 2014). The researcher can only know of these topics through intimate familiarity with the community.

Conversation around locally critical issues and "areas of disputed knowl-edge" enhances the possibility of capturing the vernacular – "more involve-ment of the speaker, longer discussions, and more narrative" (Labov 1984: 42). Participants are sensitive to researchers having local knowledge and appreciation for their own knowledge, even in direct elicitation of linguistic structures. A poignant illustration comes from elicitation sessions for single, dual, and plural forms with a speaker of the Australian indigenous language Malyangapa. Over the years linguists had repeatedly asked this speaker to produce sentences about dogs (one dog, two dogs, three dogs). The speaker eventually objected: "I haven't got a bloody dog. I know all the stories from Western New South Wales and all that people ask me about is dogs" (Gara and Hercus 2005: 7).

The following examples illustrate narratives of personal experience in NMSEB. Example (22) is an excerpt from Manuel's story of going after a bear in a cave. In (23) Clara tells of being caught smoking as a child and Dolores gives her take on the incident.

(22)

Manuel:	... áhi donde iba mirando,	'... where I was moving along looking,
	... con mi flashlight,	... with my flashlight,
	... uh=,	... uh,
	...(1.3) vide un agujero poquito m- --	...(1.3) I saw a hole a bit m- --
	.. como del tamaño donde pudiera cabido un --	.. like the size where there would have fit a --
	.. un oso,	.. a bear,
	...(0.9) y dije,	...(0.9) and I said,
	voy a chequear ese,	I'm going to check this out,
	.. y luego me voy a revolver .. pa'trás.	.. and then I'm going to turn .. back.
	...(1.0) y= uh=,	...(1.0) and uh,
	...(0.8) y --	...(0.8) and --
	voy a salirme.	I'm going to get out.
	Ya me estaba dando,	I was already starting to feel,
	...(0.7) uh=,	...(0.7) uh,
	porque había estado adentro muy --	because I had been inside very --
	... mu- --	... a lo- --
	.. mucho tiempo.	.. a long time.'
Carrie:	.. mhm.	'.. mhm.'
Manuel:	... so fui=,	'... so I went,
	.. áhi cuando iba a chequear,	.. just when I was going to check,
	...(1.3) a mirar,	...(1.3) to look,
	... ahí donde estaba=,	... where it was,
	el agujero ese?	that hole?
	... estaba .. el oso sentado,	... there was .. the bear sitting,
	... adentro del agujero,	... inside the hole,
	.. mirando pa' afuera.	.. looking out.'
Carrie:	.. (GASP)	.. (GASP)
Manuel:	... y me escamé poco,	'... and I got a little edgy,
	pero yo dije,	but I said,
	... vine a lo que vine.	... this is what I came for.'
		(16 Trip to Africa Pt1, 24:19–24:58)

(23)

Clara:	we would !steal the cigarettes.	'we would !steal the cigarettes.
	... and,	... and,
	we'd smoke them.	we'd smoke them.
	And one time they --	And one time they --
	.. my mom caught us.	.. my mom caught us.'
Jake:	.. @@=	'.. @@'
Clara:	.. and so=,	'.. and so,
	.. sh=e,	.. she,
	... she uh= --	... she uh --
	she told my cousin,	she told my cousin,
	.. she's like,	.. she's like,
	.. <Q and you guys,	.. <Q and you guys,
	salieron en el	were in the
	Rio Grande Sun,	Rio Grande Sun,
	and,	and,
	.. you guys made front page,	.. you guys made front page,
	they have a picture of you guys	they have a picture of you guys
	smoking,	smoking,
	by grandma's car Q>,	by grandma's car Q>,'

((22 intervening lines))

Dolores:	yeah I had seen them,	'yeah I had seen them,
	and,	and,
	no,	no,
	no dije nada,	I didn't say anything,
	I go,	I go,
	... hm=,	... hm,
	... y nomás las dejé,	... and I just left them at it,
	and then I came up with this big old --	and then I came up with this big old --
	blown story,	blown story,
	del Sun because,	of the Sun because,
	.. e- --	.. e- --
	everybody in northern New Mexico	everybody in northern New Mexico
	lee the Sun cause,	reads the Sun cause,
	they even nicknamed it	they even nicknamed it
	El Mitote,	The Gossip,
	because there you find out,	because there you find out,
	like,	like,
	way too much stuff.	way too much stuff.
	<@ [an- @>] --	<@ [an- @>] --'
Jake:	[@] .. [2way too2] --	'[@] .. [2way too2] --'
Dolores:	[2so I2] --	'[2so I2] --
	so I told them,	so I told them,
	que van a salir en	that they're going to be in
	el <@ Sun @> @.	the <@ Sun @> @.'

(22 Farolitos, 16:07–17:08)

Sociolinguistic interviews in NMSEB were conducted with single individuals or pairs, and in some cases in groups. In (24) Rubén and Victor, who
participated as a pair, reminisce together about a nun at the convent school
(overlapping at times while doing so, as indicated in [ ]).

(24)

Rubén:	*and the .. roof,*	*'and the .. roof,*
	.. was flat,	*.. was flat,'*
Carrie:	*.. mhm.*	*'.. mhm.'*
Rubén:	*... and she would get up there,*	*'... and she would get up there,*
	no?	*no?'*
Víctor:	*yeah.*	*'yeah.'*
Rubén:	*.. on t- --*	*'.. on t- --*
	.. on top of the roof,	*.. on top of the roof,'*
Víctor:	*.. puchar la nieve [pa'bajo].*	*'.. push the snow [down].'*
Rubén:	*[and]=,*	*'[and],*
	she would,	*she would,'*
Víctor:	*y nai- --*	*'and nob- --'*
Rubén:	*[shovel],*	*'[shovel],'*
Víctor:	*[y no] se caíban,*	*'[and they didn't] fall,*
	y ahora se [2caen de una vez en2] --	*and now they [2fall at once2] --'*
Rubén:	*[2eh= uh=2] --*	*'[2eh uh2] --*
	she would shovel the snow	*she would shovel the snow*
	[from the roof,	*[from the roof,'*
Víctor:	*[get hurt,*	*'[get hurt,*
	or whatever].	*or whatever].'*
Rubén:	*and] from over there,*	*'and] from over there,*
	when we were at recess,	*when we were at recess,*
	she would make snowball[s=],	*she would make snowball[s],'*
Víctor:	*[yeah],*	*'[yeah],*
	.. <@ y las tiraba	*.. <@ and she would throw them*
	pa'bajo @>.	*down @>.'*

(29 La Diploma, 24:44–25:02)

3.2.2   In-group Fieldworkers

Overall rates of linguistic variants may be affected by the status of the interviewer (Rickford and McNair-Knox 1994). Whether data are gathered by an
in-group community member made a difference, for example, in word-final
nasal velarization, more common in Salvadoran than Mexican Spanish in
Houston (e.g., *fuero*[ŋ] vs. *fuero*[n] 'they went'). The rate of velarization by
Salvadorans was four times higher with a Salvadoran than with a Mexican
interviewer (Hernández 2011: 67).

For bilingual data, we know from Poplack's reports on the East Harlem
Puerto Rican community in New York that the status of the fieldworker is
critical to obtaining samples of code-switching (Poplack 1981, 1983).

For example, the average number of other-language items by one speaker was approximately four times greater in informal situations with an in-group interlocutor than with a non-group interlocutor (Poplack 1983: 113). There was also a difference in the proportion of borrowings vs. code-switches (see Chapter 9, Section 9.2.1). Whereas the in-group member obtained mostly multi-word code-switches, the non-group interviewer obtained mostly single-word or lone nouns, as in *comprando shares que bajan y suben* 'buying shares that fall and rise' (Poplack 1983: 114).

The fieldworkers for NMSEB were community members by virtue of their ethnicity (Hispanic New Mexicans, or *Nuevomexicanos*) and relationship with the participants (extended family members or their acquaintances).[1] Audio recordings were made in the home of the participant or that of another family member or friend, and lasted on average approximately 1 hour (ranging from 30 minutes to 1 hour and 45 minutes).[2] The fieldworkers were instructed to speak as they naturally would in both English and Spanish, and neither they nor the participants were aware that the impact of code-switching on grammar was to be an object of study. On a fieldtrip from Albuquerque to northern New Mexico one weekend, four interviewers collected 14 of the 31 interviews that make up the corpus. The following excerpt from the diary of Daniel Abeyta voices the fieldworkers' appreciation of the conversations in their towns of origin:

> Although many of the people we interviewed were family friends, for many of us, it was the first time we had intentionally taken the time to sit down, have a real conversation, and hear their life stories. We even had the pleasure of meeting distant family members for the first time. .... Our eyes were opened to parts of our own communities we were previously oblivious to, mainly due to believing that we were too busy or had more important things to do. .... On our journey, we discovered treasures such as friendship, laughter, proverbs, history, and food. Each of us found ourselves feeling part of something bigger than ourselves, connected to our community in a deep and meaningful way. (Daniel Abeyta, NMSEB fieldworker; June 2011)

3.2.3   NMSEB: Spontaneous Language Switching

Thanks to the natural interactions recorded by the in-group interviewers, NMSEB is a corpus in which two languages are used by the same speaker in the same setting, with no elicitation or coercion. The corpus captures abundant code-switching, unparalleled in contact studies. An explicit measure of code-switching abundance is the presence of other-language material in the vicinity

---

[1] The fieldworkers were students of the University of New Mexico (UNM), seven pursuing undergraduate degrees in various fields and one Masters student; some had taken Spanish classes in the Heritage Language Program (for learners with a cultural connection to the language) and had travelled in Spanish-speaking countries. Their speech (approximately 5 of the 29 hours in NMSEB) is not included in the analyses.

[2] Audio recordings were made on Zoom H4N handy recorders.

of the linguistic variable of interest. In a clause-based measure for Spanish subject expression, nearly one-quarter of the tokens occur with English multi-word strings, and another one-fifth with single-word items within the same or preceding clause (see Chapter 9, Section 9.2.2). A time-based measure comes from a dataset for the comparison of voice onset time in English and Spanish in NMSEB: Balukas and Koops find that at least two-thirds of /ptk/-word tokens follow a multi-word code-switch in the other language within a 5-second window (N = 642, 2015: 431).

The fluid switching between languages occurs within, as well as across, speaker turns, allowing a test of what, if any, impact the interviewer's language use has on the code-switching of the participant. Switching at the beginning of the turn can serve as an indication of whether speakers' language choice is prompted by the language choice of their interlocutor – what is known as priming or alignment in lab-based studies (e.g., Kootstra, Van Hell, and Dijkstra 2010). Continuation of the same language at the beginning of a conversational turn could be considered a manifestation of alignment with the interlocutor, and a change in language turn-initially as lack of alignment. Both occur in the data, illustrated below: in (25) the participant begins his turn following the language of the interlocutor, and in (26) he responds in a different language. (Remember that, in the translation of the examples on the right, italics indicate speech originally produced in English and roman type indicates Spanish.)

(25)

Bartolomé:	in the Bikini Atolls in 1946.	'in the Bikini Atolls in 1946.'
Gabriel:	... dónde?	'... where?'
Bartolomé:	en= .. Bikini.	'in .. Bikini.'

                                                        (02 La Marina, 31:19–31:25)

(26)

| Gabriel: | dónde está eso? | 'where is that?' |
| Bartolomé: | that's in New York. | 'that's in New York.' |

                                                        (02 La Marina, 33:00–33:02)

Rather than interpreting individual instances, the argument is quantitative, drawing on a comparison of turn-initial and turn-medial instances. If speakers replicate the language choice of the interviewer, changes of language should appear less often at the beginning of a speaker turn, as in (26), than within the speaker turn, as in (27) where the interlocutor does not come into play.

(27)

| Bartolomé: | afuera del agua, | 'outside the water, |
| | .. they had to scrape it, | .. they had to scrape it,' |

                                                        (02 La Marina, 33:15–33:18)

Table 3.2 *Switches in language turn-initially vs. turn-internally*

	N	%
Turn-initial		
No switch:	204	83%
Spanish preceded by Spanish or English preceded by English		
Switch:	42	17%
Spanish preceded by English or English preceded by Spanish		
Turn-internal		
No switch:	795	88%
Spanish preceded by Spanish or English preceded by English		
Switch:	111	12%
Spanish preceded by English or English preceded by Spanish		

NMSEB sample, from Plaistowe (2015: Table 10), 17% vs. 12%: $p = .06$.
Switches are between Intonation Units (IUs), see Section 3.4.

Switches of language in a sample of NMSEB are tabulated in Table 3.2. Against the alignment hypothesis, the results indicate no less changing of language turn-initially than turn-internally. The evidence, then, is that the language switching and linguistic structures in the corpus did not arise in response to direct – or indirect – elicitation from the fieldworkers.

3.3   Making a Speech Corpus Utilizable

Once the recordings are made, the challenge is proper transcription. Discovering bilingual norms requires systematic quantitative analysis, as cherry-picked examples do not an empirical study make. Of a collection of recordings, available for accountable linguistic analysis is the corpus which has been thoroughly transcribed. Alignment of transcriptions with audio recordings enhances both transcription accuracy and analysis not just of phonetic features, but also of morphosyntactic and discourse structures.[3]

Transcription is done orthographically to maximize searchability (Martín Butragueño and Lastra 2011: xxv; Otheguy and Zentella 2012: 228; Poplack 1993: 265–266). While morphological variants such as *vide* vs. *vi* ('I saw') and *–nos* vs. *–mos* (first person plural), and local lexical items such as *muchitos* 'kids' are represented in the transcription, standard orthography is used for phonetic variants. For example, despite variable aspiration and deletion of /s/ in New Mexican Spanish, an *s* is transcribed where plural meaning is clear from the context (so, *los muchachos* 'the-MASC.PL boys',

---

[3] For NMSEB, the transcription was done in the software ELAN (Lausberg and Sloetjes 2009) (on the use of ELAN for corpus preparation, see Nagy and Meyerhoff 2015).

not *loh muchachoh* or *lo muchacho*). Similarly, although they are variably pronounced, English-origin items such as *grandma* and *grandpa* are consistently spelled as in English, permitting systematic extraction and calculation of their recurrence (overall frequency of use) and diffusion (use by different speakers) (Aaron 2015; Poplack et al. 1988). The other reason to use standard orthography is to deter negative perceptions of the community. Respellings have been demonstrated to demote the status of the speaker (Preston 1982, 1985), projecting to readers stigmatized identities (Jaffe and Walton 2000).

Like the data collection itself, the transcription process is community-based. Transcribers unfamiliar with the dialect may misunderstand the linguistic material. For example, even a native speaker of another Spanish dialect and a well-trained linguist thought she heard *Tierra María* instead of *Tierra Amarilla* with deleted intervocalic [j].

Accurate transcriptions require multiple rounds of revisions (cf. Martín Butragueño and Lastra 2011: xxv). The NMSEB transcriptions went through at least five rounds. The recordings were transcribed initially by a Spanish–English bilingual (currently living in New Mexico, and from New Mexico or from Mexico; in some cases, the interviewer him/herself), and then revised by a second bilingual who was more comfortable in Spanish, if the first transcriber was more comfortable transcribing English, or vice versa. A sign of the highly bilingual character of the corpus is that one transcriber often caught material which had been misheard by another, each being more proficient at capturing the content in a different language. Two more rounds of revision took place in the course of anonymizing the transcriptions and sound files, and at least one more following reading of the transcript for content. For each hour of recorded speech, at least 50 are needed for transcription (Travis and Torres Cacoullos 2013: 184–187). This large time investment is comparable to other carefully prepared corpora for similar two-party conversations (the Ottawa-Hull French project, Poplack 1989: 431, and the Santa Barbara Corpus of Spoken American English, John Du Bois and Robert Englebretson, personal communication).

Community-based data collection confronts social policy issues of respecting participants' rights (Labov 1984: 51–52). First, participants must give their permission prior to being recorded. Regardless of whether permission is obtained after the fact, surreptitious recordings are likely to be of poor sound quality and, in the long term, deception of this sort, even with family and friends, will damage linguists' contacts with (and reputation in) the community (Labov 1984: 51). For NMSEB, speakers gave explicit consent prior to any recording.

Second, care must be taken in terms of data confidentiality. Where data consist of sentence completions, story retellings, or traditional narratives, public acknowledgment of participants may be preferred (e.g., Bowern 2010: 903). For sociolinguistic interviews – with narratives of personal experience – the established practice is to protect confidentiality through the use of pseudonyms. Anonymization is essential, particularly for small, close-knit communities, such as in northern New Mexico, where participants may be identified by life details. In addition to people and locations, pseudonyms are given to nicknames, some jobs held, places of military postings or other proper nouns that might identify the participant (Travis and Torres Cacoullos 2013: 187). The corresponding sound segment is anonymized through low pass filtering. Pseudonyms in the transcript are indicated by a preceding tilde ("~"), as in (28) (all speaker names, which precede examples, are also pseudonyms).

(28)
Tomás: *I never played for ~Oñate either.*

(20 Best of Both Worlds, 59:02–59:03)

Integrity of the data is preserved by giving access to linguists undertaking replicable, scientific study who are familiar with the speech community (Labov 1984: 52). Posting speech data on the web for free access may result in misuse of two kinds. On the one hand, researchers unfamiliar with the speech community may unknowingly misunderstand linguistic material. Phonological misinterpretations may be trivial (such as hearing "Tierra María" instead of "Tierra Amarilla," standard [amarija]), or they may compromise linguistic analysis. An example is perceiving Preterit *dij-imos* 'say-PRET.1PL' ([diximos]) instead of Present tense *dec-imos* 'say-PRES.1PL' with aspirated onset /s/ ([deximos] vs. standard [desimos]). Morphological misunderstandings also arise. Researchers lacking knowledge of the community are liable to misinterpret local forms, such as assuming that *muchito* 'kid' (standard *muchachito*) is missing a syllable. More consequential for analysis is, for example, where the local first-person present perfect form *ha* 'I have' is either branded as an error, or is glossed as the third-person form 's/he has' (in northern New Mexico *ha* is a first-person variant, while in other varieties it is only a third-person form).

Lack of intimate knowledge may also make the linguist more liable to unintentionally publish examples that reinforce stereotypes of a minority community or its language variety – for example, excerpts mentioning drunkenness or featuring other-language-origin words in disproportionate amounts (England 1992). Social policy issues are pressing for speakers of non-standard varieties. The tendency to perceive speech categorically results in absorption in, and showcasing of, the forms that are most different from the standard, even if these are exceedingly infrequent. Ultimately, without knowledge of the social setting and the sociolinguistic profiles of the individuals whose speech is sampled, it is not possible to characterize the linguistic phenomenon of interest as a case of change, and if so, as due to contact.

3.4 Prosodically Based Transcription

The study of code-switching and grammatical change is enhanced by prosodically based transcription. The conventions adopted for NMSEB (following the transcription method developed at the University of California, Santa Barbara) and the motivation for their use are explained below (cf. Appendix 1).

The speech stream is segmented into prosodic units, here the Intonation Unit (IU) – "a stretch of speech uttered under a single, coherent intonation contour" (Du Bois, Schuetze-Coburn, Cumming, and Paolino 1993: 47). It is similar to the "intonation group" (Cruttenden 1986), "tone unit" (Crystal 1979), "tone group" or "information unit" (Halliday and Greaves 2008), or the "intonational phrase" (Pierrehumbert and Hirschberg 1990). However, it is not identified on the basis of its internal structure, but by its boundaries, which are delimited by a set of acoustic features. These include initial pitch reset (or rise in fundamental frequency), a change in duration with faster speech early in the IU and lengthening of the final syllable(s), and pausing between IUs (Chafe 1994: 58–60). These cues work together to signal IU boundaries; no single feature individually defines the IU nor is required for the identification of an IU boundary.

Segmenting speech into IUs is done perceptually (see Ford and Thompson 1996: 145–146). Nevertheless, the waveform and pitch tracing in Figure 3.3 serve to illustrate key acoustic features attended to by the transcriber. Here we can observe the higher pitch at the beginning of the IU, gradually dropping over the course of the IU to a fall at the end (with the final intonation), as well as the slower rate of speech at the end of the IU with *chiquita* 'small'.

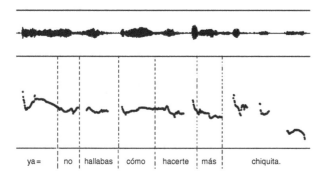

Figure 3.3 Acoustic properties of the Intonation Unit (IU) example (29)

(29)
Ivette: *ya= no hallabas cómo hacerte más chiquita.*
      'you just couldn't find a way to make yourself smaller.'
(06 El Túnico, 06:23–06:25)

Each IU is represented on a single line in the transcription (where the IU does not fit on one line, the second line is indented). IUs are marked for transitional continuity, "the degree of continuity that occurs at the transition point between one intonation unit and the next" (Du Bois et al. 1993: 53). The transcription method distinguishes between three types of transitional continuity, employing standard punctuation symbols to represent each type. In (30), for example, lines (b), (c), (d), and (e) are each marked by a period which indicates "final" intonation, characterized by a fall to low pitch; the comma in lines (a), (f), (g), (h), and (k) indicates "continuing" intonation, which comprises a class of contours, often a slight rise in pitch, but also level, or slightly falling, pitch; and the question mark in lines (i) and (l) indicates "appeal," a high rise in pitch (Du Bois et al. 1993: 54–55).[4] Finally, where the speaker breaks off before completing the prosodic contour, a double hyphen is used to represent such "truncation," as in (j).

(30)
a. Pedro: *y terminaban,* ('and they ended')
b.   *.. @@ ... @ <@ in Fraser Gym @>.*
c.   *at Española.*
d.   *.. packed.*
e.   *you couldn't even get in.*
f.   *... just packed packed pa=cked,*
g.   *and,*
h.   *... they would spend half of the time uh,*
i.   *... mopping the floor?*
j.   *because uh --*
k.   *there was so much humidity,*
l.   *no?*
(07 Basketball Teams, 01:01–01:12)

The prosodic contour is not independent from syntactic structure – while continuing intonation projects something more, final intonation suggests completion (Ford and Thompson 1996: 153). This can be seen in (a)–(b) in (30), where *y terminaban*, 'and they ended', with continuing intonation, and the prepositional phrase *in Fraser Gym*. with final intonation, together form what could be considered a "prosodic sentence"; likewise for (h)–(i) (Chafe 1994: 139). Note, however, that transitional continuity is marked on the basis of prosody not syntax; a complete syntactic unit in an IU with final intonation may

---

[4] The Spanish punctuation convention of utilizing two question marks to bracket questioned material (¿ ?) is not followed, as transitional continuity is only relevant at the end of the IU.

be subsequently extended with an "increment," as in (b)–(c) (cf. Ford, Fox, and Thompson 2002). Similarly, while appeal intonation is often used with yes/no questions, not all instances of appeal intonation are associated with questions (as in line (i)), and conversely, not all questions have appeal intonation.

IUs are clausal (i.e., contain a finite verb) about one-half of the time. This is the case for NMSEB (36,000 of the 76,000 IUs produced by participants), and has been reported for conversational data in other languages (e.g., Iwasaki and Tao 1993; Izre'el 2005; Matsumoto 2003; cf. Chafe 1994: 66). The remaining IUs mostly consist of just one word, including backchannels and discourse markers, such as *yeah* and *you know*, the tag *no?*, conjunctions, fillers such as *uh, hm*, and laughter (@), as well as constituents smaller than the clause, such as prepositional phrases and other adverbials.

3.5   Prosody and Bilingual Speech

Prosodically based transcription is of particular consequence to language contact studies. One advantage is that smooth code-switching is captured by the transcription protocols. As illustrated in Figure 3.4, English and Spanish are juxtaposed seamlessly both within a single IU (as in line (a)), and across an IU boundary linked by a comma (as in (b) and (c)).

The prosodic boundary turns out to be a major delimiter of code-switching in bilingual discourse. Code-switching sites tend to coincide with the IU boundary, rather than to occur within the IU. Table 3.3 gives the proportion of multi-word code-switching occurring across vs. within the IU in a sample from NMSEB. IUs were tagged as bilingual, with both multi-word Spanish and multi-word English; as Spanish or English, where there was no other-language item of any sort; and as containing a lone item if there were single other-language words. IUs with proper nouns, discourse markers, or backchannels such as *okay, yeah*, language-neutral fillers such as *eh, uh*, and ambiguous-language *no* were tagged as such. Counted as code-switches were bilingual IUs as well as IUs in a different language from

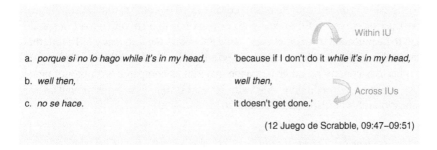

		Within IU
a. *porque si no lo hago while it's in my head,*		'because if I don't do it *while it's in my head,*
b. *well then,*		*well then,*
		Across IUs
c. *no se hace.*		it doesn't get done.'

(12 Juego de Scrabble, 09:47–09:51)

Figure 3.4 Code-switching across vs. within Intonation Units

Table 3.3 *Proportion of code-switching occurring across vs. within the Intonation Unit*

	N	%
Code-switching across IUs	152	93%
Spanish preceded by English or English preceded by Spanish IU		
Code-switching within IUs	12	7%
Bilingual IUs: multi-word Spanish and English in same IU		
No code-switching	920	
Spanish preceded by Spanish or English preceded by English IU		

NMSEB sample, from Plaistowe (2015: Table 3, Table 9).
Excluded from calculation of code-switches are cases in which the preceding IU ends in, or is constituted by, a lone other-language item.

that of the preceding IU. The great majority of code-switching occurs across IUs (cf. Shenk 2006: 188).

Transcribing prosodic features also gives the means to operationalize hypotheses about bilingualism for natural speech data. For example, a widely embraced hypothesis is that switching between languages incurs processing costs (e.g., Altarriba, Kroll, Sholl, and Rayner 1996). Disfluencies such as pauses and truncations supply a possible diagnostic test of cognitive effort in spontaneous speech (cf. Dumont 2010). Both are annotated in the transcription method employed here: pausing with dots, and truncation with hyphens. Pauses may be associated with IU boundaries (in which case they are marked IU initially), and may have interactional relevance related to turn taking (Couper-Kuhlen and Ono 2007: 514; Goodwin 1980). Pauses also occur IU internally (as in (31)), and it is here where they can most aptly be used as a measure of disfluency, where, for example, they may be a locus of corrections, such as before words of high lexical content (Croft 2007: 2).

Wilson and Dumont (2015) examine the occurrence of pauses and truncations with the bilingual compound verb [*hacer* 'do' + Verb$_{Eng}$], a device for integrating an English-origin verb into Spanish, seen in (31). They reason that if the bilingual construction serves to fill lexical gaps or responds to a cognitive load, it should tend to be preceded by disfluencies. Table 3.4 shows the frequency of IU-internal pauses. No higher incidence of pauses was found with [*hacer* 'do' + Verb$_{Eng}$] or in other IUs containing other-language material as compared with monolingual IUs, contrary to prediction. Also similar across the four environments were truncation rates (Wilson and Dumont 2015: 446–450).

(31)
Ivette: *es cuando .. hicimos decide de,*   'that's when .. (we) decided to,'
                    do.PRET.1PL

(06 El Túnico, 43:57–43:59)

Table 3.4 *Pauses in Intonation Units with other-language material vs. in monolingual IUs*

	%	IU-internal pauses
Monolingual IUs		
All Spanish	4%	(115/2,589)
All English	4%	(59/1,376)
IUs with other-language material		
hacer 'do' + Verb$_{Eng}$	4%	(4/105)
At least one other-language-origin word*	4%	(22/529)

NMSEB sample, from Wilson and Dumont (2015: Table 2).
* Established borrowings in monolingual dictionaries were not counted as other-language-origin items (Wilson and Dumont 2015: 452).

3.6   Prosody and Syntax

The demarcation of prosodic units is not only relevant to bilingual speech, but also sharpens the analysis of linguistic structure more generally, as syntax is linked with prosody. A manifestation of such a link is that words in the same IU tend to have a tighter syntactic relationship than material across different IUs (Croft 1995: 849–864). Take the prosodic positioning of complement clauses. While main clauses tend not to co-occur in the same IU, complement clauses tend to be in the same IU as their main clause. This generalization follows from several findings. Fewer than one-fifth (6,400) of all clauses in NMSEB occur with another clause in the same IU (and an even lower proportion in elicited narrative data, Croft 1995: 845; Du Bois 1987: 813). In contrast, finite clausal complements are mostly realized in the same IU as the main verb, as in (32) (78%, N = 844, and 68%, N = 328, respectively, in conversational English and Spanish data, Steuck 2016: 80). Prosodic and syntactic separation go together: the strongest factor *dis*favoring occurrence in the same IU is material intervening between the main and complement clause, for example, *Yo no creo, pues, que eso sea lo mejor* 'I don't think, then, that that would be best' (Steuck 2016: 88). The rate of same-IU occurrence appears to be higher still for non-finite complement clauses (92 percent, N = 286, in a conversational corpus recorded in Madrid, Spain, Sánchez-Ayala 2001: 211).

(32)
Betty: ... *I guess she didn't hurt herself in the accident,*

(13 La Acequia, 13:16–13:18)

Given the correlation between prosodic integration and syntactic relationship, one familiar problem that prosodically based transcription can address is the status of first-person-singular *I* + verb collocations, including *I think, I don't know,*

I guess. These may be main verbs that take a complement clause, or conventionalized formulas akin to epistemic adverbials such as *maybe* (e.g., Thompson
2002). For example, *I guess* is frequent, by virtue of constituting nearly all
occurrences of the verb *guess* (99 percent, N = 165), and is often used formulai-
cally, appearing with complementizer *that* less than 5 percent of the time (four
times below the average for complement-taking predicates, N = 2,820, in a corpus
of spoken Canadian English; Torres Cacoullos and Walker 2009: 20–21).

Prosodically based transcription provides a replicable way to determine if
a non-parenthetical token of *I guess* counts as a proper clause or as a discourse
formula. Drawing an association between prosodic and syntactic independence, we can treat tokens of *I guess* (and *I think, I don't know*) that occur on
their own in an IU, as in (33), as discourse markers rather than main clauses
(compare (32)). Their formulaic status is supported by lack of stress on
I (Travis and Torres Cacoullos 2014: 363–366).

(33)
Ivette: *I don't know,*
          I guess,
          .. I enjoy it better like .. in the cold.

(06 El Túnico, 39:20–39:24)

3.6.1   *Prosody and the Study of Subject Expression*

Prosody is decisive for assigning pronouns to verbs. Given variability in both
subject pronoun expression and position in Spanish, two verbs are sometimes
candidates for the one subject pronoun. For example, in *allá nací yo allá mi crié,*
'I was born there I was raised there' the 1sg pronoun *yo* could be a postverbal
subject on *nací yo* ('was born I'), or a preverbal subject on *yo allá me crié* ('I was
raised there'). Once IUs are identified, as transcribed in (34), the clauses are
clearly demarcated: *yo* is revealed to be a postverbal subject on *nací* – as there is
no prosodic break between them – while *me crié* has an unexpressed subject
(indicated with a Ø preceding the verb in the original and parentheses around the
pronoun in the translation).

(34)
Javier: ... *allá nací yo,*   '... I was born there,
          .. *allá Ø me crié.*   .. (I) was raised there.'

(17 La Comadreja, 1:13:43–1:13:45)

The IU is pivotal to the interpretation of examples such as (34), because, in
accordance with the correlation between syntactic and prosodic units, there is
a strong tendency for subject pronouns and verbs to occur in the same IU.
In Spanish, over 98 percent of subject pronouns are realized in the same IU as
their verb (NMSEB, N = 5,571; CCCS, N = 2,802). Croft proposes that

breaking of clauses between subject and verb in different IUs may reflect complexity; for example, subject noun phrases with a relative clause are more likely than simple lexical subjects to occur in a distinct IU from the verb (1995: 856–859).

When a pronoun occurs in a different IU from the verb, it is not always possible to tell whether it should be considered its subject (and thus a candidate for inclusion in a study of subject expression). For example, the "dislocated" *yo* 'I' in (35) could be associated with both, or neither, of the two verbs in the following IUs, functioning as a "topic" (Davidson 1996: 546–547; Otheguy and Zentella 2012: 237–238).

(35)
Bartolomé: *.. fui a trabajar en California y=,*   '.. I went to work in California and,
            ... y yo,   ... and I,
            todo lo que aprendí,   everything (I) learned,
            lo aprendí ... con el radio=,   (I) learned it ... with the radio,'
                                                    (02 La Marina, 30:28–30:36)

IU-based transcription provides an objective procedure for coding pronouns detached from the verb. While pauses have been recognized as undercutting the subject-verb association (e.g., Otheguy and Zentella 2012: 236–237), IU-based transcription supplies the criterion of type of intonation contour, or transitional continuity, to guide decisions on the status of pronouns or nouns. Pronouns in an IU that is prosodically linked to the IU of the verb via a continuing intonation contour, as in (36), are potential expressed subjects of that verb. Those separated from the verb by final intonation or truncation (double hyphen), as in (37), where the speaker breaks off and restarts, are excluded from the study of subject expression.

(36)
Leandro: *... they bought it from that guy from,*   '... they bought it from that guy from,
          de mi tío pues él,   from my uncle well he,
          se la había vendido a un gabacho.   had sold it to a Yankee.'
                                                     (25 El Servicio, 57:46–57:50)

(37)
Inmaculada: *porque él --*   'because he --
             ... trabajaba y,   ... (he) worked and,'
                                  (08 Graduación Familiar Pt2, 23:08–27:05)

Similarly, in (38), we count the noun *hermano* 'brother' as the subject of the verb, on the strength of the linking between the IUs of noun and verb by continuing intonation. In (39), however, *hija* 'daughter' is separated from the verb by final intonation (here, appeal, indicated with a question mark) and therefore may or may not be the subject; such indeterminate cases are best excluded from analysis of subjects.

(38)
Rocío: ... *y mi hermano el mayor,*   '... and my <u>brother</u> the oldest,
          .. dormía en la sala.   .. slept in the lounge room.'

                                              (05 Las Tortillas, 05:02–05:05)

(39)
Mariana: ... *la hija que vive aquí?*   '... our <u>daughter</u> who lives here?
          nos mandó una tarjeta.   (she) sent us a card.'

                                              (19 School Bus, 1:08:57–1:09:01)

In sum, prosodically based transcription is useful for the identification of syntactic units in speech, where the notion of the sentence is not readily applicable (Croft 1995: 841; Miller 1995: 132). We saw, for example, how formulaic instances of frequent collocations such as *I guess* can be distinguished from main-clause uses with the aid of prosodic position. And for pronouns, when separated from verbs, transitional continuity between prosodic units provides an objective criterion to determine their status as subjects.

3.7   Conclusion

Whereas we write in sentences, in spoken discourse the basic unit is prosodic. In this chapter we have seen that the reliability of grammatical analyses will be affected by the reliability of the transcription. Transcription based on the IU responds to this problem, by providing a replicable way to demarcate structural units in speech. The IU is particularly valuable in *bilingual* speech, serving as a major delimiter of code-switching, which tends to occur at IU boundaries. Prosodic features, including pausing and truncation, also allow testing of hypotheses about bilingual processing in spontaneous production data.

The compilation of a bilingual corpus amenable to systematic quantitative analysis is a prerequisite for probing contact-induced change as, in the absence of replicable analysis, categorical perception will exacerbate the predilection for spotlighting the expedient colorful example. Bilingual norms are discernible in a corpus that is community based, in terms of both the speaker sample and the data collection and handling. Natural bilingual interactions in two languages – from the same speaker in the same setting – are recorded here by building on the foundation of sociolinguistic corpus compilation and the strategy of the sociolinguistic interview, conducted by in-group fieldworkers. The result is copious amounts of code-switching. This, it bears stressing, was neither directly nor indirectly elicited, as verified by a test of speaker alignment with the interlocutor in language choice. The sociolinguistic interviews themselves verify participants' highly accomplished bilingualism, as discussed in the following chapter.

4   Characterizing the Bilingual Speaker

The contact-induced change hypothesis is that bilinguals' use of two languages spawns similarity between their grammars. If language change is due to contact as opposed to other sources, it should be first and foremost observable in similarities between the languages *as spoken by the bilinguals*. Differences between the same speakers' two languages, on the other hand, would provide the strongest kind of evidence against convergence between their two language varieties.

Testing the hypothesis of contact-induced grammatical change thus requires copious amounts of the two languages produced by the bilingual speakers themselves, the locus of the contact. Testing the hypothesis of the role of code-switching in such change requires copious amounts of code-switching. Yet, with few exceptions (Poplack, Zentz, and Dion 2012b), in the absence of truly bilingual speech corpora, stringent tests of the contact-induced grammatical change hypothesis have been lacking. The NMSEB corpus fulfills both requirements by purposefully sampling highly bilingual speakers.

Even highly bilingual individuals may have different *degrees* of contact with the majority language. If contact-induced grammatical change is in progress, linguistic behavior should show correlations with some external measure of contact. Extralinguistic characterization of the bilingual speakers is therefore indispensable.

How to assess speakers' bilingualism? An important tool is the composite sociolinguistic profile (Section 4.1), which integrates different sources of information. We begin with quantitative analysis of speaker self-reports (4.2), and go on to demonstrate the benefits of a content analysis of the recordings for accurate understanding of bilingual experience (4.3). In revealing linguistic attitudes, the content analysis also lays bare the use of language alternation as a discourse mode rather than a rhetorically moti-vated phenomenon in this community (4.4). A final measure to assess individuals' degree of bilingualism is provided by their very production data (4.5).

4.1   Constructing a Sociolinguistic Profile

Choosing a sample of bilingual speakers by subjecting them to a battery of proficiency tests such as those administered for experimental studies is often inappropriate, given the association of such tests with just the kinds of educational institutions that have demoted minority-language varieties. Moreover, outside the university context, proficiency tests are dubious since performance in experimental tasks is correlated with formal education (Dąbrowska 2012). For NMSEB we required instead that participants all meet the criterion of *regular use* of both languages, with the same interlocutor in the same setting, as observed over time by the fieldworkers or as reported to the fieldworkers by other acquaintances (cf. Poplack 1993: 254). Participants thus defined may still of course differ in degree of contact. But how can this information be reliably obtained? Here, we construct a sociolinguistic profile of the participants by triangulating data from:

(1) Self-reports in response to questionnaire items

Following the recorded sociolinguistic interview (Chapter 3, Section 3.2.1), fieldworkers filled in responses to a short questionnaire on participants' demographic background (Chapter 2, Table 2.1) and linguistic history: self-ratings of their Spanish and English, and self-reports on domains of use of, and contact with, the two languages.

(2) Content analysis of the recordings

We systematically extracted from the transcribed recordings sociodemo-graphic, linguistic-history, and language-attitude information that arises naturally in the course of the conversations. Content analysis contextua-lizes questionnaire responses – supplementing, in some cases correcting, and more generally allowing for the interpretation of self-reports – and brings to light topics not anticipated by the questionnaire.

(3) The production data themselves

These comprise stretches of both Spanish and English. The distribution of clauses between the two languages for each participant complements extralinguistic measures of degree of contact.

4.2   Principal Component Analysis of Self-reports

To obtain measures of degree of contact with English, we tabulated speakers' responses to 10 questionnaire items on: first language and where English was learned (home, school or both); preferred language; self-rating of English and Spanish; language(s) spoken with family, among friends, and at work; and the preferred language for listening to the radio, watching TV, and reading books. This provided an indication of the highly bilingual lifestyles of the partici-pants. In the aggregate, NMSEB speakers stated that their first language was

Spanish (35 of 40 participants) and that they learned English at school (32/40). They report using both languages not just in the home (31/40), but also with friends (31/40) and at work (24/40). All NMSEB participants rated themselves as either a four or five for both languages on a scale from one to five, and most rated both languages equally (25/40) (Travis and Torres Cacoullos 2013: 182).

Responses to the questionnaire were tabulated by assigning a score from one to three to each item, 3 indicating more English, 1 more Spanish, and 2 somewhere in between, such as when a response of "both" was given. While we could sum each speaker's scores as a measure of contact (Travis and Torres Cacoullos 2013: 183), responses may not be independent of each other or may not contribute equally to the mean score. To address this, we carried out data optimization using PCA to reduce the multidimensional space made up of the 10 questionnaire items to a smaller number of orthogonal components, which partition that space (as described in Chapter 2, Section 2.5) (cf. Hoffman and Walker 2010: 47–48).

PCA reduced the 10 responses to four principal components that accounted for 73 percent of the total variance in the dataset. We interpret these as: preferred language overall (PC1), preferred language for TV (PC2) and radio (PC3), and relative self-rating of the two languages (PC4). Table 4.1 shows the associations (loadings) of each of the 10 questions with these

Table 4.1 *Loadings of questionnaire items on Principal Components*

Questionnaire item	PC1 Preference	PC2 TV	PC3 Radio	PC4 Self-rating
Preferred language	0.64	−0.37	0.17	0.32
First language	0.23	−0.07	0.34	−0.52
Self-rating (relative English–Spanish)	0.17	−0.11	0.34	0.53
How English learned	0.24	−0.07	0.39	−0.56
Preferred language				
... radio	0.53	0.37	−0.49	−0.09
... TV	0.13	0.81	0.42	0.17
... books	0.09	−0.05	0.11	0.05
Language spoken				
... with family	0.005	−0.21	0.07	−0.004
... with friends	0.23	−0.02	−0.32	−0.09
... at work	0.30	−0.01	−0.22	−0.02
Variance accounted for	32%	16%	14%	11%

principal components; cell shading indicates questions with relatively stronger associations (with a magnitude greater than 0.4, cf. Horvath and Sankoff 1987: 194).

The first principal component (PC1), preferred language, alone accounts for 32 percent of the variance (given in the bottom row). One-half of the speakers report preferring English (20/40), close to one-third Spanish (12/40), and the remainder state "both" (8/40). Note that preferred language scores show at best a weak correlation with self-rating scores using a Pearson correlation test ($r = 0.32$, $p = .045$). While fewer than one-fourth (8/40) of NMSEB speakers report that they prefer both languages, most (25/40) self-rate their English and Spanish as equal; the rest are evenly divided between rating their Spanish (7/40) or their English (8/40) higher. Nor does preferred language correlate with reported first language ($r = 0.33$, $p = .038$). Speakers listing Spanish as their first language are just as likely to rate Spanish (6/35) as English (7/35) as their stronger language, with most indicating that both are equal (22/35). In fact, self-rating and first language load onto a distinct principal component from preferred language (PC4), and do so with opposite signs from each other. Preferred language and relative self-rating can be used, then, as two independent measures of degrees of bilingualism.

4.2.1   Language Preference and Self-rating

The hypothesis of grammatical convergence would predict that contact-induced change should be more visible or more advanced among speakers with a higher degree of bilingualism. For Spanish subject pronoun expression, comparison of speaker groupings is expected to reveal higher subject pronoun rates for speakers who state a preference and/or a higher rating for English. Recall that social factors do not influence NMSEB bilinguals' Spanish subject pronoun rate (Chapter 2, Section 2.5.2). Here we see that neither is it affected by preferred language score, as shown in Figure 4.1, nor by self-rating, in Figure 4.2. These measures of degree of bilingualism, then, fail to support contact-induced grammatical change.

Two other factors that emerge in the PCA are language preferred for TV and radio. NMSEB speakers mostly prefer to listen to the radio in Spanish (27/40) but to watch TV in English (30/40). How to explain the discrepancy? Apart from some local TV news, television programming comes from Los Angeles, Miami, or other national and international sources. Beyond the content of the programming, from Diana and Marco's remark in (40) below that "they talk very fast" we gather that television Spanish is seen as distinct from the local variety. On the other hand, there are local radio stations that

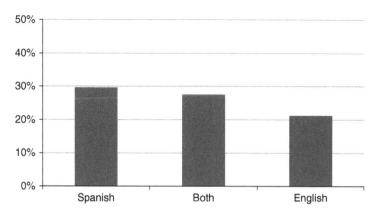

Figure 4.1 Rate of subject pronouns according to reported preferred language
12 speakers prefer Spanish (N = 1,191; *M* = 30%, *SD* = 17.1),
8 both languages (N = 1,544; *M* = 28%, *SD* = 12.8),
20 English (N = 2,836; *M* = 21%, *SD* = 8.7), *F* = 1.91, *p* = .163.

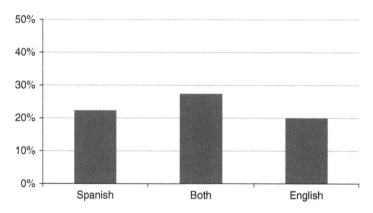

Figure 4.2 Rate of subject pronouns according to relative self-rating
7 speakers rate their Spanish higher than their English (N = 1,141; *M* = 22%,
SD = 11.8),
25 both languages the same (N = 3,762; *M* = 27%, *SD* = 13.9),
8 English higher than Spanish (N = 668; *M* = 20%, *SD* = 9.0), *F* = 1.21, *p* = .310.

play New Mexican music, and we infer positive affect toward New Mexican
language and culture from speakers' mentions of local stations such as
KDCE (Española) and KDNM (Reserve), and New Mexican bands such as
Cuarenta Y Cinco.

(40)

Diana:	... *y hay en veces me pongo a*	'... and there are times when I start
	escuchar áhi el televisión.	listening to the television.
	... en español,	... in Spanish,
	y me quedo no más con que,	and I am just,'
Marco:	*@[@@]*	'@[@@]'
Ricardo:	*[@@]*	'[@@]'
Diana:	*@*	'@
	.. qué está hablando ésa,	.. what is she saying,
	le digo a [éste].	I ask [him].'
Ricardo:	*[qué está hab-] --*	'[what is she sa-] --'
Diana:	*@@*	'@@'
Marco:	*.. hablan muy rápido.*	'.. they talk very fast.'

(24 La Floresta, 48:50–49:03)

Solving the discrepancy between TV and radio language preferences illustrates how content analysis allows us to use – together with our intimate knowledge of the community – the participants' own comments to properly interpret the measures of degree of contact that are suggested by the PCA based on the questionnaire responses.

4.3   Growing Up Bilingual, Defying L1 vs. L2 Dichotomies

Content analysis of the sociolinguistic interviews is carried out through systematic extraction of all comments arising in the course of the conversations that provide information relevant to the sociolinguistic profile of the participants. These are categorized as responses to "virtual" questions (Poplack, Walker, and Malcolmson 2006: 196–207). Compiling such comments goes beyond questionnaires in a number of ways.

The content – what people actually say in their own words – brings to the analyst's attention issues and attitudes relevant to the community beyond the pre-determined categories imposed by the questionnaire. It is telling that not all the categories resulting from the content analysis correspond to those in the questionnaire, some examples being the stigmatization of New Mexican Spanish, contact with Mexicans, and language choice in younger and older generations (illustrated in examples given in Chapter 2, Section 2.3). Moreover, questionnaire responses can be interpreted in the context of the community, as in the preference for Spanish radio but English TV described above.

Of particular relevance is speakers' bilingual experience, elicited in the questionnaire items concerning first language, how English was learned, language preference, and self-ratings, but elucidated through the course of the recording.

The speakers' own remarks corroborate that it is misleading to transpose into the setting of the bilingual community constructs that are applied to university students learning a second language or individual nuclear families moving to a new country. For example, language dominance (e.g., Silva-Corvalán and Treffers-Daller 2015), though an intuitive notion, is not straightforwardly operationalizable outside the lab setting, given the standard-language bias of most (proficiency) tests. Preference and self-rating, as we saw, are not correlated. Grosjean has argued that the construct of global dominance glosses over different domains of use of each of a bilingual's languages (2015). Furthermore, were we able to arrive at language dominance scores, these still provide no window on bilinguals' actual experience with their two languages.

Widely evoked dichotomies in second language acquisition research, such as first vs. second language (L1 vs. L2) and simultaneous vs. sequential, or early vs. late, bilinguals, are also not readily applicable to members of bilingual communities. Even self-reports of bilingual ability and responses to direct, apparently simple questions such as "What was your first language?" or "What language do you prefer?" may not be reliable. Some responses from NMSEB participants challenge the very legitimacy of such questions. For example, Inmaculada, who was recorded twice, self-rated her Spanish a 5 both times, but her English a 4 the first time and a 5 the second, a year later; and while she gave English as her first language the first time, she gave Spanish the second. Another speaker, Rocío, rated both her languages a 4, clearly conducting her self-assessment under a normative lens. To the questionnaire item on how English was learned, Leandro responded that it was at school and in the military, but in the course of the sociolinguistic interview, he said that when he first attended school in the south of the state while his dad worked in the mines, he didn't know Spanish (*mexicano*) either (example (41)).

(41)

Leandro:	*allá aprendimos a hablar inglés nosotros.*	'it was there we learned to speak English.'
Ricardo:	*Yeah.*	'Yeah.'
Leandro:	*pues no sabíanos ni el inglés ni el mexicano.*	'well we didn't know English or Spanish.
	Porque,	Because,
	los a- --	the --
	los --	the --
	los mexicanitos esos,	those Mexican guys,
	they --	they --
	.. hablaban muy diferente el mexicano que nosotros,	.. spoke Spanish very differently from us,'
Ricardo:	*Yeah.*	'Yeah.'

Leandro:	*y nosotros hablábanos otra class de*	'and we spoke another kind of
	language sandwich	*language sandwich*
	<@ que [le dicen @>,	*<@ as [they say @>,*
	@@@	*@@@*
	de Nuevo México].	of New Mexico].'
Ricardo:	*[@@@@]*	'[@@@@]'
Leandro:	*pero cuando fuimos allá,*	'but when we went there,'
Ricardo:	*uh [huh].*	'uh [huh].'
Leandro:	*[pues] estábanos como mudos ahí*	'[well] it was like we were mute
	sí ve.	you know.
	@ no sabíanos ni inglés,	@ we didn't know English,
	y no sabíanos el mexicano !bien.	and we didn't know Spanish !well.'

(25 El Servicio, 05:07–05:31)

Notions such as order of acquisition or early vs. late bilinguals, and even the L1-L2 distinction, are blurred where alternating between languages is a fact of daily life. Most NMSEB speakers responded on the questionnaire that Spanish is their "first" language and that they learned English at school. But it is clear from the content analysis that there was English in the community and in the home, from siblings and, in some cases, parents and other adults. It also transpires that they did not necessarily start school knowing no English. Sandra, for example, reports having learned English at school, but she must have had some English at home and in the neighborhood, since she recalls that her brother taught her the ABCs (42), that her sister listened to English radio series (43), and that her mother spoke to English-speaking neighbors (44). In light of the indeterminacy of "order of acquisition" in this bilingual community, Inmaculada's apparent uncertainty over her first language in response to the questionnaire described above comes to make sense.

(42)

Sandra:	*you know my brother was my teacher.*	'you know my brother was my teacher.*
	... we would --	*... we would --*
	.. coming back from the school?	*.. coming back from the school?*
	There in the arroyo?	*There in the arroyo?*
((10 intervening lines))		
	and he would make --	*and he would make --*
	a blackboard out of the sand.	*a blackboard out of the sand.*
	...(0.7) mira,	*...(0.7) look,*
	me decía,	he would say to me,
	...(0.8) lo=s --	*...(0.8) the --*
	.. el --	*.. the --*
	los ay bee cees, ((ABCs))	the ABCs,
	... son .. puros palitos,	*... are .. just little sticks,*
	.. y bolitas.	*.. and little balls.'*

(03 Dos Comadres, 58:01–58:25)

(43)

Sandra:	.. *my sister Rita was into the soap operas.*	'.. *my sister Rita was into the soap operas.*
	.. *on the radio.*	.. *on the radio.*'
Adriana:	.. *mhm.*	'.. *mhm.*'
Sandra:	*y ahí estaba The Romance of Helen Trent.*	'and there was *The Romance of Helen Trent.*
	... *[You=ng Doctor Malone].*	... *[Young Doctor Malone].*'
Adriana:	*[@@@@]*	'*[@@@@]*'
Sandra:	.. *The Edge of Night.*	'.. *The Edge of Night.*
	.. *y quién sabe qué tanto.*	.. and who knows what else.
	...*(1.1) qué tanto más.*	...(1.1) whatever else.'

(03 Dos Comadres, 15:04–15:11)

(44)

Sandra:	.. *so cuando entramos,*	'.. so when we came in,
	oh muy gente la Mrs. Johnson,	oh she was very nice Mrs. Johnson,
	<Q come on in,	*<Q come on in,*
	come on in Q>,	*come on in Q>,*
	y entró mamá,	and mom went in,
	and she could --	*and she could --*
	...*(0.7) she could explain herself,*	...*(0.7) she could explain herself,*
	you know,	*you know,*
	she could speak English.	*she could speak English.*'

(03 Dos Comadres, 1:03:55–1:04:03)

The words of Rocío, who ranked herself as a 4 out of 5 in both languages, starkly evince linguistic insecurity: despite describing herself as someone who entered school knowing only Spanish (as we saw in example (9) in Chapter 2), she claims that she learned Spanish by translating letters from Mexico for her aunt's boss (45). She describes the Spanish in her own family as *mocho* (broken) (46); as an adult, she improved her Spanish while hosting Mexican visitors whom she helped learn English (47). Rocío's use of the label *Spanglish* (in conjunction with *mocho*) in (46) encapsulates the negative view of the local variety (on the term *Spanglish*, see Lipski 2008: 38–74; Otheguy and Stern 2010).

(45)

Rocío: ... *and he used to write letters.*
...*(1.4) to my tía's boss.* ('my aunt's boss')
... *a=nd,*
...*(1.5) eh he .. decided,*
... *that .. I was going to learn how to read them,*
... *and that I was going to have to .. learn how to write.*
... *and I was going to translate them.*
...*(0.9) and that's how I learned how to speak Spanish.*

(05 Las Tortillas, 57:45–58:05)

(46)

Rocío:	.. *mis= hermanos hablaban poquito,*	'.. my brothers and sisters spoke some,
	.. *pero muy <@ mocho @>.*	.. but very <@ broken @>.'
Adriana:	.. *[mocho]?*	'.. [broken]?'
Rocío:	*[@@]*	'[@@]'
Adriana:	*mhm.*	'mhm.'
Rocío:	*[yeah].*	'[yeah].'
Adriana:	*[hm lo] hablaban.*	'[hm they] spoke it.'
Rocío:	...*(0.7) [2the Spanglish2].*	'...(0.7) [2the Spanglish2].'
Adriana:	*[2XXX2]*	'[2XXX2]'
Rocío:	*@*	'@'
Adriana:	.. *sí.*	'.. yes.'
Rocío:	.. *yeah.*	'.. yeah.
	... *they still do.*	... they still do.'

(05 Las Tortillas, 01:39–01:49)

(47)

Rocío: ... *your boys learned how to speak English,*
.. *the same way that they're teaching me,*
the proper way.
... *of speaking Spanish.*

(05 Las Tortillas, 59:32–59:38)

Rather than a regime of ordered first and second language acquisition, the content analysis of the sociolinguistic interviews underscores the pervasiveness of both languages in daily life. There is regular interaction with English speakers, notwithstanding possibly distancing terms for Anglos such as *güero* 'literally: fair skinned' or *gabacho* 'foreigner (Yankee)', seen in (48). Spanish and English are used in public and private gatherings, bilinguals' adapting their language choice (49) and even their name accordingly (50).

(48)

Enrique: *de cuando estaba en el eh- --*   'when I was in the uh --
eh,   uh,
.. *trabajando en la sierra,*   .. working in the mountains,
... *<X in the X> skiing equipment,*   ... <X in the X> skiing equipment,
andaba un gabachito   there was a Yankee
!nosing around.   !nosing around.'

(23 El Pacific, 07:29–07:35)

(49)

Eduardo: *I know=,*
...*(2.0) what we call=,*
los güeros, ('Anglos', literally 'fair skinned people')
Carrie: ... *@@*

Eduardo: .. *if,*
          uh=,
          ... I know if they're arou=nd,
          ... and we are all in a group like that.
          ... I try to s- --
          ... speak to where everybody understands.

(27 Climate Change, 18:00–18:12)

(50)
Enrique: *cada rato me digo ~Henry,*   'I often call myself Henry,
          o ~Enrique,   or Enrique,
          any <@ way @>,   any <@ way @>,'

(23 El Pacific, 31:42–31:45)

4.4 Alternating Between Languages . . . Just Because: Code-switching as a Discourse Mode

In the corpus, the same speakers produce clauses in each of the languages. This is illustrated in the excerpt in (51): Ivette speaks Spanish in lines (c) and (k)–(p), and English in (a)–(b) and (e)–(j). Coding each clause for language (based on the language of the verb) revealed that the two languages are used with equal proportions in the corpus overall, as depicted in Figure 4.3. The even distribution of both languages nullifies notions such as that of an overall "matrix language" (Myers-Scotton 1993) or its obverse, a less-frequently-used "more salient language" (Myslín and Levy 2015: 871).

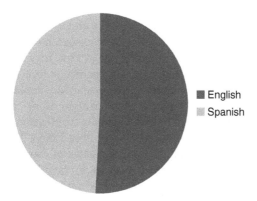

Figure 4.3 Even distribution of clauses between bilinguals' two languages (Spanish N = 17,689, English N = 18,322)

(51)
a.	Ivette:	.. *I've done that.*	'.. *I've done that.*
b.		*not only that one time,*	*not only that one time,*
c.		*e- ahora cuando trabajaba en el Penney's.*	e- now when I was working at Penney's.'
d.	Rafael:	*... por [qué]?*	'... [why]?'
e.	Ivette:	*[I]* --	'*[I]* --
f.		*I set,*	*I set,*
g.		.. *I guess I didn't see the time right,*	.. *I guess I didn't see the time right,*
h.		*and I thought it was* --	*and I thought it was* --
i.		... *right,*	... *right,*
j.		*it was an hour early?*	*it was an hour early?*
k.		...*(0.8) y,*	...(0.8) and,
l.		... *me alisté y todo,*	... I got ready and everything,
m.		.. *y luego me fui,*	.. and then I left,
n.		... *y vi el parking lot todo oscuro,*	... and I saw the parking lot all dark,
o.		*y dije pues,*	and I said well,
p.		... *dónde están .. todos?*	... where is .. everyone?'

(06 El Túnico, 22:26–22:44)

Now, a widely embraced idea is that particular elements of the linguistic or extralinguistic context precipitate code-switching. Over the decades, a variety of sociocultural, interactional, or discourse determinants of code-switching have been put forward, often involving the bilingual abilities of the interlocutor, the topic, the establishment of identity, particular rhetorical functions, or the information status of the other-language item (e.g., Auer 1995; Bhatt and Bolonyai 2011; Gumperz 1976/1982; Myslín and Levy 2015). Switching to another language may serve metalinguistic functions such as marking direct speech or excluding a participant who does not know the language, as is reported to be the case, for example, for Tariana and Tucano in northwest Amazonia in Brazil (Aikhenvald 2002: 190–191).

Unlike locally motivated code-switching, "intra-situational" code-switching is where two languages are brought to bear in a single speech event with no change in interlocutor, situation, or even topic, i.e., no external trigger (Poplack 2015). Here the alternation between languages lacks particular local rhetorical goals, but functions globally as a community discourse mode (Poplack 1998, 2000 [1980]). Code-switching in northern New Mexico is of the intra-situational kind, described as "the appropriate code for the Hispano community" by Gonzales, based on ethnographic participant-observation (1999: 29).

The NMSEB conversations strongly support the status of code-switching between Spanish and English as a discourse mode in northern New Mexico, with the content analysis laying bare a striking lack of particular motivations for alternating between languages. This is evident, on the one hand, in that not a single participant makes mention of any particular value attached to one or the other language. It was only in relation to Spanish church hymns and prayers that one language was singled out as more expressive than the other. This point arose fleetingly, and just 3 times, in 2 of the 31 conversations. Example (52) illustrates.

(52)

Victoria:	*they= .. sing a song called Madre Morena.*	'*they .. sing a song called Madre Morena.*
	...(1.0) está bien suave,	*...(1.0) it's really nice,*
	it's beautiful.	*it's beautiful.*'
		(12 Juego de Scrabble, 33:08–33:15)

In contrast to the stark lack of comments on motivations for switching, many NMSEB participants make reference to the ease with which they switch between the two languages. Eduardo in (53) describes doing so unintentionally, as the two languages 'get crossed' (*la lengua se atraviesa*), just speaking 'whatever language comes up' (*lo que venga*), as Bartolomé puts it in (54). The facility in using either language can also be seen here, where Bartolomé states that he will simply respond in the language he is addressed in.

(53)

Eduardo:	*...(1.0) we can=,*	'*...(1.0) we can,*
	... be talking in English,	*... be talking in English,*
	y=,	*and,*
	...(1.0) en media conversación,	*...(1.0) in the middle of the conversation,*
	estamos hablando españo=l.	*we're speaking Spanish.*
	.. yo=,	*.. I,*
	hay veces que me hallo,	*sometimes I find myself,*
	... donde estoy hablando inglé=s,	*... where I'm speaking English,*
	...(1.4) y cuando menos acuerdo,	*...(1.4) and before I know it,*
	la persona,	*the person,*
	que estoy ha- --	*who I'm --*
	.. con la que estoy platicando o algo,	*.. who I'm speaking to or whatever,*
	.. se= me en=traviesa el español,	*.. Spanish crosses over,*
	la lengua se atraviesa y,	*the language crosses over and,*
	y ahí estoy hablándole en mexicano,	*there I am speaking to them in Spanish,*'
		(27 Climate Change, 21:54–22:18)

(54)

Bartolomé:	*...(1.2) lo que venga.*	'*...(1.2) whatever comes out.*'
Gabriel:	*...(1.3) sí=.*	'*...(1.3) yes.*
	...(1.1) y cuál prefiere hablar en español o en inglés?	*...(1.1) and which do you prefer to speak in Spanish or in English?*'
Bartolomé:	*...(2.0) pues sabes que yo nunca ha puesto at- --*	'*...(2.0) well you know I have never paid at- --*

...(0.7) atención,	...(0.7) attention,
...(0.8) si me hablan en español les	...(0.8) if they speak to me in
hablo .. les respondo en español.	Spanish I speak to me in .. answer
	them in Spanish.
Si me hablan en inglés les respondo	If they speak to me in English I
en inglés.	answer them in English.'

(02 La Marina, 57:17–57:36)

There is also good indication that NMSEB participants switch equally well from one language to the other – just as Spanish may pop in to the conversation when speaking English, as we saw for Eduardo in (53), English may pop in to an otherwise Spanish conversation. Mónica, in (55), talks of speaking "half-half" English and Spanish, a sentiment echoed by Miguel in (56).

(55)

Mónica:	*siempre estábanos hablando,*	'we were always talking,
	... mitad y mitad español,	... half and half Spanish,
	y mitad inglés=.	and half English.'

(11 El Trabajo, 00:44–00:48)

(56)

Rafael:	*...(2.6) what do you think you'd know*	'...(2.6) what do you think you'd
	better?	know better?
	.. as far as language?	.. as far as language?
	.. do you think you know more	.. do you think you know more
	English?	English?
	Or do you think you know more	Or do you think you know more
	Spanish?	Spanish?'
Miguel:	*...(1.0) X XX.*	'...(1.0) X XX.'
Rafael:	*... or would you say you're equal?*	'... or would you say you're equal?
	... what do you think?	... what do you think?'
Miguel:	*... I'd say that I'm equal.*	'... I'd say that I'm equal.'
Rafael:	*...(0.7) really?*	'...(0.7) really?'
Miguel:	*...(1.7) yeah.*	'...(1.7) yeah.
	...(2.7) porque like I say,	...(2.7) because like I say,
	you know,	you know,
	like I was telling you,	like I was telling you,
	...(1.1) cuando estoy con mexicanos,	...(1.1) when I'm with Mexicans,
	o algo que --	or something that --
	.. son de México?	.. they're from Mexico?
	.. como que entonces quiero hablar	.. it's like then I want to speak
	es- --	Span- --
	.. <@ inglés @>.	.. <@ English @>.
	.. como que se me sale más easy.	.. it's like it's more easy for me.
	.. y --	.. and --
	... y como que no <@ me hallo las	... and it's like I don't <@ find
	words @> pa' Spanish.	the words @> for Spanish.
	.. muy curioso.	.. very strange.'

Rafael:	.. how [funny].	'.. how [funny].'
Miguel:	[y] --	'[and] --
	... y en inglés,	... and in English,
	when I'm speaking,	when I'm speaking,
	... hay veces que quiero poner	... there are times when I want to put
	una .. Spanish word in there.	a .. Spanish word in there.'

(04 Piedras y Gallinas, 1:10:38–1:11:24)

4.5 A Linguistic Gauge of Degree of Contact

Earlier in this chapter we considered extralinguistic measures of degree of bilingualism, obtained through self-reports, which were driven largely by stated language preference (English, Spanish, or both) and also by self-ratings of language ability. We saw that neither measure of contact with English correlates with Spanish subject pronoun expression, and both provide but a superficial view of linguistic experience for members of this bilingual community.

Linguistic distributions in the production data can be used as alternative measures of speaker differences. However, note that even measures of an individual's bilingualism based on overall rates of linguistic features are not unfailingly decisive. To illustrate, we could appeal to the normalized frequency of other-language words spontaneously produced by a speaker. This would be a plausible measure were it not for the fact that overall rates are susceptible to fluctuation according to conversational topics or other situational parameters. For example, Inmaculada, who was recorded twice, had a standardized count of 7 English-origin nouns per 10,000 words in one recording and 51 in the other (Aaron 2015: 480), a seven-fold increase!

Here we take a linguistic gauge of degree of contact based on the distribution of clauses between the two languages for each participant, what we refer to as language predominance. The even distribution of Spanish and English clauses in the corpus is an aggregate measure that can vary from speaker to speaker. While language predominance is not an absolute measure of language dominance since it, too, is susceptible to situational parameters, it could be taken as a proxy for the speaker's relative amounts of use of the two languages in their daily lives. Alternatively, it could be seen as an operationalization of relative "activation" level of each language (e.g., Kroll, Bobb and Wodniecka 2006), or of language "modes" in a situational continuum (Grosjean 1998; 2001). A greater proportion of English clauses would be consistent with greater activation of that language, or a more bilingual mode.

Speakers were categorized as "English predominant" if fewer than one-third of their clauses (finite verbs) were Spanish (N = 13 speakers), "Spanish-predominant" if more than two-thirds of their clauses were Spanish (N = 12), and "both" if the proportion of Spanish clauses was more than one-third but

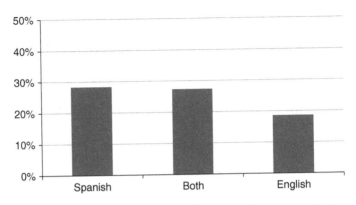

Figure 4.4 Rate of subject pronouns according to language predominance
12 speakers produce more than two-thirds of their clauses in Spanish
(N = 2,448; *M* = 29%, *SD* = 11.2),
15 between one and two-thirds (N = 2,428; *M* = 28%, *SD* = 16.4),
13 fewer than one-third (N = 695; *M* = 19%, *SD* = 6.4), *F* = 2.61, *p* = .087.[1]

less than two-thirds of their total clause count (N = 15). Language "predominance" is an independent measure of degree of contact. It does not correlate with participants' stated language preference ($r = -0.01$, $p = .96$), nor strongly with self-rating ($r = 0.31$, $p = .05$). Both Mónica and Molly, for example, report that they prefer to speak Spanish but rate their English as higher. And while Mónica uses the two languages equally in the recording, Molly uses Spanish more than she does English.

For subject expression, the hypothesis of contact-induced grammatical change would predict a higher rate of Spanish subject pronouns for "English predominant" speakers. Pronoun rates by language predominance as depicted in Figure 4.4 are not significantly different.

4.6   Conclusion

While bilingual speakers are often categorized according to degree of bilingualism or degree of contact with majority language speakers on the basis of proficiency tests or questionnaire responses, such measures are easily misinterpreted, especially for speakers of non-standard varieties. Instead, a sociolinguistic profile characterizing the linguistic experiences and attitudes of the community can be constructed with systematic content analysis of recorded conversations. What bilinguals say in their own words brings out

---

[1] Only 12 percent (N = 695) of the subject expression tokens corresponds to the third group, so the (non-significantly) lower rate should not be over-interpreted.

issues and attitudes beyond the categories imposed by the questionnaire. It is misleading to transpose constructs such as language dominance or dichotomies such as first vs. second language (L1 vs L2) into the community setting, where alternating between languages is a fact of daily life.

Though individuals appear to vary in the degree of contact they have with English, when different measures deriving from optimization of questionnaire responses are applied, the measures do not correlate with each other nor do they show systematic correlation with subject expression. Thus, neither self-reported preference nor a higher self-rating for English leads to a higher rate of Spanish subject pronouns. The proportion of English clauses produced by a speaker does not affect rates of Spanish subject pronouns either. All three – independent – measures of degree of contact counter a hypothesis of contact-induced grammatical change.

NMSEB is a true bilingual corpus. Testimony to the bilingual character of the speakers, and the unrivalled corpus recording their natural use of both languages, is the overall even distribution of Spanish and English clauses. This will allow thorough comparisons for both of the bilinguals' languages. Critically, NMSEB records abundant smooth multi-word code-switching, the discourse mode of the northern New Mexican community. This sets it apart from corpora in which material from the other language is sparse and rhetorically motivated or is restricted to single-word items. The bilingual speech that is faithfully captured constitutes the most apposite data source for putting grammatical change instigated by code-switching to the test. In the next chapter we dissect the linguistic structure that has featured in many a claim of contact-induced change: subject pronoun expression.

5   Subject Pronoun Expression: Reconsidering the Constraints

A claim of grammatical change in a bilingual variety must rest on comparison with a quantitative monolingual benchmark. A *quantitative* benchmark shields the analysis from comparisons with idealized states and supplies discerning criteria in terms of distribution and co-occurrence patterns. In this chapter, we establish such an operational benchmark for subject pronoun expression in Spanish. We know from over four decades of studies that Spanish variable subject expression – with pronominal and unexpressed (or null) subjects as competing variants – is probabilistically constrained by a number of language-internal factors. Here, we revisit these factors, considering their interpretation in cross-linguistic perspective as cognitive, communicative, and interactional constraints.

In accounting for the use of subject pronouns, grammarians and linguists have long privileged the functions of contrast or emphasis (Section 5.1) and ambiguity resolution (5.2), yet instantiations of these functions account for small proportions of the data. The most replicated effect is that of accessibility configured as subject continuity (5.3). Also robust is priming, or repetition of the most recently used variant (5.4). Differences among main, subordinate, and coordinate clauses turn out to reflect strength of prosodic and syntactic linking between the target and the previous subject in coreferential contexts (5.5). The much-debated effects of verb tense may have less to do with syncretism in person morphology and more to do with temporal sequencing (5.6). We also observe an interaction with verb class, such that effects and data distributions according to tense-aspect depend on aspectual characteristics of verbs (5.7). On the other hand, more pertinent than general semantic classes of verbs or apparent lexical frequency effects are lexically particular constructions such as quotative *decir* 'say' and person- and tense-specific *yo creo* 'I think' (5.8). Finally, widely reported person differences partly reflect the availability of a lexical option for third person and the impact that has on the accessibility effect within the envelope of variation (5.9).

For a reliable monolingual benchmark we draw on previously published reports, supplemented by our own analyses of data from the Corpus of

Conversational Colombian Spanish (CCCS; cf. Travis 2005: 9–25), and in some cases the NMSEB corpus (see Table 1.1).

5.1 Contrast and Emphasis

Cross-linguistically, expressed subject pronouns are widely held to mark "contrast," "emphasis," or "focus" (e.g., Chafe 1994: 37; Haegeman 1994: 217; Payne 1997: 43). This has been claimed for a range of languages with variable subject expression, including Romance languages (Mayol 2010), as well as Finnish (Helasvuo 2014: 454), Japanese (Lee and Yonezawa 2008: 741–739), Javanese (Ewing 2014: 55–56), and so on. For Spanish, this view is widespread among both linguists and grammarians (e.g., Butt and Benjamin 2004: 130; Gili y Gaya 1964: 23–34; Luján 1999: 1277; RAE and AALE 2010: 645).

Yet contrast and emphasis, though intuitive notions, are rarely established in a replicable manner. Without operationalizations, circularity sets in, whereby expedient examples are interpreted as contrastive because of the presence of a subject pronoun, and then the pronoun is designated a marker of that contrast.

First of all, subject pronoun expression is not required to mark contrast between verbs with different subjects, such as in the constructed pair of examples *Nosotros / Ø queríamos que asistiera pero ella / Ø no quiso ir* 'We / Ø wanted her to attend but she / Ø didn't want to go' (where Ø indicates an unexpressed subject) (Otheguy, Zentella and Livert 2007: 775–776). Contrast in different-subject pairs of verbs can be marked by expressions other than subject pronouns, such as topic-introducing adverbials associated via metonymic inferencing to the subject referent, as in *Mis padres veranean en la playa. Por mi parte, yo / Ø prefiero ir a la montaña* 'My parents spend the summer at the beach. As for me, I / Ø prefer to go to the mountain.' (Amaral and Schwenter 2005: 121).

More importantly, once operationalized via co-occurring contextual elements, contrast turns out to account for miniscule portions of the data (for tests of contrast, see Travis and Torres Cacoullos 2012: 714–723; 2014: 367–371). The failure of a surmised global contrastive function to account for variable subject expression emerges from the handful of studies that have quantified contrast or emphasis.

One measurement that can be adapted for subject pronoun expression is "double contrast" (Myhill and Xing 1996). Double contrast, or converse predicates, is illustrated in (57), where different-subject verbs with opposite meanings are juxtaposed ('she comes' in (c), 'he doesn't' in (k)). The double-contrast subject in line (k) is expressed, as were the great majority of double-contrast subjects in a sample of first-person-singular from conversational data (Travis and Torres Cacoullos 2012: 718). But qualifying as cases of double contrast were only 4 percent of all subjects (6/162), and only 6 percent (5/81) of those that were expressed!

(57)
a. Leandro: *she's a nice little girl.*
b. Ricardo: *oh= yeah.*
c. Leandro: *... she comes to help your dad.*
d.   *.. [work] --*
e. Ricardo: *[she's] --*
f. Leandro: *work in the <@ ditch @>.*
g.   *@[@@*
h. Ricardo: *[yeah,*
i.   *ella] --* ('she')
j. Leandro: *@]@@*
k.   *pero él no viene casi nunca.* ('but he hardly ever comes')

(25 El Servicio, 01:23–01:31)

Criteria for contrastiveness by Paredes Silva included verbs with opposite meanings, negative versus affirmative polarity, and different complements for the same verb. She found that such "emphasis" did favor pronoun expression, but that just 13 percent (N = 2,085) of 1sg and 2sg subjects in Brazilian Portuguese letters met the criteria. Alternatively, one could consider lexically marked contrast, for example, with a "contrastive morpheme" (Li and Thompson 1979: 332) or what Givón refers to as "contrastive quantifiers" (2001: 233), as with *sólo* 'only', *sí* literally 'yes', or *mismo* 'oneself', literally 'same' (Fernández-Soriano 1999: 1226). But lexically marked contrast appears to be similarly infrequent in spontaneous discourse. Bentivoglio (1987: 46–48) counted instances of 1sg and 1pl co-occurring with *mismo* 'oneself', adversative connectives such as *pero* 'but', *mas* 'yet', *sin embargo* 'however', or adverbs such as *justamente* 'precisely', in Caracas sociolinguistic interviews. Though the subject pronoun rate for these contrastive tokens was 56 percent, compared with 39 percent in the absence of such markers, all contrastive tokens thus classified added up to only 4 percent of the data (N = 892). In conversational Colombian (CCCS) data, out of more than 1,500 1sg and 3sg subject pronouns, there are no tokens co-occurring with *mismo* 'oneself', and only ten with *sí* 'yes'.

The conclusion is that rather than being general markers of contrast in and of themselves, subject pronouns are favored in particular constructions with contrastive elements, which, furthermore, are rare.

5.2   Ambiguity Resolution

The other oft-ascribed function of subject pronouns is one of disambiguation. The ambiguity-resolving hypothesis is based on the observation that, while subject person-number is generally indicated in agreement marking on the verb in Spanish, 1sg and 3sg take the same form in some tenses, for example the Imperfect (past imperfective). It is hypothesized that the need to resolve ambiguity with such syncretic forms results in an increased rate of expressed subjects (we take up tense effects in Section 5.6.1).

Consider example (58), where, having asked who looked after the children, Fabiola is trying to be clear on who worked day shift and who night shift, Molly or her husband. While the syncretic Imperfect used throughout this example does not distinguish between a 1sg and 3sg subject, the presence of the subject pronouns in Fabiola's question in line (f) and in Molly's answer in (i), (n), and (o) does.

(58)

a.	Fabiola:	*...(1.8) y quién cuidaba a los muchitos?*	'...(1.8) and who looked after the kids?'
b.	Molly:	*...(0.9) pues el Flavio trabajaba de noche y se quedaban con él no.*	'...(0.9) well Flavio worked at night and they stayed with him you know.
c.		*... <@ pero @>,*	... <@ but @>,
d.		*[@]*	[@]'
e.	Fabiola:	*[él]* --	'[he] --
f.		*.. o él <u>pepenaba</u> betabel en la noche?*	.. or did <u>he pick</u> beets at night?'
g.	Molly:	*.. en el día.*	'.. during the day.
h.		*... él* --	... he --
i.		*... él <u>trabajaba</u> de=,*	... <u>he worked</u> during,
j.		*... [de]* --	... [during] --'
k.	Fabiola:	*[de] día y tú de noche?*	'[during] the day and you at night?'
l.	Molly:	*...(1.3) n=-* --	'...(1.3) n- --
m.		*.. no él,*	.. no he,
n.		*... él <u>trabajaba</u> de noche y yo de día,*	... <u>he worked</u> at night and I during the day,
o.		*él se dormía,*	he slept,
p.		*y las cui-* --	and look- --
q.		*los cuidaba no.*	looked after them you know.'

(09 La Salvia, 08:39–09:01)

The ambiguity hypothesis is consistent with the view that "the subject can be dropped" in Spanish and other languages because their verbs carry person-number agreement marking (Chomsky 1981 [1993]: 241). This view is at odds with the fact that there are many languages that do not mark grammatical person, but which nevertheless have variable subject expression, including for example, Mandarin (Jia and Bayley 2002; Li and Thompson 1979), Indonesian (Englebretson and Helasvuo 2014: 1), and Japanese (Ono and Thompson 1997).

Ambiguity may be popular in linguistic theorizing (students of linguistics will recall constructed examples of syntactic ambiguity such as *Mary saw the man with the binoculars* and "garden path" sentences such as *The horse raced past the barn fell*), but it is a marginal phenomenon on the ground. Ambiguity leading to wrong interpretations (e.g., that *raced* is the main verb rather than a past participle) is unlikely outside of experimental settings and ambiguity-avoidance is not a prime motivator of speaker choices (Christiansen and Chater 2016: 7; cf. Ferreira 2008; Jaeger 2010: 53; Roland, Elman, and Ferreira 2006).

In corpus data, cases of apparent ambiguity are no longer so once the wider discourse context and the participants' background knowledge are taken into account. Consider now example (59), where the syncretism in the 1sg and 3sg person of the Pluperfect in line (f) allows for two possible interpretations: "I had arrived" or "my mom had arrived," *my mom* just having been mentioned in line (b). But the discourse context leaves no doubt that the referent is the speaker, who had arrived at her mother's house for a family gathering.

(59)

a.	Sandra:	*she's so cute.*	'she's so cute.
b.		*my mom.*	my mom.'
c.	Adriana:	*... @@[@]*	'... @@[@]'
d.	Sandra:	*[u]=m,*	'[u]m,
e.		*... u=m,*	... um,
f.		*... Ø había llegado y iba a ser --*	... (I) had arrived and it was going to be --
g.		*... uh,*	... uh,
h.		*.. Thanksgiving,*	.. Thanksgiving,
i.		*.. or Christmas I'm not sure.*	.. or Christmas I'm not sure.
j.		*... y me dice,*	... and she says to me,
k.		*anda mijita,*	come on honey,
l.		*ayúdame a quitar este mantel y poner mi mantel de=,*	help me take this tablecloth off and put on my tablecloth,'

(03 Dos Comadres, 49:10–49:24)

At the same time, it is also the case that the presence of a subject pronoun does not guarantee disambiguation of a referent. When multiple same-sex referents are present (e.g., when family members are talking about other family members), a pronominal subject makes little difference to interpretation. In (60), expressed *ella* 'she' in line (k) by itself does not identify the referent; only patient reading of the transcript tells us that this pronoun refers to Otilia, the sister of the speaker's mother-in-law (pseudonyms in the transcript are indicated with a preceding ~). It is also evident that instances of ambiguity in reference are likely to be fewer when the interlocutors are long-standing acquaintances than in conversations with an outside interviewer (e.g., the knowledge that Hilda is the speaker's wife helps to make sense of the relationships here).

(60)

a.	Leandro:	... *él trabajó mucho tiempo allá en ~Valencia en las minas.*	'... he worked for a long time there in Valencia in the mines.'
b.	Ricardo:	*.. yeah.*	'.. yeah.'
c.	Leandro:	*mi tío ~Arturo.*	'my uncle Arturo.'
d.	Ricardo:	*... awesome.*	'... awesome.'
e.	Leandro:	*.. su uncle XX,*	'.. her uncle XX,
f.		*su padrino de ella.*	her godfather.'
g.	Ricardo:	*... uh huh.*	'... uh huh.'
h.	Leandro:	*.. uh huh.*	'.. uh huh.'
i.		*...(1.2) [ella era]* --	...(1.2) [she was] --'
j.	Ricardo:	*[awesome].*	'[awesome].'
k.	Leandro:	<u>*ella era*</u> *hermana de mi .. suegra.*	'she was a sister of my .. mother-in-law.'
l.	Ricardo:	*... yeah.*	'... yeah.'
m.	Leandro:	*y él de mi* --	'and he of my --
n.		*you know mi grandma?*	you know my grandma?
o.		*.. de mi grandma ~Otilia?*	.. of my grandma Otilia?'
p.	Ricardo:	*... [~Otilia]?*	'... [Otilia]?'
q.	Leandro:	*[mi] mama ~Otilia,*	'[my] mom Otilia,
r.		*le digo=.*	I call her.
s.		*ella era* --	she was --
t.		*.. la mamá de la ~Hilda?*	.. Hilda's mother?
u.		*they were sisters.*	*they were sisters.*
v.		*.. ella.*	.. her.
w.		*.. mi tía ~Ofelia y mi .. grandma.*	.. my aunt Ofelia and my .. grandma.
x.		*.. y mi suegra.*	.. and my mother-in-law.'

(25 El Servicio, 49:48–50:10)

In fact, ambiguity in spontaneous language use is conspicuously rare once context is taken into account, both linguistic (preceding and following discourse) and extralinguistic (speakers' background knowledge). For example, in a study of 12,000 tokens of variable plural /-s/ and verbal /-n/ expression in Puerto Rican Spanish, Poplack found that, through the interplay of morphological, syntactic, semantic, and cultural information, "no case in which ambiguity as to number resulted from marker deletion" (1980a: 378). For subject expression, Ranson (1991: 148) finds that when contextual elements are considered, grammatical person is relevant but unmarked linguistically in just 2 percent (N = 1,035) of verbs (all person-numbers). In a NMSEB sample, only 6 out of 1,002 unexpressed 1sg tokens are contextually ambiguous. In three of these, furthermore, the identity of the subject makes no difference to the interpretation of the event. For example in (61), the subject of *tenía que meter el dedo* could be 1sg ('I had to stick in my finger'), but it could just as well be 3sg ('one had to'). This is a case of what Ranson (1991: 145) refers to as "person irrelevant" and Ono and Thompson (1997: 488) describe as the "referent" being left "open."

(61)

Inmaculada:	*y ella me decía ándale lava los trastes y yo te doy lipstick.*	'and she would say to me go and wash the dishes and I'll give you lipstick.'
Lucy:	*<@ oh= @>.*	'<@ oh @>.'
Inmaculada:	*so lavaba los trastes y yo muy contenta con lipstick.* *pero ya= estaba bien gastado,*	'so I would wash the dishes and I'd be all happy with lipstick. but it was already really used up,'
Lucy:	*[uh huh].*	'[uh huh].'
Inmaculada:	*[Ø tenía] que meter el dedo <@ pa' adentro pa' agarrar el lipstick @>.*	'[(I/she/one) had] to stick a finger <@ inside to grab the lipstick @>.'

(14 Proper Spanish, 40:59–41:12)

Tokens that are truly ambiguous such that the analyst cannot identify the subject referent must of course be excluded from the analysis of variation. But these are distinct from both indeterminate cases, where the referent is irrelevant as in (61), and instances where the intended subject is unknown when speakers cut short what they were saying. For example, because of the truncation in line (b) in (62) (captured with the two dashes at the end of the IU) it is not possible to know what the speaker might have intended to say.

(62)

a.	Benita:	*estaba una=,*	'there was a,
b.		*...(1.2) vivía --*	...(1.2) (there/she/I) lived --
c.		*... uh --*	... uh --
d.		*you don't know,*	you don't know,
e.		*las Bacas,*	the Bacas,
f.		*.. las conoces?*	.. do you know them?'

(31 Speed Limit, 01:36–01:41)

In sum, accounts of variable subject expression that appeal to an ambiguity-resolving function of subject pronouns are at odds with the low incidence of ambiguity of reference in everyday speech. Pronouns can serve that function, but the occasions on which they are called upon to do so are too few to account for the bulk of the data.

5.3   Accessibility as Subject Continuity

A widely reported cross-linguistic constraint on subject expression is "accessibility," pioneered in Givón's work on topic continuity. The cross-linguistic generalization is that less "coding material" (or less phonetic bulk) corresponds to more accessible referents and more coding material to less accessible referents (Givón 1983: 18). For subject pronouns, the likelihood that they are unexpressed (less coding material) is greater when the referent is more accessible, as determined by *subject continuity*. Subject continuity is usually operationalized as "same" vs. "switch" reference – that is, whether or not the subject referent of the target clause is the same as, or different from, that of the immediately preceding clause (Silva-Corvalán 1982: 104). Same reference, or continuity of subjects across clauses, is exemplified in (63), and switch reference in (64) where the target subject of interest is in line (f).

(63)
a. Celia: *Yo la pongo encima de la mesa?*   'I put it on top of the table?
b.   *... Se la pelo,*   ... I peel it for her,
c.   *y Ø le quito así el piquito,*   and (I) pull out the tip,'
                                                         (CCCS 01, 1494–1496)

(64)
a. Ángela: *Voy a grabar.*   'I am going to record.'
b. Sara: *... [Sí]?*   '... [Yes]?'
c. Ángela: *[Si no] te importa.*   '[If it doesn't] bother you.'
d. Sara: *[2@@@2]*   '[2@@@2]'
e. Ángela: *[2Pero no es por nada2],*   '[2It's nothing2],
f.   *Ø ahorita te explico,*   (I)'ll explain to you in a minute.'
                                                         (CCCS 04, 1–6)

An alternative operationalization of subject continuity is the gradient measure of distance. This considers the number of clauses intervening between the target subject and the previous mention of the same referent in subject position – henceforth *previous mention*. The distance measure is inspired by the general measurement of topic continuity known as Referential Distance, which assesses the lapse from the previous mention of the referent (Givón 1983: 13; Myhill 2005: 473), as depicted in Figure 5.1. For example, in (64), there are two clauses intervening between the target in line (f) and the previous mention in line (a) (in lines (c) and (e)). Compare this with (65), where there are three intervening clauses between the target in (g) and the previous mention in (a) (in lines (c), (d), and (f)). By this measure of distance in clauses, though the target

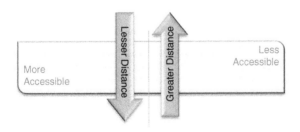

Figure 5.1 Distance as a measure of subject continuity: Number of intervening clauses between the target subject and previous mention

subjects in (64) and (65) both qualify as switch reference, that in (64) is more accessible than that in (65).

(65)

a.	Betty:	... *le fajé una nalgada.*	'... I gave her a slap on the bottom.'
b.	Carrie:	.. *@@@*	'.. @@@'
c.	Betty:	.. *she was starting to walk,*	'.. she was starting to walk,
d.		... *and she wanted to go to the fireplace,*	... and she wanted to go to the fireplace,
e.		*sit on the mantel,*	sit on the mantel,
f.		*...(1.0) y no la dejaba la ~Bobbie.*	...(1.0) and Bobbie wouldn't let her.
g.		*yo no sé qué estarían haciendo allá.*	I don't know what they were doing there.'

(13 La Acequia, 18:16–18:28)

5.3.1   Human Switch Reference (Intervening Human Subjects)

As a refined measure of subject continuity, Givón put forward the notion of "potential interference" (1983: 14). Building on this, Travis and Torres Cacoullos found that, for the expression of subject pronouns, the presence of another human subject between the target and previous mention interferes with subject continuity more than a non-human subject does (2012: 727–729). The refinement, then, is *human* switch reference. The difference can be seen in examples (64) and (65) above: (64) illustrates a switch reference context where the clauses intervening between the target and the previous mention do not have human subjects ('if it doesn't bother you' and 'it's nothing'), while (65) illustrates switch reference with intervening human subjects ('she' and 'Bobbie').

The following pair of examples juxtaposes human switch reference and canonical switch reference with respect to the subject of the immediately preceding clause. In example (66) we have switch reference with an intervening human subject ('I' in line (e)), while (67) is a switch reference context with only a non-human subject intervening between the target and the previous mention (an apartment, in line (c)).

(66)   ✓ Human switch reference (Intervening human subject present)
        ✓ Switch reference

a.	Omar:	... *Ø Tenía un=a pintura de=* --	'... (She) had a picture of --
b.		.. *De un ángel.*	.. Of an angel.'
c.	Rocío:	... *Mhm.*	'... Mhm.'
d.	Omar:	... *en blanco y negro,*	'... in black and white,
e.		*y yo simplemente le eché color.*	and I just added color to it.
f.		... *Y ella quedó feliz.*	... And she was happy.'

(CCCS 18, 82–87)

(67)   ✗ Human switch reference (Intervening human subject absent)
        ✓ Switch reference
a.   Santi: *Entonces,*   'So,
b.   *Ø lo miro,*   (I)'ll look at it,
c.   *.. si tiene alcoba del servicio,* .. if it has a maid's room,
d.   *.. entonces te --*   .. then --
e.   *.. Ø Te aviso.*   .. (I)'ll let you know.'
                                        (CCCS 05, 1332–1338)

Table 5.1 shows subject expression rates according to both human switch reference and canonical switch reference. When there is no intervening human subject there is little difference between same, in (63), and canonical switch reference contexts, in (64) and (67) (39 percent and 41 percent respectively, top row). Meanwhile, within switch reference contexts, the rate of subject expression is significantly higher if there is a human subject in the intervening clause(s), in (65) and (66), than if there isn't, in (64) and (67) (55 percent vs. 41 percent, right column). In other words, what makes the most difference is a switch vis-à-vis the preceding clause subject with a *human* referent.

The more discerning measure of human switch reference accords with cross-linguistic switch reference systems. In languages with grammaticalized switch reference, coreference and disjoint reference are marked morphologically, typically on the verb, "as a device for referential tracking" (Haiman and Munro 1983: ix). For example, in (68) the suffix *–k* on the verb indicates that the subjects of the adverbial and the main clause are the same (SS = same subject) and *–m* that they are different (DS = different subject). DS marking is typical for the introduction of "agentive, fully referential" subjects (Stirling 2006: 320), which on the whole would be specific humans.

Table 5.1 *Rate of subject pronouns according to switch reference and human switch reference*

Human Switch Reference	**Same Reference** (previous mention in immediately preceding clause)	**Switch Reference** (previous mention at distance of 1 or more intervening clauses)
Intervening human subject absent	39% (113/289)	41% (31/76)
Intervening human subject(s) present	No cases	55% (283/519)

(41% vs. 39%, p = .79; 55% vs. 41%, p < .05, by Fisher's exact test; 1sg, CCCS, from Travis and Torres Cacoullos 2012: 728)

(68)   Switch reference system in Mojave (Mohave) (Munro 1980: 145)
         nya-isvar-k   *iima-k*
         when-sing-SS   dance
         'when he$_i$ sang he$_i$ danced'

         nya-isvar-m   *iima-k*
         when-sing-DS   dance
         'when he$_i$ sang he$_j$ danced'

5.3.2   Distance Between Mentions vs. Local Coreferentiality

Does it matter for Spanish subject pronoun expression how far back the previous mention of the subject referent is? Local switch vs. same reference looks only to the immediately preceding clause, whereas the gradient measure of distance looks further back into the preceding discourse. Table 5.2 gives rates of expression at different degrees of distance measured in clauses, as well as in the presence and absence of intervening human subjects. Considering distance (top half of the table), the subject pronoun rate is lowest at zero intervening clauses (with, by definition, no intervening human subjects) and is highest at five or more clauses (with at least one intervening human subject), rising from 18 percent to 42 percent. In between, there are step-by-step increases (to 22 percent and then 28 percent), not merely a jump between zero and one clause followed by a leveling off.

Attending now to intervening human subjects (bottom half of Table 5.2), the measure of human switch reference is confirmed: the difference between zero and one clause is lost in the absence of intervening human subjects (with near-identical rates at 18 percent and 17 percent), but emerges in their presence (where the rate rises to 26 percent). Human switch reference thus provides a keener measure for subject expression than traditional switch reference does when the previous mention is at a distance of just one intervening clause.

Table 5.2 *Rate of subject pronouns according to distance from previous mention (number of intervening clauses) and presence of intervening human subjects*

	0 clauses	1 clause	2–4 clauses	5+ clauses
Intervening clauses				
	18% (507/2,846)	22% (168/766)	28% (209/757)	42% (433/1,042)
Intervening human subject(s)				
absent	18% (507/2,846)	17% (54/321)	25% (39/153)	–
present	No cases	26% (114/438)	28% (168/592)	42% (433/1,042)

(NMSEB)

At a greater distance, the two measures converge (with rates of 25 percent and 28 percent), because it is more likely that there will be an intervening human subject anyway.

The conclusion is that there is both an effect of distance – the number of clauses interposed between coreferential mentions – and an effect of local coreferentiality – human switch reference. Another local accessibility measure, as we will see, is clause linking (Section 5.5).

5.3.3   Other FAQs Concerning Accessibility

5.3.3.1   What Counts as a Clause?   Included in a clause count are finite clauses produced by any speaker participating in the conversation. Non-finite clauses are not counted; thus, the non-finite 'sit on the mantel' in line (e) in (65) above is skipped over for the purposes of determining subject continuity. Speech overlapping with the target clause is also not considered to interrupt subject continuity. In (69), the overlapped clause in (c) is skipped over, and the previous mention is considered to be in the adjacent clause, at a distance of 0.

(69)

a.	Dora:	.. *Clarita la vi más bonita ahora*	'.. Clarita looked prettier to me
		que Ø estuvo aquí.	when (she) was here just now.'
b.	Ángela:	*Ah sí,*	'Oh yes,
c.		*[ahí estaba todavía más niña].*	[she was younger then].'
d.	Dora:	*[en la fotografía no Ø salió=]* ..	'[in the photo (she) didn't come
		tan linda.	out] .. so pretty.'

(CCCS 24, 1719–1722)

Expressions that derive from clauses but which cannot be rightfully considered clausal are excluded. Such deverbal expressions are, for example, temporal phrases (e.g., *hace tres años* 'it's been three years / three years ago', *el año que viene* 'the coming year / next year'), certain fixed subjunctive forms (e.g., *lo que venga* 'whatever (may come)'), and some impersonal expressions (e.g., *es que* 'it's that', *pueda que* 'may be') (cf. Cameron 1992: 144; Otheguy and Zentella 2012: 262).

Discourse markers that lack clausal status include the invariable *o sea* 'that is, I mean', *dale* 'there you go', and *qué sé yo* 'what do I know' (Company Company 2006; Schwenter 1996). Discourse markers are often community specific (e.g., Rivas and Brown 2009), and their clausal status may vary from study to study. In the data examined here, (*yo*) *no sé* 'I don't know' and (*yo*) *creo* 'I think' have clausal status by the measure of shared constraints on *yo* 'I' expression with other instances of variable subject expression (see Section 5.8).

5.3.3.2   Does the Syntactic Role of the Previous Mention Matter?   A previous mention of the referent may occur as subject, object, or another syntactic role. Accessibility is operationalized as *subject* continuity because previous subject mentions affect more the workings of coreferentiality than non-subject mentions. Subjects are expressed less often when there is a previous subject mention than when there is a non-subject mention in the immediately preceding clause (29 percent, 245/858 vs. 34 percent, 60/149; $p = < .01$, 1sg and 3sg CCCS data). Furthermore, the occurrence of a subject mention in the immediately preceding clause is much more frequent than a non-subject mention, occurring five times as often (858 vs. 149). Both rates and data distribution confirm, then, that accessibility is most meaningfully measured as subject continuity (Silva-Corvalán 1994: 157). The primacy of the subject agrees with the typological topic hierarchy, which places subjects above other syntactic roles as having greater continuity in discourse (Givón 1983: 22). It also agrees with psycholinguistic accessibility, in that subject referents are "the most easily retrieved from memory" (Bock and Warren 1985: 61).

5.3.3.3   How Do We Treat Partial Coreferentiality Between Plurals and Singulars?   Target plural subjects can be treated as coreferential with previous singular mentions of one of the set. Cameron (1995: 20) determined that pronouns were disfavored for plural subjects in contexts where one member of the set making up the plural referent had been referred to previously, as in (70). The effect is substantial, because the vast majority (total N = 900) occurred with one of the set elements mentioned within the previous five clauses. This contextual distribution accounts for a lower rate of expression of plural over singular subjects.

(70)
a.   *Entonces Ø me invitó a ver Jaws*
b.   *y esta noche Ø nos hicimos novios.*

a.   'Then (he) invited me to see Jaws
b.   and that night (we) became boyfriend and girlfriend.'

(from Cameron 1995: 18)

The reverse is not necessarily the case; that is, partially coreferential previous plurals do not behave as coreferential with target singular subjects. In this context, the rate is not lower than average (48 percent, 29/61, as compared with 41 percent overall; CCCS data). Furthermore, partially coreferential previous plurals account only for a miniscule proportion of the data (just 3 percent). Thus, unlike plural subjects, what counts as the previous mention of a singular subject should be limited to another singular subject.

5.3.3.4 Do Mentions by an Interlocutor Count As Coreferential Previous Mentions?   Another issue that arises in conversational data is how to handle previous mentions produced by an interlocutor. In the dialogic CCCS data, the rate of expression when the immediately preceding clause has a coreferential subject produced by the interlocutor, as in (71) and (72), is higher than when it was produced by the same speaker (38 percent, 114/300, in interlocutor coreferential contexts vs. 29 percent, 245/858 in same speaker coreferential contexts). Nevertheless, it is lower than that in non-coreferential contexts (48 percent, 767/1,587). Thus, interlocutor-produced mentions would seem to have an intermediate effect.

(71)

Omar:	*Pero él vivió en Gorgona mucho tiempo.*	'But he lived in Gorgona for a long time.'
Milena:	*[Hm].*	'[Hm].'
Omar:	*[Como] nativo de Gorgona.*	'[Like] a native of Gorgona.'
Milena:	*...(2.0) Y=,*	'...(2.0) And,
	él le hace limpieza a la playa,	he cleans the beach,
	no?	right?'

(CCCS 20, 914–919)

(72)

Fabio:	*Vos,*	
	viste clase con él?	'Did you have class with him?'
Nury:	*Ø Estaba viendo Análisis con él ahora.*	'(I) had Analysis with him just now.'

(CCCS 11, 1189–1191)

However, 1sg and 3sg may not behave in the same way. In the CCCS, for example, for 3sg, instances as in (71), where the previous mention is produced by the interlocutor, have a similar pronoun rate as non-coreferential contexts (38 percent, 81/214, and 37 percent, 250/680). For 1sg, in contrast, the interlocutor's 'you', as in (72), results in a similar rate of pronominal *yo* 'I' as speaker-produced previous mentions, lower than non-coreferential contexts (38 percent, 33/86, as opposed to 57 percent, 517/908, for non-coreferential contexts). The status of 1sg as representing the speaker in face-to-face interaction with the interlocutor, as opposed to 3sg referring to an external party, may be what motivates this difference. What we take from this for subject continuity is that while interlocutor mentions count toward accessibility as previous mentions, they should be categorized separately.

5.3.3.5 What About Subject Mentions in Quoted Speech?   Subject pronouns are favored when shifting into quoted speech, illustrated in line (b) (73) and (74). For 1sg, the subject pronoun occurs at a rate over twice the average of coreferential contexts (46 percent, 49/106 vs. 21 percent, 326/1,584, NSMEB data), and actually higher than that of non-coreferential contexts (36 percent, 600/1,664).

Subject expression may be favored more when the speaker is quoting themselves, as in (73), than when quoting a third party as in (74) (58 percent (21/36) for a self-quote vs. 40 percent (28/70) for quotes of others, which involve a deictic shift, here from third to first person). As subject continuity does not hold for quoted speech, it would well be excluded from analysis.

(73)   Quoted speech: 1sg quotative > 1sg quoted speech
a. Diana: *Yo les digo,*   'I say to them,
b.   ... *Yo tengo* mi biblia,   ... I have my bible,'
                                  (24 La Floresta, 08:42–08:45)

(74)   Quoted speech: 3sg quotative > 1sg quoted speech
a. Santi: *Él dice,*   'He says,
b.   *Yo me graduo,*   I'm going to graduate,
c.   *y yo me dedico a eso.* and I'll follow that profession.'
                                  (CCCS 03, 1411–1413)

In summary, pronoun expression rates are impacted by the accessibility of the subject referent. At greater distances from the previous mention the subject pronoun rates are higher, though not all intervening clauses have the same impact on subject expression. Intervening human subjects disrupt subject continuity more than do intervening clauses with non-human subjects. Most disfavorable to pronouns are *coreferential contexts*: where a previous mention occurs as the subject of the immediately preceding clause or of a prior clause without an intervening human subject.

5.4   Coreferential Subject Priming

Near ubiquitous in speech is structural priming, also known as persistence or perseveration, whereby the use of a certain structure in one utterance "primes" or prompts the same structure to be subsequently repeated. Analyses of morphosyntactic variables as early as Sankoff and Laberge (1978), Poplack (1980a), Weiner and Labov (1983), and Scherre and Naro (1991) have reported that choice of variant is influenced by the variant last chosen by the speaker. For Spanish subject expression, priming was first demonstrated in Cameron's (1992) pioneering dissertation and is drawing renewed attention (e.g., Flores-Ferrán 2002; Shin 2014: 312; Travis 2007: 120–122).

The pertinent effect is that of *Coreferential subject priming*, seen in the tendency to repeat the form of the previous mention: a previous pronoun favors a subsequent pronoun, as in (75), lines (a) and (d), and a previous unexpressed subject favors a subsequent unexpressed subject, as in lines (c), (e), and (h) of (76). The coreferential subject prime shares the same referent as the target subject. It need not occur in a coreferential context (i.e., in the immediately preceding clause), but can be separated from the target by intervening clauses (as is the case in (75) and (76)). This is not to be confused with what can be called adjacent-clause subject priming, which looks to the immediately preceding clause subject (be that coreferential or not) (Cameron 1994). Coreferential subject priming is stronger than adjacent-clause subject priming, though it decays with increasing distance between prime and target (see Travis, Torres Cacoullos, and Kidd 2017: 288–289).

(75)
a.	Ángela:	*yo ahorita no estoy trabajando.*	'right now I'm not working.
b.		*... Entonce=s,*	... So,
c.		*Es de ahorros.*	It's from savings.
d.		*de unos ahorritos que yo tengo.*	from some savings that I have.'

(CCCS 04, 687–690)

(76)
a.	Santi:	*Yo me averiguo,*	'I'll find out,
b.		*y,*	and,
c.		*Y Ø te digo si hay algún apartamento,*	And (I)'ll tell you if there's an apartment,
d.		*Entonces,*	So,
e.		*Ø lo miro,*	(I)'ll look at it,
f.		*.. si tiene alcoba del servicio,*	.. if it has a service room,
g.		*.. entonces te --*	.. then --
h.		*.. Ø Te aviso.*	.. (I)'ll let you know.'

(CCCS 05, 1332–1339)

Priming is not the same as repetition with interactional functions related to turn taking or rapport building (Tannen 1987: 583–584). Evidence is that speakers are primed more by themselves than by their interlocutor: priming is stronger "production-to-production" than "comprehension-to-production" (Gries 2005: 374). It is a "mechanical" effect in the sense that it is immune to communicative needs (Labov 1994: 547–568). For example, priming constrains plural marking in Puerto Rican Spanish, where the realization of word-final /-s/ depends on its realization on preceding elements in the same noun phrase. In a phrase such as *unas nenas bonitas* 'some beautiful girls', once /-s/ is marked on one element, it is more likely to be marked on subsequent elements, such that "One marker leads to more, but zeros lead to zeros" (Poplack 1980a: 378).

From a psycholinguistic perspective, structural priming is "the unintentional and pragmatically unmotivated tendency to repeat the general syntactic pattern of an utterance" (Bock and Griffin 2000: 177). Outside of language, priming from previous experience applies to human behavior more generally, for example with motor control (van der Wel, Fleckenstein, Jax, and Rosenbaum 2007). As a domain-general mechanism, it is compatible with functional explanations of grammatical structure based on the cognitive processes brought into play in language use (Bybee 2010).

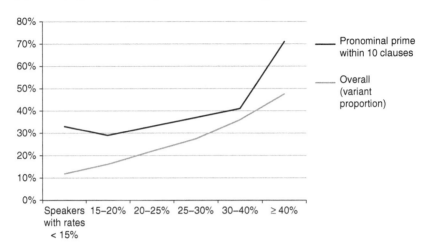

Figure 5.2   Rate of subject pronouns under coreferential subject priming
Individuals binned according to their overall rate; N = 5,571 (NMSEB).

Priming holds across the board. Figure 5.2 compares overall subject pronoun rates of individuals with their rates when they have produced a coreferential subject pronoun within the preceding five clauses. The rates under coreferential subject priming are clearly above the variant proportions, regardless of whether individuals have lower or higher overall rates (cf. D. Sankoff and Laberge 1978: 122).

5.4.1   Subject Continuity in Interaction with Priming

We can appreciate the effect of coreferential subject priming by considering how it interacts with subject continuity. For a previous unexpressed subject in a coreferential context, priming and subject continuity work synergistically, each disfavoring a subject pronoun with the target verb. They also work together for a pronominal prime in a non-coreferential context, each favoring a subject pronoun with the target verb. As a result, the lowest rate of subject expression obtains in the first configuration – with an unexpressed prime in a coreferential context – and the highest rate in the second – with a pronominal prime in a non-coreferential context. However, with a pronominal prime in a coreferential context, priming and subject continuity work antagonistically, since the former feature favors, while the latter disfavors, subject pronoun expression. The two independent variables also work against each other for an unexpressed prime in a non-coreferential context. The result of these antagonistic configurations is intermediate expression rates.

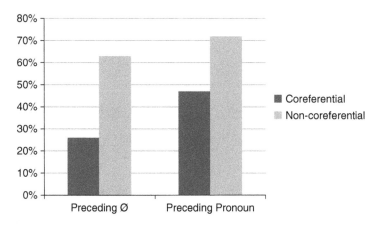

Figure 5.3 Rate of subject pronouns according to subject continuity, with unexpressed and pronominal primes
Subject continuity is stronger with unexpressed primes (where the rate more than doubles, 63% vs. 26%, N = 778) than with pronominal primes (where the rate is one-and-a-half times higher, 72% vs. 47%, N = 534) (singular persons, San Juan, from Cameron 1994: 39).

The strength of subject continuity is thus moderated by priming, as seen in Figure 5.3, which compares the effect of subject continuity according to the form of the immediately preceding clause subject. The difference in subject pronoun rate between non-coreferential and coreferential contexts is greater when the preceding clause subject is unexpressed (the left pair of bars) than when it is expressed (on the right).

In sum, subject pronouns beget subject pronouns, a repetition effect that is strongest for coreferential pronouns (*yo* to *yo* 'I', *él* to *él* 'he', *ella* to *ella* 'she').

5.5 Clause Type: Coordination, Subordination, and Clause Linking

It has been claimed that non-expression is categorical in coreferential-subject coordinate and subordinate clauses (e.g., Bayley, Greer, and Holland 2013: 25; Luján 1999: 279). There is, however, variability in such contexts, as illustrated in (77) and (78) for coordinate, and in (79) and (80) for subordinate, clauses. Where clause type has been tested for subject expression, coordinate clauses are consistently found to have a lower pronoun rate than non-coordinate main clauses, whereas subordinate clauses are variously reported to have an intermediate rate, a higher rate than main clauses, or no significant effect (Enríquez 1984: 257; Orozco 2015: 22; Otheguy and Zentella 2012: 164; Shin 2014: 211; Travis 2007: 115). What might be behind these results?

(77)
Diana: *al menos soy de Trujillo,*   'at least I am from Trujillo,
        vivo en Palmira,   I live in Palmira,
        y Ø estudio en Cali.   and (I) study in Cali.'
                                                  (CCCS 10, 216–218)

(78)
Ángela: *... Yo a los dos quiero,*   '... I love both of you,
        y=,   and,
        ... y yo tengo que ser imparcial.   ... and I have to be impartial.'
                                                  (CCCS 02, 356–358)

(79)
Patricia: *... Éste,*   '... This one,
          sí,   yes,
          no lo voy a botar,   I'm not going to throw it out,
          porque Ø lo necesito.   because (I) need it.'
                                                  (CCCS 09, 257–260)

(80)
Dora: *Me decía la odontóloga que ella*   'The dental surgeon told me that just
        estuvo ahorita e=n --   now she was on --
        .. En vacaciones de semana santa?   .. On vacation for Easter?'
                                                  (CCCS 24, 2411–2412)

Despite the consistent effects reported for coordination, it has not been well defined. Otheguy and Zentella (2012: 268) operationalize it as "any second clause after *y* ['and'] or *ni* ['neither'], and in a sequence of clauses separated by a comma," thus relying on criteria of conjunction presence and prosodic connectedness. A first stipulation is coreferentiality. The presence of a coordinating conjunction (mostly *y* 'and' and *pero* 'but') in fact only makes a difference in coreferential contexts, where the subject pronoun rate with a conjunction is half that without a conjunction (16 percent, 30/186 vs. 34 percent, 174/516; CCCS data). In non-coreferential contexts the rate of expression is similar with and without a coordinating conjunction (45 percent, 94/207 vs. 49 percent, 655/1,333). Clearly *y* 'and'-clauses in coreferential contexts should not be lumped together with clauses following *y* 'and' in non-coreferential contexts (as in example (65), line (f)) or where the previous coreferential subject was produced by the interlocutor (as in (71)). *Coordinate clauses*, then, are those joined via a coordinating conjunction to a coreferential-subject clause.[1]

---

[1] Coordinate clauses may rather rarely be separated from the first conjunct by intervening IUs containing subordinate or parenthetical main clauses (see, for example, (96)), representing under 10 percent of coordinate clauses in English conversational data (Torres Cacoullos and Travis 2014: 27).

It may be asked whether the favoring of unexpressed subjects in coordinate (and subordinate) clauses is simply an artifact of a higher occurrence of subject continuity with such clause types, because, as operationalized just above, coordinate clauses have coreferential subjects. To test this, we therefore need to compare pronoun rates according to clause type in coreferential contexts only.

Spontaneous speech data spotlights the role of prosody in connecting grammatical elements, alongside syntactic linking. *Prosodically linked* clauses are those produced by the same speaker that occur either in the same IU, as in (80), or in IUs connected by continuing intonation, as in lines (a) and (b) in (81). This can be contrasted with non-prosodically linked clauses that occur in IUs that are separated by final intonation or by one or more intervening prosodic units, as in the clauses in lines (b) and (d) in (81).

(81)
a.   Julia: *Él se levantó de la poltrona,*   'He got up off the couch,
b.   *y Ø se fue a= --*   and <u>(he) went</u> to --
c.   *A la cama.*   To bed.
d.   *... Y ahí Ø quedó.*   ... And there <u>(he) stayed</u>.'

(CCCS 12, 613–616)

Subordinate and coordinate clauses are necessarily linked syntactically to the preceding coreferential-subject clause, by virtue of the presence of a conjunction. But they may or may not be prosodically linked. Figure 5.4 depicts the incidence of prosodic linking in each of the three clause types (for coreferential contexts only). As can be seen, main clauses are about half as

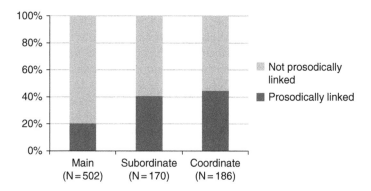

Figure 5.4 Proportion of data in prosodically linked vs. non-linked coreferential contexts by clause type
Prosodic linking is more frequent in subordinate (41%) and coordinate (45%) than in main clauses (20%) ($p < .0001$ in both cases) (CCCS).

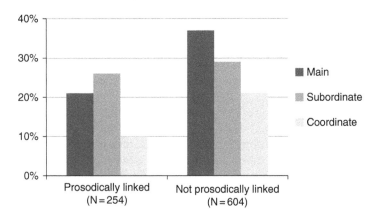

Figure 5.5 Rate of subject pronouns by clause type and prosodic linking in coreferential contexts
Differences between subordinate and main not significant (prosodically linked: 26 percent vs. 21 percent; p = .46; non-linked: 29% vs. 37%; p = .16). Coordinate clauses retain a lower rate of expression than main clauses both in prosodically linked (10%; p < .05) and non-linked contexts (21%; p < .01) (CCCS).

likely to be linked prosodically to the preceding coreferential-subject clause than are subordinate and coordinate clauses. Thus, though main and subordinate clauses occur with a similar rate in coreferential contexts (approximately one-third of the time), they differ in their prosodic connectedness: prosodic linking occurs more where there is also explicit, syntactic linking in the form of a conjunction.

Figure 5.5 gives the rate of subject expression across the three clause types according to prosodic linking. Coordinate clauses retain a lower subject pronoun rate than main clauses both in prosodically linked and in non-linked contexts. The disfavoring effect of coordination via a conjunction seems to be a genuine effect, which is enhanced by prosodic linking (Chapter 6, Section 6.6.1). Nevertheless, for subordinate vs. main clauses, when we consider prosodically linked and unlinked contexts separately, there are no significant differences. The effect of subordinate clauses sometimes reported is likely, then, to be a broader effect of clause linking rather than of subordination per se.

In this section, we have seen that differences in subject pronoun rate according to clause type are tied to subject continuity combined with clause linking. Linking – prosodic connectedness together with conjunction presence – disfavors subject pronoun expression.

5.6 Tense-aspect and Temporal Sequencing

Tense-Aspect-Mood (TAM) has been widely explored for Spanish subject expression. Three tenses – Present, Preterit, and Imperfect – generally constitute the bulk of the data, in the area of 90 percent (e.g., Cameron 1993: 317; Erker and Guy 2012: 535; Shin 2014: 309). The most consistent, though largely unremarked, finding is that Preterit (perfective) forms disfavor subject pronouns (Claes 2011: 202; Erker and Guy 2012: 541; Lastra and Butragueño 2015: 43; Shin 2014: 311; Silva-Corvalán and Enrique-Arias 2017: 181; Torres Cacoullos and Travis 2015: 84). In contrast, subject expression is favored by the Imperfect (past imperfective) more than the Present, in most (though not all) studies. The Imperfect effect has monopolized attention and its interpretation is hotly debated, with one account being based on ambiguity resolution and another on the discourse function of different tenses.

5.6.1 Limits on Ambiguity as an Account for Tense-aspect Effects

The ambiguity-resolving hypothesis predicts a higher rate of expressed subjects with verb tenses involving syncretism in person morphology, such as the Imperfect Indicative, Conditional, and all tenses of the Subjunctive. Syncretism in person morphology can be seen in, for example, *trabajaba* 'work-$_{\text{IPFV-IND-1/3SG}}$'(I/he) worked' (cf. example (58), Section 5.2).

To deconstruct the proposed syncretism effect, a first consideration is that it would mostly be an effect of the Imperfect (Indicative), which accounts for the majority of the incidences of syncretism (e.g., 80 percent in studies by Erker and Guy (2012: 540) and Claes (2011: 202)). Second, the syncretic tenses do not behave uniformly. For example, the Imperfect has nearly twice the pronoun rate of the Subjunctive (Present and Imperfect) for 1sg in one study (Enríquez 1984: 351); and, in another, the Conditional has a higher rate than the Imperfect, which in turn does not differ from the Present (Claes 2011: 202).

Three-way ambiguity would occur in Caribbean Spanish varieties, which are known for variable expression of word-final /-s/, including in 2sg verb forms. For example, *trabajabas* 'you worked', with /-s/ deletion would be realized identically to 1sg and 3sg *trabajaba* 'I/he worked'. These same varieties also generally show higher rates of subject pronouns than non-deleting varieties (e.g., Cameron 1993: 306; Otheguy and Zentella 2012: 72). Compensation for word-final consonant reduction has been put forward as an explanation for dialect differences, on the basis of the argument that increased use of subject pronouns in Caribbean varieties is motivated by the ambiguity resulting when word-final /-s/ is deleted.

This account, formalized as the "functional compensation" hypothesis, was put forward in the framework of the more general proposal that language change is constrained such that relevant information is preserved in some linguistic form (Hochberg 1986: 609; Kiparsky 1982: 87). The preservation of meaning may be illustrated by the evolution of French, in which word-final /-s/ distinguished 2sg from 3sg, for example, in *tu vas* 'you go' vs. *il/elle va* 's/he goes'. It has been conjectured that with the loss of final consonants and the ensuing erosion of agreement marking on the verb, variably expressed subjects became obligatory in the diachrony of French, and more recently in Brazilian Portuguese (e.g., Kato 1999). Against functional compensation, however, Ranson demonstrates a lack of correlation between potential ambiguity and higher rates of subject pronouns in Old and Middle French (1999: 39). Furthermore, the increase in use of subject pronouns in French did not follow the loss of final consonants, but was related, rather, to word order change (Fleischman 1991: 277; Harris 1978: 112). For Brazilian Portuguese, Naro (1981) presents compelling evidence against a disambiguating role for subject pronouns in his apparent time study of the loss of agreement marking across age groups. He reports no increase in expressed subjects with third-person plural verbs that have dropped the agreement marking, and which are rendered "ambiguous" with this change (1981: 355).

How might we determine whether information preservation is at work in present-day Spanish subject expression? On the one hand, we would expect uniformly higher subject pronoun rates in (/-s/ deleting) Caribbean varieties. This is, however, not the case. For example, the rate of just 28 percent expression reported for Castañer, Puerto Rico, by Holmquist (2012: 208, N = 2,882) is more similar to (non-/-s/ deleting) Peninsular Spanish rates than those typically reported for Caribbean varieties.

On the other hand, if the grammar of Caribbean varieties is different, then this should be seen minimally in distinct tense effects. However, Cameron (1993), in a comparison of San Juan (Puerto Rico) and Madrid (Spain), found that, despite higher subject pronoun rates in San Juan than in Madrid, the probabilistic constraints were identical. Table 5.3 depicts three-way comparisons between forms with no syncretism in either variety (the Preterit), forms with two-way syncretism in San Juan (between 2sg and 3sg due to /-s/ deletion, primarily the Present), and forms with three-way syncretism in San Juan and two-way syncretism in Madrid (primarily the Imperfect). The three TAM classes are compared by subject continuity and by dialect. We see an intersection of TAM classes and subject continuity which holds in both dialects, such that a higher rate with the syncretic Imperfect emerges in non-coreferential contexts. From this comparison we learn, then, that tense interacts with subject continuity, and that it does so in the same way regardless of /-s/ deletion and potential morphological ambiguity. The conclusion is that "despite the difference in the rates ... the grammar of the two dialects ... is the same" (Cameron 1993: 315).

Table 5.3 *Subject pronoun rates and probabilistic constraints, by subject continuity and tense (morphological ambiguity) – Madrid and San Juan*

		Coreferential			Non-coreferential		
		Preterit	Present	Imperfect	Preterit	Present	Imperfect
Madrid	**%**	13%	14%	13%	34%	37%	44%
N=1,464	**Prob.**	.32	.34	.39	.61	.63	.76
San Juan	**%**	32%	32%	38%	55%	64%	73%
N=1,708	**Prob.**	.33	.30	.39	.57	.61	.74

Counted with Present are Future and Perfect forms; counted with Imperfect are Conditional and Subjunctive (singular persons, from Cameron 1993: 317–319). The Probability values are from variable rule analysis (D. Sankoff 1988b).[2]

5.6.2 The Discourse Function of Tense-aspect

An alternative interpretation of the tense effect is that the use of a TAM with expressed or unexpressed subjects is motivated by its discourse function, as proposed by Silva-Corvalán (1997; Silva-Corvalán and Enrique-Arias 2017: 180–181): the Imperfect, Conditional, and Subjunctive express backgrounded, non-factual, non-assertive verbal situations whereas perfectives (the Preterit) foreground events, and subject pronouns may be more consonant with backgrounded than foregrounded clauses.

An interpretation appealing to discourse function is consistent with the role of *temporal sequencing* in subject expression. Unexpressed subjects are favored in "discourse connected" clauses expressing a "sequence of events centered on the same referent" (i.e., with the same subject and the same tense) (Paredes Silva 1993: 43). More broadly, unexpressed subjects are favored in the subset of coreferential contexts in which the adjacent clauses have a temporal relationship, either of sequentiality, as in (82), or of simultaneity, as in (83).

(82)
Patricia: *Ø lo destapé,*   '(I) opened it,
             Ø lo miré,   (I) looked at it,
             .. y tiene casi lo mismo.   .. and it's almost the same.'

                                              (CCCS 09, 447–449)

(83)
Rocío: *.. Ø entró,*   '.. (he) came in,
          y Ø venía llorando,   and (he) was crying,'

                                              (05 Las Tortillas, 44:02–44:03)

---

[2] Probability values in variable rule analysis (D. Sankoff 1988b) indicate the strength of constraints relative to the "input probability" (which in turn reflects the overall rate of subject pronoun expression in each variety).

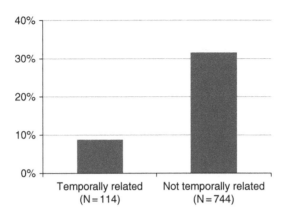

Figure 5.6 Rate of subject pronouns by temporal relationship
The rate is markedly lower in temporally related clauses than in clauses
lacking a temporal relationship, 9% vs. 32% (coreferential contexts, CCCS).

Temporal relationship applies to subject expression in coreferential mentions. Among these, it does not apply to subordinate clauses, nor to previous mentions by the interlocutor or in quoted speech, and so is relevant to only a portion of coreferential instances (approximately two-thirds). Even where applicable, coreferential-subject main clauses most often lack a temporal relationship, as is the case, for example, with stative predicates (Travis and Lindstrom 2016: 117–118). Yet though temporally related clauses make up only a small proportion of all coreferential instances, their effect is very strong: the rate of subject expression where there is a temporal relationship is nearly four times lower than where there is none (9 percent vs. 32 percent), as captured in Figure 5.6.

An appreciable difference between the tenses lies in their distributions precisely with respect to this sub-context – coreferential-subject clauses that have a temporal relationship. In Figure 5.7 we see that the Preterit is approximately twice as likely as the Imperfect to be used in a temporally related context (26 percent vs. 14 percent).[3]

On balance, despite the attention lavished on the tense effect in subject expression, it is usually weaker than subject continuity and, where included, priming, and person (Bentivoglio 1987: 60–61; Erker and Guy 2012: 547;

---

[3] The magnitude of tense effects is susceptible to genre. The Preterit more strongly favors unexpressed subjects in monologic narratives than in dialogic conversations, perhaps because of its association with temporally related contexts (Travis 2007: 119; cf. Givón 1990: 943ff on the genre dependence of TAM distributions).

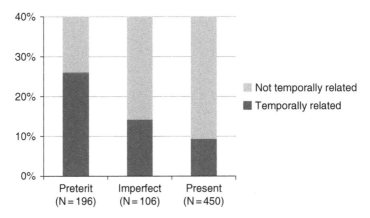

Figure 5.7 Distribution of tenses according to temporal relationship
26% of verbs in the Preterit appear in a temporally related clause compared with 14% of Imperfect verbs ($p < .05$) (and 9% of the Present) (coreferential contexts, CCCS).

Lastra and Butragueño 2015: 43; Otheguy and Zentella 2012: 181–182; Shin 2014: 311; Torres Cacoullos and Travis 2011: 253). The literature has privileged favoring of subject pronouns with the Imperfect (past imperfective), and this has been widely interpreted as serving to resolve ambiguity. However, the most consistent finding is the *dis*favoring effect of the Preterit (perfective), which may be propelled by the higher proportion of temporally related clauses with this tense, consonant with a discourse function interpretation of the tense effect.

5.7 Verb Class: Dynamic vs. Stative Verbs

A dynamic predicate involves change, whereas a stative situation continues as is unless something happens to change it (Comrie 1976: 48–50). A handful of verbs usually makes up datasets of statives, highly frequent being copulas *ser* and *estar* 'be', *querer* 'want, love', and *tener* 'have'. Dynamic verbs are more diverse, frequent types being *decir* 'say', *hacer* 'do', *ir* 'go', *ver* 'see', *dar* 'give', and *trabajar* 'work'.[4] The general result for subject expression is that dynamic ("external action" or activity) verbs disfavor subject pronouns, or favor *un*expressed subjects (e.g., Claes 2011: 205; Enríquez 1984: 240; Erker and Guy 2012: 541).

---

[4] Dynamic verbs comprise seven times as many distinct lexical types as stative verbs, 300 dynamic vs. 40 stative, in 1sg and 3sg subject expression data (CCCS).

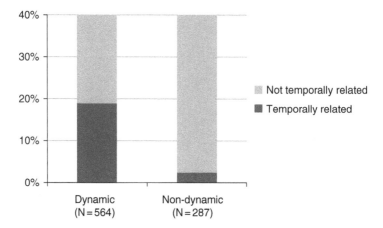

Figure 5.8 Distribution of dynamic vs. non-dynamic verbs according to temporal relationship
Coreferential contexts where temporal relationship is applicable: Proportion in temporally related clauses is 17% of dynamic verbs, 2% of non-dynamic verbs (CCCS).

This effect is at least in part due to a favoring of unexpressed subjects in clauses that are temporally related to the preceding clause, or, conversely, a favoring of pronouns in non-temporally related contexts (as seen in the previous section). Dynamic verbs occur proportionally more often in clauses that have a temporal relationship with a preceding coreferential-subject clause. Considering those instances in which temporal relationship applies, dynamic verbs occur in temporally related contexts nearly one-fifth of the time while non-dynamic verbs very rarely do so (Figure 5.8). Another piece of evidence supporting the contribution of temporal relationship is that it makes a difference even *within* dynamic verbs, where the subject pronoun rate is substantially lower in temporally related than in non-temporally related clauses (7 percent vs. 27 percent).

More generally, verb class intersects with tense-aspect. Table 5.4 shows subject pronoun rates (percent pronoun) and data distributions (percent data) by tense-aspect and verb class, here breaking down non-dynamic into stative verbs and cognition verbs such as *creer* 'think', and *saber* 'know' (which are aspectually stative). The rates of pronouns (shaded columns) tell us that tense differences do apply to dynamic verbs (first row), but that the difference is really one of aspect – perfective vs. imperfective – with the Preterit disfavoring subject pronouns much more than both the Imperfect and Present. For stative verbs (second row), however, tense-aspect is not of import for subject expression: differences between the Preterit and the Imperfect as well as the Present

Table 5.4 *Rate of subject pronouns by tense and verb class (% pron) and distributions of verb classes according to tense (% data)*

	Preterit		Present		Imperfect		
N	1,712		1,963		1,439		
	% pron	% data	% pron	% data	% pron	% data	N
Dynamic	12%	47%	19%	27%	22%	26%	3,326
Stative	31%	11%	28%	43%	30%	46%	1,103
Cognition	62%	4%	50%	87%	59%	9%	685

(NMSEB)

are negligible. Likewise, for cognition verbs (third row) there is virtually no difference between Preterit and Imperfect.

Also of consequence are the data distributions, or percentage of data (unshaded columns). First is the fact that cognition verbs are overwhelmingly used in the Present (87 percent). Second is the distributional skewing of lexical aspect, also known as Aktionsart: dynamic verbs are more associated with perfective aspect, whereas statives are more associated with imperfective (47 percent of dynamic verb tokens occur in Preterit forms whereas 46 percent of statives occur in Imperfect) (cf. Hopper 1979: 215).

In sum, the effect of lexical aspect helps us understand the role of tense-aspect in subject expression. The cross-tabulations of the intersecting variables of verb class and tense show clearly that verb class has a consistent effect such that subject pronouns are most favored by cognition verbs, much less by other statives, and least by dynamic verbs. Tense effects, on the other hand, are not consistent across verb classes. Given the association of dynamic verbs with temporal sequencing and with perfective aspect seen here (and cross-linguistically), their favoring of unexpressed subjects supports the interpretation of TAM effects – where actually found – as motivated by their discourse functions.

5.8   Verb Class: Cognition-Verb Constructions and Quotative 'Say'

Across different studies and different varieties, cognition verbs, also referred to as mental (activity) or estimative verbs, are the class that most favors subject pronouns (e.g., Bentivoglio 1987: 48–53; Claes 2011: 205; Enríquez 1984: 152, 235–245; Erker and Guy 2012: 541–542; Otheguy and Zentella 2012: 189; Posio 2013: 270; Silva-Corvalán 1994: 162; Travis 2007: 116–117).

Note that the strong favoring of subject pronouns with cognition verbs such as 'think' or 'know' really concerns only the 1sg subject *yo* 'I'. Close to 90 percent of cognition-verb tokens occur with 1sg subjects, and this group of verbs represents one-fifth of 1sg, but less than 3 percent of 3sg data (CCCS data). The skewed distribution of verb class and grammatical person means that the widely replicated favoring of Spanish subject expression with cognition verbs is specific to 1sg, not a general effect. The reason that it surfaces when the grammatical persons-numbers are analyzed together is that, in studies of personal pronoun use, 1sg is usually the most frequent subject to occur, alone constituting from one-third to one-half the data (e.g., Bayley et al. 2013: 27; Claes 2011: 199; Erker and Guy 2012: 540).

Cognition verbs with 1sg subjects constitute a class, as verified by their distinct linguistic conditioning of the pronoun *yo* 'I'. In the CCCS, 1sg subject expression with cognition verbs is conditioned by the position of the verb in the speaker turn (Travis and Torres Cacoullos 2012: 734–737) (cf. Bentivoglio 1987: 38–40). Per this local interactional effect, *yo* 'I' is favored in turn-initial position, as in line (c) in (84). Cognition verbs are also more likely to occur in non-coreferential contexts, which are favorable to *yo* 'I' (cf. Brown and Raymond 2012). The divergence in subject expression patterns, in addition to divergent rates, bolsters the evidence for a class of cognition verbs.

(84)

a.	Santi:	*De todos los carros que han comprado,*	'Of all the cars that they have bought,
b.		*es el más regularcito.*	it's the most mediocre.'
c.	Ángela:	*Yo creo que fue por=* --	'I think that it was --
d.		*.. Por el pre=cio.*	.. Because of the price.'

(CCCS 03, 408–411)

The class can be defined as comprising those items filling the schematic verb slot in a construction of the form [(*yo*) + COGNITION VERB$_{1SG}$]. In usage-based theory, constructions are form-meaning pairings that are usually partially schematic morphosyntactic structures. As Bybee (2010: chapter 5) characterizes them, constructions describe the relations between specific lexical items and specific grammatical structures. High-frequency exemplars are likely to be interpreted by language users as central members of categories, such that categorization is similarity based and can take place by reference to the central member. For example, the class of adjectives defined by the schematic slot in the [*drive* someone ADJ] construction is based on analogical comparison with the lexically particular [*drive* someone *crazy*]. Other less frequent adjectives, such as *insane* or *nuts*, are classified based on similarity to the central members, *crazy* (in American English) or *mad* (in British English).

The productive [(*yo*) + COGNITION VERB$_{1SG}$] construction is centered on the lexically particular constructions *(yo) creo* 'I believe/think' and *(yo) no sé* 'I don't know'. As conventionalized strings, lexically particular constructions have been called prefabs (Bolinger 1976: 1; Erman and Warren 2000), reusable fragments (Thompson 2002: 141), or formulaic language items (Corrigan,

Moravcsik, Ouali, and Wheatley 2009). Alone, *(yo) creo* and *(yo) no sé* account for a major portion of 1sg cognition-verb occurrences (56 percent, 165/296, in the CCCS). These 1sg Present-tense expressions qualify as lexically particular constructions, on the grounds of (1) frequency, (2) distributions across linguistic contexts, and (3) rates and conditioning of the pronoun *yo* (Travis and Torres Cacoullos 2012: 738–742).

(1) *Frequency*: Lexically particular constructions constitute a large proportion of their respective lexical types. For example, the forms *creo* 'I think' and *no sé* 'I don't know' comprise the majority of all tokens – all persons and tenses – of *creer* 'think' and *saber* 'know' respectively.

(2) *Contextual distributions*: Lexically particular constructions have distinct contextual distributions. For example, negated *no sé* 'I don't know' occurs at least half the time without a direct object, whereas the majority of affirmative *sé* 'I know' tokens occur with a complement clause.

(3) *Rates and conditioning*: Lexically particular constructions may retain variable elements, but differ both in rates of use and conditioning from the general construction. For example, *(yo) creo* 'I think' has a subject pronoun rate substantially above the overall average. Separate logistic regression analysis of Present-tense *creo* showed that while 1sg subject pronoun *yo* is still sensitive to priming, it is immune to subject continuity.

Frequency leads to the *chunking* of word sequences as single processing units, in the manner that repetition leads to the fusing of sequential experiences outside of language, as with tying one's shoelaces (Bybee 2010: 34 and references therein). For example, the vowel of *don't* is more likely to reduce to a schwa in *I don't know* than with a less frequent main verb, as in *I don't inhale*, even though the two expressions are apparently of the same syntactic structure (Scheibman 2000: 114). In subject expression, chunks would behave more as single units than as analyzable combinations of pronoun and verb (or of pronoun and negation and verb).

Nevertheless, chunk status is a gradient property. Formulaic lexically particular constructions retain patterns of, and interact with, their more general cognate constructions in synchronic variation and diachronic grammaticalization (Bybee and Torres Cacoullos 2009; Torres Cacoullos and Walker 2009, 2011). Thus, in comparing the linguistic conditioning of *(yo) creo* with the aggregate patterns of subject expression, there is dissimilarity for some probabilistic constraints (e.g., the lack of a subject continuity effect) and similarity for others (e.g., coreferential subject priming is retained). The difference in probabilistic constraints provides evidence for its status as a particular construction that is partially, but not wholly, autonomous from other instances of the more schematic [(yo) + Cognition Verb$_{1SG}$] construction.

The status of *yo creo* 'I think' as a particular construction favoring the subject pronoun appears to hold across several varieties – for example,

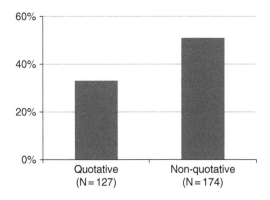

Figure 5.9 Rate of subject pronouns with verb *decir* 'say', by quotative vs. non-quotative uses
The rate is lower for quotative *decir*, 33% vs. 51% (CCCS).

Dominican, Mexican, (Erker and Guy 2012: 539), and Peninsular Spanish (Aijón Oliva and Serrano 2010: 6; Posio 2015: 67). This is not the case for *no sé* 'I don't know', which differs across varieties; in Puerto Rico it appears without the pronoun and so has been excluded from variable subject expression studies (e.g., Cameron 1992: 102), whereas in Cali, Colombia (CCCS data) its pronoun rate is higher than average.

Particular construction effects are also evident for speech verbs. Of notable frequency is the verb *decir* 'say' (Bayley et al. 2013: 26; Erker and Guy 2012: 536). *Decir* 'say' has been reported to occur with relatively high rates of expression, for example, in Colombian Spanish spoken on the coastal region of Barranquilla (Orozco 2015: 24), but with low rates of expression in Peninsular Spanish (Posio 2015: 65).

Higher or lower rates of expression for *decir* 'say' mask distinct tendencies for this verb in quotative vs. non-quotative uses. In the CCCS, the rate of expression of *decir* 'say' overall (43 percent) is similar to that in the dataset as a whole (41 percent). However, as seen in Figure 5.9, the subject pronoun rate for quotative *decir*, as in line (b) in (85), is lower than that in non-quotative uses, as in line (a). This disfavoring of subject pronouns with quotative *decir*, an effect that would pass unnoticed without breaking down the uses of this verb, again highlights the role of particular constructions in subject expression.

(85)
a. Javier: *Así Ø me dijo hoy.*   'That's what (he) said to me today.
b.   *... Porque Ø me dijo,*   ... Because (he) said,
c.   *y en qué anda papá?*   and what are you going in dad?'
                                                                    (CCCS 05, 1060–1062)

In conclusion, dialect-specific preferences for frequent expressions – with either higher or lower than average subject pronoun rates – recall what Clark (1996: 107) has called "communal lexicons." It is to be expected that prefabs, which "represent the conventional way of expressing an idea" (Bybee 2010: 81), may be specific to a speech community.

What do we gain by thinking of subject expression patterns as contoured by constructions? First, rather than lexical types or lemmas, relevant are particular constructions or chunks. It is not the frequency of individual verbs that matters, but individual verbs in specific grammatical structures (person, tense, polarity) associated with specific discourse contexts – for example, *(yo) creo* 'I think', or *(yo) no sé* 'I don't know' and quotative *decir* 'say'. Second, lexically particular constructions display idiosyncrasies – for example, lack of a subject continuity effect for *(yo) creo* – but also retain an association with, and contribute to, general subject pronoun expression patterns. And third, lexically particular constructions can have noticeably higher rates of subject expression, but also noticeably lower rates. The fact that particular high-frequency forms tend to conventionalize either with or without a subject pronoun lies behind the contradictory findings on lexical frequency effects on pronoun use in synchronic studies (e.g., Bayley et al. 2013; Erker and Guy 2012). The lack of uniform frequency effects for lexical items per se is just as would be predicted by usage-based theory.

5.9   Grammatical Person Differences

Grammatical person is often reported to be among the strongest factors conditioning subject expression. One consistent finding is that plural subjects have a lower rate of expression (e.g., Alfaraz 2015: 10; Bayley and Pease-Alvarez 1997: 363; Bentivoglio 1987: 36; Otheguy et al. 2007: 791). This result is a byproduct of linguistic contextual distributions, namely the greater propensity of plural than singular subjects to occur in the context of a previous partially coreferential mention (Cameron 1995: 21; see Section 5.3). Another result concerns the distinct behavior of 2sg subjects according to specificity of reference, though the direction differs across varieties. Non-specific 2sg referents (e.g., *tú llegas ahí* 'you get/one gets there') favor expression more than specific referents in Caribbean and some other Latin American varieties, while the opposite is the case in Madrid Spanish (Cameron 1993: 326; Lastra and Butragueño 2015: 44; Silva-Corvalán and Enrique-Arias 2017: 183). Non-specific 2sg is another example of community-specific norms of subject expression in particular constructions.

In most studies, 1sg favors pronominal expression more than 3sg does. Why is 'I' more likely to be expressed than 'he' or 'she'? The persons differ in their distribution with respect to verb class. As noted earlier, cognition verbs favor

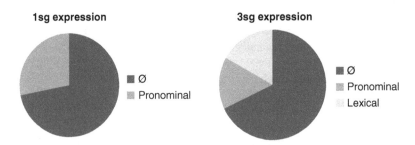

Figure 5.10 Form of 1sg and 3sg subjects: Ø vs. pronominal vs. lexical
1sg: 72% unexpressed, 28% pronoun (N = 3,296);
3sg: 68% unexpressed, 15% pronoun, 17% lexical (N = 2,737) (NMSEB).

pronominal subjects in Spanish and are overwhelmingly 1sg (Section 5.8). Cognition verbs make up notable proportions of 1sg and tiny proportions of 3sg subjects – for example, in conversational data from Swedish and American English, as well as in Spanish (Dahl 2000: 54; Scheibman 2001: 69, 82; Shin 2014: 311; Travis and Torres Cacoullos 2012: 726).

Beyond the contextual distribution difference with respect to cognition verbs, subject pronouns are thought to highlight the referent, so that greater expression of 1sg subjects would be consistent with the "egocentric nature of verbal communication" (Silva-Corvalán and Enrique-Arias 2017: 184, our translation). A problem is that egocentricity has been proposed to account for the contrary, i.e., lesser subject expression for 1sg. This is attributed, for example in Javanese, to speakers' desire not to put themselves forward, an assumption in turn questioned with the argument that 1sg pronouns are in fact widely used, but not in subject position (Ewing 2014: 59).

What is certain is that the lower rate of subject pronouns for 3sg is at least in part due to the fact that there exists a third form, namely a lexical subject. Figure 5.10 gives the rate of subject pronouns, on the left, for 1sg with the two-way breakdown (pronoun vs. unexpressed), and, on the right for 3sg, with the three-way breakdown. Pronominal tokens make up proportionally more of the 1sg than of the 3sg data (28 percent for 1sg vs. 15 percent for 3sg). Yet once we include both pronominal and lexical subjects, the difference between the persons in the proportion of *un*expressed subjects virtually disappears (72 percent vs. 68 percent).

5.9.1   *Grammatical Person and Accessibility*

It makes sense that there would be a true difference between first and third person in relation to their accessibility: while a first-person referent is always accessible as a discourse participant the same is not so of third-person referents,

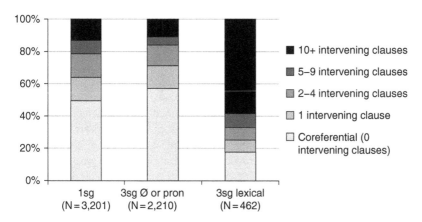

Figure 5.11 Distribution of 1sg and 3sg subjects according to distance from previous mention (Ø and pronominal vs. lexical)
1sg: 49% in coreferential contexts, 21% at 5+ distance;
3sg Ø and pronominal: 57% in coreferential contexts, 16% at 5+ distance;
3sg lexical: 18% in coreferential contexts, 58% at 10+ distance (NMSEB).

which are typically made accessible through a mention in the discourse (Chafe 1994: 78–79; Dahl 2000: 64–66). The difference is grammaticalized in some languages. For example, in languages with split ergative marking, third person may be treated differently from first and second person (Delancey 1981). And in languages with switch reference marking, this is sometimes applied only on third-person verbs (Haiman and Munro 1983: xi).

The two grammatical persons differ in the distribution of subject forms according to distance from the previous mention, as seen in Figure 5.11. The first two bars give the breakdown for 1sg and 3sg pronominal and unexpressed subjects and the third bar for 3sg lexical subjects. Comparing the first two bars, we see that 3sg pronominal and unexpressed subjects tend to occur closer together than 1sg subjects, appearing proportionally more in coreferential contexts and less with a previous mention at five or more intervening clauses. 3sg lexical subjects, however, occur the bulk of the time at a distance of ten or more intervening clauses from their previous mention. Full noun phrases are the favored 3sg form to introduce a new referent, or to return to a prior referent that hasn't been mentioned for some time (Travis and Torres Cacoullos 2018; cf. Dumont 2016: 84).[5] The conclusion is that lexical subjects are appropriately left outside the envelope of variation for

---

[5] Analyzed are lexical subjects in pre-verbal position, as for the pronouns (see Chapter 7, Section 7.2).

subject expression, but nevertheless impact patterns within it. The occurrence of unexpressed and pronominal targets at greater degrees of distance from their previous mention is depressed for 3sg precisely because speakers have the option of using a lexical subject.

This greater clustering of 3sg (unexpressed and pronominal) than 1sg subjects – more tokens occurring with a distance of 0 and fewer with 5+ intervening clauses from their previous mention – can be explained by the deictic properties of these subject persons: as external parties, 3sg subject referents are introduced as topics of discussion, and then abandoned, while 1sg subject referents can be referred to at any time without introduction. Dahl similarly finds greater "clustering" for third person than for first- and second-person referents in Swedish conversation, and remarks that "once you have started talking about a third-person referent, the chance that you will continue doing so also in the following clause is much higher than in the case of egophoric referents, other things being equal" (2000: 65). This contextual distribution provides a partial account for the higher rate of pronouns with 1sg subjects, when we consider the effect of subject continuity – 1sg subjects tend to occur with greater degrees of distance between coreferential mentions, while 3sg (unexpressed and pronominal) subjects occur proportionally more often in coreferential contexts.

Person differences go beyond the contextual distribution, however. 1sg and 3sg subjects also differ in how the effect of subject continuity applies. Figure 5.12 shows that for both persons there is a distance effect, with the rate of subject expression greater when there are ten or more intervening clauses than when there is just one intervening clause from the previous mention. This effect, however, kicks in earlier for 1sg, with a steady rise from zero through to five and then a sharper rise at 10 or more intervening clauses. For 3sg, on the other hand, the rate of subject pronouns vs. unexpressed subjects is basically constant up to four intervening clauses, at which point it increases modestly. Consistent with the pattern in Figure 5.12, it has been found that when all 3sg subject forms are considered in a single analysis, switch reference is pertinent for the choice of lexical, but not pronominal, over unexpressed subjects (Gudmestad, House, and Geeslin 2013: 287). The conclusion is that unexpressed and pronominal 3sg subject referents are treated as remaining locally accessible for a longer chunk of discourse than 1sg are.

In sum, grammatical person differences in rates of pronominal vs. unexpressed subjects are in part attributable to the availability of lexical subjects for 3sg. Evident are different distributions according to contexts impinging on subject expression, with 1sg subjects tending to occur more than 3sg subjects (setting aside full noun phrases) in environments that are propitious to subject pronouns, namely with cognition verbs and at greater distance from the previous mention. In contrast, 3sg subjects (again setting aside full noun phrases)

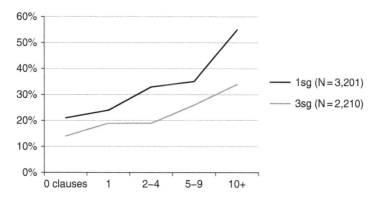

Figure 5.12 Rate of subject pronouns by distance from previous mention for 1sg vs. 3sg Ø and pronominal
1sg: 0 = 326/1,584; 1 = 109/458; 2–4 = 154/471; 5–9 = 93/268; 10+ = 229/420;
3sg: 0 = 181/1,262; 1 = 59/308; 2–4 = 55/286; 5–9 = 29/112; 10+ = 82/242 (NMSEB).

tend to cluster together and accessibility via previous mention has minimal impact at low degrees of distance, such that the rate of subject pronouns remains flat. Because 3sg unexpressed and pronominal subjects cluster together and are treated as accessible at low degrees of distance, the ratio of unexpressed to pronominal subjects is greater than it is with 1sg.

5.10   Conclusion

This chapter has reviewed and reinterpreted the principal probabilistic con-straints on Spanish subject pronoun expression. First, rather than functioning as markers of contrast generally, subject pronouns are favored in particular contrastive constructions, such as with converse predicates (which, however, are very uncommon). Second, though subject pronouns may serve functions of ambiguity resolution, contexts for such uses arise rarely and, though they may be of prime concern for linguistic theorists, they do not appear to be so for interlocutors.

Instead, the two most robust general effects are subject continuity and priming. Pronominal expression is favored at greater distances from the pre-vious mention of the subject referent, especially in the presence of intervening human subjects. This effect of subject continuity on Spanish subject expression is in agreement with the cross-linguistic tendency for less accessible referents to be coded with more linguistic material. As to priming, the pertinent effect is coreferential subject priming – favoring pronominal expression is previous mention in pronominal form, in line with the domain-general tendency to repeat structural patterns. The two probabilistic constraints interact, such that the effect of subject continuity is strongest when the previous mention is unexpressed.

Disfavoring pronominal expression within coreferential contexts is linking with the clause of the previous mention, syntactically by way of a conjunction and prosodically by means of a single IU or continuing intonation contour. Clause linking is reflected in clause type effects: pronominal subjects are least favored in coordinate clauses, followed by subordinate clauses, and are most favored in non-coordinate main clauses.

Also disfavoring subject pronouns are perfective aspect and dynamic verbs, both of which are associated with temporal sequencing in coreferential contexts. This pair of results concords with the interpretation of reported tense effects as driven by discourse function.

The role of semantic classes of verbs is an effect of lexically particular constructions, which idiosyncratically favor or disfavor subject pronouns. Such conventionalized units constitute a locus of community-specific norms. A candidate pan-Spanish construction is the frequent 1sg Present-tense *(yo) creo* 'I think', which is partially autonomous from the more schematic [*(yo)* + COGNITION VERB$_{1SG}$] construction and highly favorable to subject expression. On the other hand, the quotative *decir* 'say' construction disfavors expression, at least in some dialects.

Finally, grammatical person differences largely follow from data distributions impinging on subject continuity. In comparing the two most commonly used persons, 1sg subjects occur more often with greater distance between them, while 3sg pronominal and unexpressed subjects are more likely to cluster close together and to be treated as accessible at low degrees of distance, as new mentions tend to be introduced with full noun phrases.

In sum, behind familiar probabilistic constraints lie broader principles of variation. Spanish subject expression is most satisfyingly understood from tendencies found cross-linguistically, following from general cognitive mechanisms and wider discourse usage patterns. It is on this foundation that comparisons between language varieties can be insightful. In Chapter 7 we will see whether New Mexican Spanish subject expression shows departures from the monolingual benchmark, as quantitatively established here. But first, in Chapter 6, we turn to English subject expression, which has until now been only superficially considered in attributions of change to contact. The English benchmark will allow us to address whether bilinguals' Spanish subject expression evidences any English-particular tendencies, as predicted by the hypothesis of contact-induced grammatical change.

6 Cross-language Comparisons: Reconsidering Language Types

If change is due to convergence, then it must go in the direction of greater similarity with the contact language, as revealed by comparison of linguistic structures. A linguistic structure is a candidate for convergence if it is the locus of enough overlap between the languages in contact for bilinguals to make "interlingual identifications" (Weinreich 1953/1968: 7). These in turn would enable transfer from one language to the other of its distributions or functions, or "grammatical replication" of the superficially similar structure (Heine and Kuteva 2005: 2; Matras and Sakel 2007: 836). To verify that the provenance of any new distributions or functions is indeed the contact language, we must rule out common cross-linguistic tendencies of change. Thus, also required are interlingual differences: we have to know how monolingual varieties differ at the given structural site.

Subject pronoun expression is a candidate for grammatical convergence because Spanish and English subject pronouns are thought to be associated for bilinguals due to the overlap in their person-number categories and deictic meaning – referring to the speaker, interlocutor, and third persons. To date, however, no cross-language comparison has been carried out. The goal of this chapter is to pinpoint interlingual differences in the structure of variable subject expression, which will yield predictions to test contact-induced change in bilinguals' Spanish.

We begin by reconsidering the familiar distinction between null and non-null subject languages (6.1), leading us to put forward *variationist typology* (6.2). To see how postulated differences between language types play out in discourse, we rely on comparable speech corpora (6.3). The conversational data allow for a test of whether VP coordination is, as widely assumed, a discrete category that distinguishes English as a non-null-subject language. Instead, coordination turns out to be a gradient category of syntactic and prosodic linking and a locus of similarity between English and Spanish (6.4). Comparison of the variable context – where speakers have a choice between an unexpressed and a pronominal subject – brings to the fore a prosodic-initial-position restriction on unexpressed subjects in English, a key diagnostic difference between the two languages (6.5). Comparison of the probabilistic constraints operative within each of the variable contexts exposes remarkable similarities across the two languages in direction of effect, consistent with shared cross-linguistic patterns. But further differences are identified in effect strength (6.6). A third site of measurable cross-language differences is contributed by language-specific lexically particular constructions (6.7).

6.1   Null- vs. Non-null-subject Languages

The distinction between null and non-null-subject language types has been a staple of linguistics for decades. Functionalist typologists, seeking to identify linguistic universals, and formalist syntacticians, in the tradition of Universal Grammar, largely converge on a classification of language types according to the expression of pronominal subjects. Languages such as English (as well as, for example, French and Icelandic) with "obligatory pronouns," or "non-null-subject" languages, are contrasted with those "in which the normal expression of pronominal subjects is by means of affixes on the verb," or "null-subject" languages – for example, Spanish (and Greek and Arabic, among others) (Dryer 2013; Roberts and Holmberg 2010).

The following example from the Santa Barbara Corpus of Spoken American English (SBCSAE; see Section 6.3) illustrates variability in English. The pronominal subject has been underlined, and a Ø has been inserted to indicate an unexpressed subject.

(86)
Jeff: *So=,*
          ... he= .. took off for .. Big Bear.
Jill: *... You're kidding.*
Jeff: *Ø Had no idea where he was going,*

(SBCSAE 28: 630–633)

Though unexpressed subjects do occur in English, they are rare in everyday speech, in line with the classification of English as a non-null-subject language. Comparing Spanish and English conversation, overall rates of non-expression for 1sg and 3sg human specific subjects are indeed conspicuously different: 60 percent in Spanish (1,726 out of 2,879), but approximately 3 percent in English (329 unexpressed out of an estimated 10,000). The considerable rate difference has led many to assume that Spanish and English must also be fundamentally different in the patterns of variation between pronominal and unexpressed subjects (e.g., Otheguy et al. 2007: 772; Sorace 2004: 144), or that unexpressed subjects in English have "special properties that distinguish them from the canonical null subjects" (Roberts and Holmberg 2010: 5). This difference has also been the basis of the prediction that US Spanish varieties will evince higher rates of subject expression than non-contact varieties.

One problem in testing the hypothesis of disparate rates is that, beyond significance according to a statistical test, a linguistically meaningful threshold for "higher" (or lower) rate would have to be determined. When it comes to subject expression, there are non-negligible differences in overall rate among null-subject languages. For example, Polish and European Portuguese are both considered null-subject languages, yet showed a 27 percentage point difference in non-expression rates, at 79 percent and 52 percent respectively for first-person singular (1sg) (Chociej 2011: 52, N = 536; Posio 2013: 269, N = 704) (see Chapter 1, Figure 1.2). Moreover, within a single null-subject language we also find overall rate differences. For example, for third-person singular (3sg) subject pronouns with human specific referents, rates of unexpressed subjects vary strikingly in Spanish: compare 68 percent in conversational Colombian data (see below) with 73 percent (N = 450) in sociolinguistic interviews in Mexico City (Lastra and Butragueño 2015: 43) and 97 percent (N = 285) in narratives by Peninsular Spanish speakers (Comajoan 2006: 60). These differences may be due to situational circumstances that in turn affect data distributions – for example, high proportions of coreferential contexts in narratives – which raise the rate of non-expression (Travis 2007: 130).

Fundamental is that such blatant differences in overall rates of use cannot be taken as evidence of differences in grammatical structure (Chapter 1). In Spanish, for all the differences in rates of expression, the constraints identified across varieties have been found to correspond. For example, even though Otheguy, Zentalla, and Livert found a 12 percentage point difference between speakers of Mainland vs. Caribbean dialects, the top five probabilistic constraints were ranked identically according to magnitude of effect (setting aside "set phrases") (2007: 785, 789). And even though Cameron found a 24 percentage point difference between San Juan and Madrid, the probability values for subject continuity and other constraints were "startlingly similar" (1993: 319), as they were for Caracas and Los Angeles (Silva-Corvalán and Enrique-Arias 2017: 175–176).

That is, by the criterion of uniformity in the conditioning of variability, the grammar of subject expression across Spanish varieties is one and the same (cf. Chapter 5, and summary in Chapter 7, Table 7.1).

6.2   Variationist Typology

To pinpoint cross-language similarities and differences in actual language use, we look not just to rates, but to the structure of variability. The variationist comparative method adds a quantitative component to the comparative method of historical linguistics, by incorporating the inherent variability characteristic of speech (Poplack and Meechan 1998: 129–132). Variationist comparative analysis considers, together with the overall frequency of some feature, details of co-occurrence and distribution in discourse. Cross-linguistic tendencies may be manifested as putative categorical constraints in some languages and as "statistical preferences" in others (Bresnan, Dingare, and Manning 2001; cf. Givón 1979: 22–43). Building on this idea, here we apply what we call variationist typology (Torres Cacoullos and Travis (To Appear)).

Variationist typology: Cross-linguistic tendencies are manifested in shared aspects of the variable structure internal to each language. Methodologically, similarities and differences across languages are identified through comparisons of intra-linguistic variability. The locus of such comparisons is both the set of *probabilistic constraints* on the variation and the delimitation of the *variable context* within which the probabilistic constraints are operative.

The proposed dynamic approach directs attention to the factors shaping linguistic structure and giving rise to similarities and differences among languages. Rather than a focus on linguistic forms as static structures, consideration is given to the processes shaping them and the functions they serve (Bybee 2009; Croft 2001: 60). Variationist typology elucidates cross-language similarities and differences that have been obscured by the time-honored classification into null-subject vs. non-null-subject language types. It also allows us to develop criteria to distinguish contact-induced from internal change, the basis for the comparisons in Chapters 7 and 8.

6.3   Data for Comparative Analysis of Monolingual Benchmarks

To explore the locus of cross-language similarities and differences in language use, we examine 1sg and 3sg subjects in conversational data from two directly comparable corpora. The English data are extracted from the SBCSAE (Du Bois et al. 2000–2005), which consists of 60 recordings made 1988–1996. We make use here of the 50 transcripts that have tokens of unexpressed 1sg or 3sg human specific subjects (N = 329). This subcorpus totals approximately 207,000 words, and includes 88 speakers who produce unexpressed subjects. The Spanish data are drawn from the CCCS (cf. Travis 2005: 9–25), which consists of 30 conversations recorded in 1997 and 2004. The CCCS comprises a total of approximately 100,000 words, or nine hours of speech, from 37 speakers (the corpora are presented in Chapter 1, Table 1.1).

Crucially, as we will shortly see, these corpora, like the bilingual (NMSEB) corpus, are prosodically transcribed following the same precise protocols (Chapter 3, Section 3.4). The speech is broken down into prosodic units. Each IU appears on a distinct line followed by punctuation representing its prosodic contour. In example (87), the last IU is marked with a period, which indicates "final" intonation (a fall to low pitch), while the preceding IUs are marked with commas, which indicate "continuing" intonation (Du Bois et al. 1993: 53). The sequence of IUs in (87) forms a "prosodic sentence" (Chafe 1994: 139–140) and illustrates the role of prosody in the linking of clauses.

(87)

Tom: *And finally,*
        when I ran out of money,
        uh=,
        I wrote home to my family and said,
        would you be kind enough to uh,
        please send me a passage ho=me.

(SBCSAE 32: 508–513)

6.4   VP Coordination

The main observation regarding subject expression from grammars of English is that the subject can be left unexpressed under coordination (e.g., Quirk, Greenbaum, Leech, and Svartvik 1985: 910). Unexpressed subjects in what is known as VP coordination are said to not be true null subjects, based on the understanding that verbs under coordination involve a single clause with two predications, rather than two clauses with a null subject in the second (cf. Haspelmath 2004: 31; Huddleston and Pullum 2002: 238). In this vein, scholars have appealed to Conjunction Reduction as a rule according to which two sentences are reduced to one under coordination (e.g., Akmajian and Heny 1980: 261–262). Such claims have been made, however, in the absence of an operational definition of VP coordination. More generally, the notion of coordination remains nebulous, with unclear or inconsistent criteria applied. Thus, a first question is whether English has genuine null subjects. To answer this, we look beyond theory-internal convictions and test empirically whether VP coordination is a discrete category, and whether it is a distinguishing feature of English as a non-null-subject language.

In general, English VP coordination is applied to the occurrence of an unexpressed subject that is coreferential with a preceding subject. Beyond coreferentiality, two sets of features to consider are conjunction presence and prosodic relation (Chapter 5, Section 5.5).

We probe first conjunction presence, which embodies *syntactic* linking. Verbs with coreferential subjects may be coordinated with or without a conjunction, in so-called syndetic as opposed to asyndetic coordination (cf. Biber, Johansson, Leech, Finegan, and Conrad 1999: 156; Haspelmath 2004: 4). The coordinating conjunctions in the dataset are *and, but*, and *or*, and these in combination with an adverb (e.g., *and then*). Figure 6.1 compares coreferential main-clause contexts with *and*, other coordinating conjunctions, and no conjunction. One finding from quantifying the use of these conjunctions in

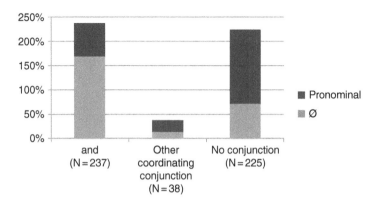

Figure 6.1 Syntactic linking: Coreferential main-clause contexts according
to the presence of a conjunction (number of occurrences and proportion
of Ø)
Overall sample rate of Ø is artificially high; see Section 6.5.1 (SBCSAE).

speech data is that *and* is by far the most frequent, occurring over six times as
often as all other coordinating conjunctions combined. Another is that coordination with *and* appreciably has the highest rate of unexpressed subjects –
double that both with other coordinating conjunctions and in the absence of
a conjunction (71 percent, 169/237, vs. 35 percent, 13/38, and 32 percent, 72/
225, respectively, in a dataset with an artificially high rate of unexpressed
subjects, see Section 6.5.1).

Thus, in operationalizing VP coordination, we can establish that not all
forms of coordination are equal in discourse: coordination with *and* is pre-
ponderant and distinct from both asyndetic coordination and syndetic coordination with other conjunctions. The conclusion is that it is *and*-coordination
that realizes maximal *syntactic* linking between coreferential-subject main
clauses.

Second, in speech, *prosodic linking* is integral to coordination. Verbs with
coreferential subjects may be prosodically connected or not. To specify the role
of prosody in coordination, we can measure prosodic connectedness by relying
on the boundary and contour of the prosodic unit. Defined as prosodically
linked are clauses that occur in the same IU or in adjacent IUs connected with
a continuing intonation contour (see Chafe (1988: 10) for English and Mithun
(1988: 332) cross-linguistically). Not prosodically linked are clauses that are
separated by final (period) or appeal (question mark) intonation, truncation, or
intervening IUs.

Let us consider now prosodic linking together with syntactic linking (via
and). For two verbs with coreferential subjects, there are four possible linking
configurations:

1) maximally linked, both syntactically (via *and*) and prosodically (in the same IU, (88), or across IUs connected by continuing intonation, (89));
2) linked only syntactically (90);
3) linked only prosodically (91);
4) no prosodic nor syntactic link (92).

(88)
✓ syntactic linking (*and*),
✓ prosodic linking (same IU)
a. ... *that's when he came* .. *and Ø s=at b=y me,*   (SBCSAE 08: 495)
b. *So this man walked up to him and he said,*   (SBCSAE 08: 1224)

(89)
✓ syntactic linking (*and*),
✓ prosodic linking (continuing intonation contour)
a. ... *Dad called him,*
    and Ø told him he had to.   (SBCSAE 31: 363–364)
b. *so he came,*
    and he stood opposite me,   (SBCSAE 55: 161–162)

(90)
✓ syntactic linking (*and*),
✗ prosodic linking (e.g., final intonation contour)
a. *and he ran them off.*
    ... *And Ø saved their lives.*   (SBCSAE 30: 572–573)
b. *he's a broker.*
    ... *And he buys hay,*   (SBCSAE 56: 803–804)

(91)
✗ syntactic linking (no *and*)
✓ prosodic linking (continuing intonation contour)
a. *A=nd then I worked for a rancher over there for a while,*
    ... *Ø followed the rodeos for a while,*   (SBCSAE 32: 1587–1588)
b. *That's what I did all day today,*
    I had ... three or four different kids come up,   (SBCSAE 43: 156–157)

(92)
✗ syntactic linking (no *and*),
✗ prosodic linking (e.g., final intonation contour)
a. ... *And yesterday was the first day she used it.*
    Ø Put a bunch of stuff in it to read,   (SBCSAE 43: 34–35)
b. .. *I do the hard labor.*
    I build barns and,   (SBCSAE 56: 84–85)

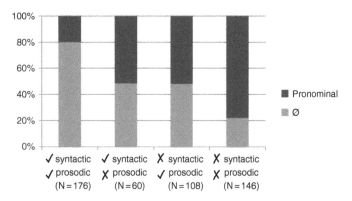

Figure 6.2 Prosodic and syntactic linking: English
Rate of Ø according to prosodic link to preceding clause & *and*-coordination
(coreferential main clause contexts)

Looking for verification that transcends theoretical orientations, and recognizing the circularity of the argument that the presence of the subject pronoun itself annuls VP coordination, we make a prediction that can be quantitatively falsified. If coordination is a discrete category of false null subjects, and the second verb is not a genuine clause, we expect categorical behavior – 100 percent unexpressed subjects – in at least the configuration with the tightest linking. But in fact, none of the configurations is exclusive of either variant: both unexpressed subjects, illustrated in (a) in each pair of examples in (88) through (92), and pronominal subjects, illustrated in (b), occur in each configuration.

Figure 6.2 gives the rates of subject expression across the four configurations. Instead of categorical behavior we find gradience: the tighter the link – *prosodic* and *syntactic* – between the target and the preceding clause coreferential subject, the higher the rate of unexpressed vs. pronominal subjects.

Furthermore, if VP coordination were a property specific to English as a non-null-subject language, we would expect to observe differences with Spanish, a bona fide null-subject language. Figure 6.3 shows that instead there is a similar, graded effect of linking in Spanish as there is in English.

In sum, contrary to what has been widely assumed, once operationalized and tested against the data, VP Coordination in English shows neither categorical nor patently special behavior. These facts compel us to conclude that VP Coordination must be abandoned as a discrete category and as a property of English that sets it apart as a non-null-subject language: English does have genuine null subjects. And, as in Spanish, coordinate clauses, including those that are

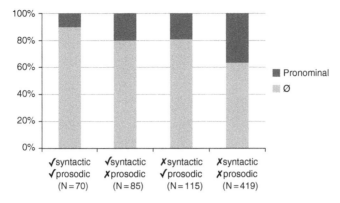

Figure 6.3 Prosodic and syntactic linking: Spanish
Rate of Ø according to prosodic link to preceding clause & *y* coordination
(coreferential main clause contexts)

maximally linked (with conjunction *and* along with prosodic connection) belong
to the variable context.

Unlike Spanish, however, outside coordinate clauses the variable context in
English is restricted, primarily by considerations of prosody.

6.5   Differences in the Variable Context: The English Prosodic-Initial Restriction

The two loci of cross-language comparisons in variationist typology are first,
the *variable context*, and second, the *probabilistic constraints* on the variation
within that variable context. We begin with delimitation of the envelope of
variation.

The variable context is the broadest domain in which speakers have a choice
between variants – for subject expression, the set of linguistic contexts where
both pronominal and unexpressed subjects occur. By delimiting the variable
context, we can follow the principle of accountability: "that reports of the
occurrences of a variant must be accompanied by reports of all non-occurrences"
(Labov 2004: 7). In order to identify the probabilistic constraints on speakers'
choices, the analysis must be limited to contexts where the two variants are
alternatives, and contexts where either unexpressed or pronominal subjects are
used all or none of the time must be accounted for separately.

Outside of coordinate clauses, unexpressed subjects in English occur solely
in prosodic-initial position, preceded in the IU by at most non-speech material
such as fillers (*um*), laughter or pausing (Torres Cacoullos and Travis 2014:
25–26). In the data under study here, there are no tokens of unexpressed

subjects in non-IU-initial position. Therefore, non-IU-initial pronouns must be excluded. In (93), for example, the IU-initial pronoun in *he doesn't* occurs in the variable context; the non-initial *he* in *he's gay* does not.

(93)
Cam: .. <u>*He₁ doe=sn't know* that *he₂'s gay?*</u>
Lajuan: .. *Hm-mm.*
            .. *Ø₁ <u>Has</u> no idea.*

(SBCSAE 44: 250–253)

The restriction to initial position has been interpreted as a syntactic constraint under the formalist view of English null subjects as a "root" (main-clause) phenomenon (e.g., Haegeman 2013). It has alternatively been considered a phonological constraint, under what has been termed "left-edge deletion" of sentence initial material (Weir 2012; cf. Napoli 1982; Quirk et al. 1985: 896; Sigurðsson and Maling 2010). Apparent support for the clause as the unit of analysis is that, of the 329 unexpressed 1sg and 3sg subjects in the SBCSAE, none occur in subordinate clauses nor in interrogatives.[1] However, while unexpressed subjects are favored in clause-initial position, they are not restricted to that position (cf. Harvie 1998: 21; Leroux and Jarmasz 2005: 4).

Prosodically based transcription makes a decisive difference here. Thanks to transcription in IUs we can tease apart clause type and prosodic position. In subordinate clauses (N = 96) and interrogatives (N = 16), pronominal subjects virtually always occur in non-IU initial position, preceded by a subordinating conjunction, relative pronoun, *wh*-word, or a form of *do*. So, we can't tell whether the absence of unexpressed subjects here is due to clause type or to prosodic position. However, subject pronouns in main-clause declaratives occur in both prosodically initial and non-initial position – for example, preceded by *well, oh, of course* in the IU (approximately one-quarter of the time in non-initial position, 99/388). If the restriction were a purely syntactic one, then unexpressed subjects in declarative main clauses should mirror pronominal subjects and also occur in both initial and non-initial IU position. But in fact, outside of coordinate clauses, unexpressed subjects never occur in non-prosodic-initial position. Thus, we can establish that the lack of variability in subordinate clauses and interrogatives is bound up with prosody, and therefore the pertinent unit is not the clause or sentence. The initial-position restriction of non-coordinated unexpressed subjects is prosodic. In English, then, non-coordinated non-IU-initial pronouns fall outside the variable context.

Spanish is not similarly restricted, showing robust variability in both IU-initial and non-IU-initial position, and, correspondingly, in both main and

---

[1] In a sample of subject pronouns made up of the first 10 occurrences in each of the 50 SBCSAE conversations with unexpressed 1sg and/or 3sg subjects.

subordinate clauses. It is important, too, that what is a categorical restriction in English is not even a statistical preference in Spanish, as unexpressed subjects are not favored in IU-initial over non-IU-initial position (55 percent, 972/1,761, and 66 percent, 541/823, respectively). The prosodic-initial position restriction represents a clear *diagnostic difference* between English and Spanish. As a context in which the two languages in contact display contrasting patterns, the diagnostic difference, or "conflict site," provides a hard test for convergence in bilingual varieties (Poplack and Meechan 1998: 132).

What other sub-contexts are excluded from the variable context in each language? Non-variable formulaic expressions must be set aside. In English this includes *I mean, I guess, I think* when used as discourse markers, for which we treat the pronoun as an integral part of the chunk. Discourse marker uses are defined as instances that are prosodically independent (occupying their own IU) or that occur as parentheticals (Travis and Torres Cacoullos 2014: 366). Also invariable are quotatives, such as *I said, she goes* (outside coordinate clauses). And, finally, pronouns with contracted auxiliary forms (e.g., *he's, I'm*) are also excluded.

In Spanish, frequent cognition-verb expressions, such as *yo creo* 'I think', and quotatives, such as *dije* 'I said', are variable and therefore are included (though their status may differ across varieties; see Chapter 5, Section 5.8). Falling outside the variable context are subjects in *wh*-interrogatives, which either are unexpressed or expressed in postverbal position. Postverbal subjects are not an alternative variant for subject expression because they are sensitive to different conditioning factors from unexpressed and preverbal pronominal subjects (see Chapter 7, Section 7.2). An additional but small set of excluded items are so-called emphatic constructions in which the pronoun is followed in the same IU by *mismo* 'same' (e.g., *yo mismo* 'I myself') or *sí* 'yes' (e.g., *yo sí* 'I do', literally 'I yes'; see Chapter 5, Section 5.1).

Figure 6.4 depicts the set of environments constituting the variable context in English and Spanish. While in Spanish nearly all finite verb tokens occur within the variable context, in English the proportion of subject pronouns occurring within the variable context is less than one-half. Our first finding, then, is that one locus of difference can be precisely pinpointed in the much narrower variable context in English, driven primarily by the prosodic position restriction.

6.5.1   Principled Sampling of Non-occurrences

To account for the patterning of unexpressed subjects, we have to consider their non-occurrences – that is, pronominal subjects. In English, because unexpressed subjects are so outnumbered by pronouns, we create a higher relative frequency of the unexpressed variant for the statistical analysis by taking a principled sample of pronominal subjects (e.g., Harvie 1998: 18).

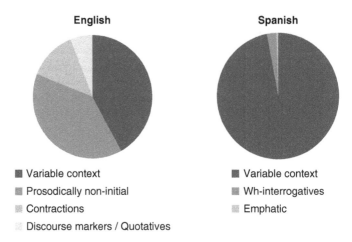

English

- ■ Variable context
- ■ Prosodically non-initial
- ▨ Contractions
- ░ Discourse markers / Quotatives

Spanish

- ■ Variable context
- ▨ Wh-interrogatives
- ▨ Emphatic

Figure 6.4   The variable context for subject pronoun expression in English vs. Spanish
English (SBCSAE) N = 500, sample of subject pronouns; Spanish (CCCS) N = 2,879
English tokens belonging to more than one category of non-variable context were classified following the order indicated, thus proportions of Contractions and Discourse markers/Quotatives under-represent their occurrences.

For each unexpressed subject we extracted the closest preceding and following subject pronoun of the same grammatical person produced by the same speaker, and falling *within the variable context*. Because of the narrow variable context, in more than half of the instances we had to go past the immediately preceding or following pronoun to extract an eligible one for the sample. By way of illustration, in example (94), of the four 1sg subject pronouns in the proximity of the target unexpressed subject in line (a), only one falls within the variable context. The pronoun in (c) occurs with a quotative (and not in a coordinate clause), and neither of those in lines (a) and (d) occur in IU-initial position or in a coordinate clause. Note that the pronoun in line (a) also occurs in a subordinate clause, and that in line (d) also in an interrogative. Thus, we extract the pronoun in (e) as the closest eligible token following the unexpressed subject in (a).

(94)   pronoun in variable context
a. Jim: *... And even if I go out and Ø a=sk for it.*   ✗
b.   *you know,*
c.   *I say,*   ✗
d.   *<Q can I copy that Q>.*   ✗
e.   *.. I won't feel guilty.*   ✓

(SBCSAE 17: 3–7)

This protocol resulted in an English dataset of 987 observations, and a modified rate of unexpressed subjects of 33.3 percent (329/987). This artificial rate allows us to examine the relative frequency of the variants in linguistic sub-contexts, in order to discern the effect that those sub-contexts have on speaker choice to express the subject or not. In the next section we compare the probabilistic constraints defined by these sub-contexts with those that affect Spanish subject expression. Do these differ, as do the variable contexts?

6.6   Similarities in the Probabilistic Constraints

The second step in variationist typology is to compare the internal structure of the variability. This is instantiated by the *linguistic conditioning* of variant selection in each language – that is, probabilistic statements about the co-occurrence of the variants and elements of the linguistic context in which they appear. These contextual elements embody hypothesized constraints. Candidate shared constraints cross-linguistically are accessibility, priming, tense-aspect, and person (see Chapter 5 for discussion of these probabilistic constraints in Spanish).

Table 6.1 shows the results of two identical logistic regression analyses (specifically, variable rule analyses, D. Sankoff 1988b), run independently on each dataset.[2] While in the rest of the book we take the perspective of pronominal subjects, in this chapter we take the complementary perspective, presenting the effect of the conditioning factors on non-expression (which is merely a mirror image of results for expression). The analyses identify a statistically significant subset of the factor groups, or predictors, that account for the variation in each dataset. English is presented on the left, and Spanish on the right. The first column of numbers gives the probability value for an unexpressed subject. A value closer to 1 shows the *favoring* of an unexpressed subject, and closer to 0 a disfavoring effect (or, favoring of the pronoun). The following columns give the rate of unexpressed subjects (% Ø) and the number of tokens (N).

Selected as having a significant effect (indicated in bold) are Accessibility, configured as linking to the preceding subject, Coreferential subject priming, and Verb class, while Tense-aspect is not selected as significant in either language. Person is not included for English given the sampling protocol of extracting two pronouns of the same grammatical person for every unexpressed subject. We see here that, *in both languages*, unexpressed subjects are most favored: when linked to the preceding coreferential subject, when the previous coreferential subject was also unexpressed, and with

---

[2] Variable rule analysis (VRA) draws attention to data distributions in natural speech, clearly displays direction of effect, and, in the Goldvarb application (D. Sankoff, Tagliamonte, and Smith 2015b), permits exclusion of sparse categories from particular predictors rather than excluding data points entirely. Generalized linear mixed-effects models corresponding to the VRAs in Table 6.1 are given in Torres Cacoullos and Travis (To Appear).

Table 6.1 *Two independent analyses of factors significant to unexpressed vs. pronominal subjects*

	English N=329/987; Input: .29 (Artificial rate: 33.3%)			Spanish 1,659/2,802; Input: .60 (Overall rate: 59%)		
	Prob	% Ø	N	Prob	% Ø	N
Accessibility as linking						
Coreferential and linked	.79	65%	344	.69	79%	458
Coreferential only	.42	24%	226	.52	63%	700
Non-coreferential	.27	13%	403	.44	52%	1588
Range	*52*			*25*		
Coreferential subject priming						
Previous mention unexpressed	.67	57%	116	.63	73%	841
Outside priming environment*	.46	20%	343	.47	55%	1138
Previous mention as pronoun	.49	37%	508	.38	46%	637
Range	*21*			*25*		
Verb class						
Dynamic	.55	41%	627	.57	67%	1761
Stative	.40	20%	210	.41	53%	685
Cognition	.45	20%	138	.35	35%	335
Range	*15*			*22*		

Also included in analyses: Tense-aspect (Present vs. Past in English, perfective vs. non-perfective in Spanish), not significant in either language; Person in Spanish, 3sg .57, 68%, 1,413 vs. 1sg .43, 50%, 1,389.

* Outside priming environment: for both languages, previous mentions as full NPs and relative pronouns, previous or target in quoted speech, and previous produced by interlocutor; for English, previous mentions beyond 5 clauses; for Spanish previous mentions beyond 10 clauses and previous postverbal subjects.

dynamic over stative verbs (and with 3sg over 1sg, as we will see). Overall, then, unlike the language-particular variable contexts, the probabilistic constraints turn out to be shared across the two languages.

The striking interlingual similarity, which exists despite the classification of Spanish and English into opposing language types, is our second finding in this variationist typology endeavor. At the same time, linguistic conditioning yields diagnostics for contact-induced change, derived from loci of difference. These we can precisely discern by digging deeper, to pursue detailed views of each predictor.

6.6.1   *Accessibility as Linking, Semantic and Structural*

A candidate universal conditioning factor of subject expression is what has been termed "accessibility" (Ariel 1994: 2630; Givón 1983: 17), "activation" (Chafe 1994: 75), or "recoverability" (e.g., Haegeman 2013: 89). The observation has been that the greater the "accessibility," "activation," or "recoverability" of the subject referent, the greater the likelihood that the subject is unexpressed. For subject expression, accessibility has generally been configured as subject continuity. In Chapter 5 (Section 5.3), we saw that most favorable to unexpressed subjects are coreferential contexts, namely where a previous mention by the same speaker occurs as the subject of the immediately preceding clause or of a prior clause without an intervening human subject. Coreferentiality with the preceding clause subject conditions variable subject expression in Spanish and across a range of other languages: for example, Arabic (Owens, Dodsworth, and Kohn 2013: 263), Australian Sign Language (McKee, Schembri, McKee, and Johnston 2011: 388), Bislama (a Vanuatan creole) and Tamambo (an indigenous language of Vanuatu) (Meyerhoff 2009: 308), Persian (Haeri 1989: 160), and English (Harvie 1998: 21; Leroux and Jarmasz 2005: 7; Torres Cacoullos and Travis 2014: 24; Travis and Lindstrom 2016: 112).

We refine the measure of coreferentiality by bringing in structural linking between clauses, syntactic and/or prosodic, following from what we saw in examining VP coordination (Section 6.4; also Chapter 5, Section 5.5). Here, considering both coordinate and subordinate clauses, syntactic linking is realized by means of a conjunction, coordinating or subordinating, and prosodic linking by virtue of occurrence in the same IU or in adjacent IUs connected with continuing intonation. In the proposed refinement, "linkage to antecedents" (Levinson 1987: 381) or "conjoinability" of clauses (Li and Thompson 1979: 330) comprises a combination of semantic and structural features, with the semantic link of coreferentiality being broken into two categories based on the presence or absence of structural linking. The hypothesis is that, within coreferential contexts, unexpressed subjects are favored more with structural linking than without. As can be seen in Table 6.1, the hypothesis is borne out: unexpressed subjects are most favored precisely when the preceding clause subject is coreferential and there is also a prosodic and/or syntactic link between target and preceding clause (as in examples (88)–(91) above), less so in coreferential contexts when there is no such structural linking (as in (92)), and least in non-coreferential contexts (as in (93)).

Note that structural linking with the preceding clause impacts subject expression in Spanish as well as English: beyond mere coreferentiality with the preceding subject there is a difference between coreferential contexts with vs. without structural linking between the clauses. This result confirms that it will be profitable to rethink accessibility in discourse as a composite of semantic and structural features (see Chapter 5, Sections 5.3 and 5.5). We have learned something new about subject expression in a null-subject language thanks to the analysis of a non-null-subject language!

Yet, a difference between the two languages is to be found in the relative strengths of the shared probabilistic constraint. An indication of relative

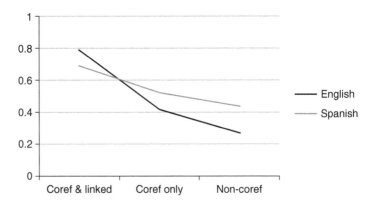

Figure 6.5 Probability of Ø according to linking with preceding clause subject (Table 6.1)

strength is the Range of probability values for each predictor. In English, Linking (accessibility) clearly is a stronger constraint than either Priming or Verb class (displaying a Range that is more than double that of the other significant predictors), while in Spanish this is not the case. Figure 6.5 displays the strength of Linking in English in the steeper drop in the probability of an unexpressed subject, from the relative favoring in structurally linked contexts to the strong disfavoring in non-coreferential contexts. In Spanish, though the tendency is identical, the decline is more gradual.

The difference in effect strength impacts the distribution of unexpressed subjects: in English, tokens in prosodically connected *and*-clauses constitute 43 percent (140/329) of all unexpressed subjects, while in Spanish, prosodically connected *y*-clauses make up just 4 percent (63/1,659) of the total. The impact of prosodically connected *and*-coordinate clauses has surely fed the presumption of a qualitatively special status for VP coordination in non-null-subject languages. Here we see how the quantitative comparative analysis of variationist typology allows us to discern a locus of difference in strength of effect, while revealing that the trend, or direction of effect, in the two languages is the same.

6.6.2   Grammatical Person

Grammatical person effects on subject expression have been reported for a range of languages, for example, Arabic (Owens et al. 2013: 268; Parkinson 1987: 356), Cantonese, and Russian (Nagy et al. 2011: 141–142). Differential behavior according to person has been widely reported for Spanish, often as the strongest constraint (see discussion in Silva-Corvalán and Enrique-Arias 2017:

183–185). The most pertinent person difference is that between 1sg and 3sg human specific subjects, as these two persons make up the bulk of the data of variable subject pronoun expression. Together they account for approximately two-thirds of Spanish data, with 1sg being two to three times more frequent than 3sg (e.g., Claes 2011: 199; Erker and Guy 2012: 540; Lastra and Butragueño 2015: 43), and are also the most frequent in English conversational data (Scheibman 2001: 68, 80).

1sg usually favors pronominal expression more so than 3sg in Spanish (e.g., Ávila Jiménez 1995: 29; Bayley and Pease-Alvarez 1997: 363; Cameron 1992: 168; Enríquez 1984: 350; Morales 1986: 93–96; Orozco 2015: 27; Posio 2015: 72; Ranson 1991: 139). The same pattern has been observed not only in the typologically similar language Brazilian Portuguese (Silveira 2011: 48), but also in Mandarin Chinese (Jia and Bayley 2002: 110). You may remember from Chapter 5 (Section 5.9), this is because the availability of lexical subjects for third person contributes to distinct contextual distributions of pronominal and unexpressed subjects. As compared with 1sg, 3sg pronominal and unexpressed subjects are more likely to occur in a coreferential context, and even in non-coreferential contexts they tend to cluster together more. They also show lesser sensitivity to subject continuity at lower distances from the previous mention. The result is greater favoring of unexpressed subjects with 3sg than with 1sg.

For English, where pronominal subjects were sampled by extracting two of the same person for every unexpressed subject (Section 6.5.1), we estimate the overall rate of unexpressed subjects within each person by taking the number of tokens of Ø as the numerator, and that of Ø + pronoun as the denominator. Based on this calculation, the rates of unexpressed subjects are 5 percent (180/3,500) for 3sg vs. 2 percent (149/6,600) for 1sg, the same pattern observed in Spanish. The greater likelihood of unexpressed subjects for 3sg human specific referents than for 1sg is a locus of similarity across the two languages. No change in grammatical person effects would therefore be predicted for bilinguals' Spanish as due to English influence.

6.6.3   Coreferential Subject Priming

Structural priming is the repetition of the same syntactic structure across clauses. A priming effect for subject expression, though not as widely tested as coreferentiality, has been observed in spontaneous speech data for Spanish (Chapter 5, Section 5.4) and several other languages, for example, Australian Sign Language (McKee et al. 2011: 388), Bislama and Tamambo (Meyerhoff 2009: 308), and for Italian, in experimental work with children (Serratrice 2009).

Coreferential subject priming is repetition of the form of the previous coreferential subject. Accordingly, in English, the unexpressed variant is favored when the previous mention was also unexpressed (Torres Cacoullos and Travis 2014: 29–30; Travis and Lindstrom 2016: 115). Unexpressed-to-unexpressed priming in a coreferential context is shown in (95), and in a non-coreferential context in (96).

(95)
Miles: *But it was like I went to Bahia,*
            ... last Sunday,
            ... Ø got there at eight,
            .. Ø left a te=n,
            ... Ø dropped this person off at home,

                                                   (SBCSAE 02: 848–852)

(96)
Fred: *... I look at my bank sta- .. bank statements.*
            And,
Wess: *Mhm.*
Fred: *... Ø look through my checks.*
            When they come in.
            .. And Ø make sure that it's fine.

                                                   (SBCSAE 59: 749–754)

Coreferential subject priming is not to be dismissed as repetition in the service of some rhetorical function, for example as a cohesive device (Fox 1987: 31–32, 54; Halliday and Hasan 1976: 282–284; Oh 2006: 830–835). For subject expression in English especially, it may be conjectured that clustering of unexpressed subjects serves to present chains of events as connected. However, while clusters of English unexpressed subjects are indeed favored in chain-like events, as in (95), equally chain-like events can be presented with expressed subjects, as in (97) (Torres Cacoullos and Travis 2014: 29).

(97)
Mary: *and I started up the engine and,*
            both !Gary and !Rita were sitting on the edges of their seat.
            ...(SWALLOW) And I turned around and I looked,
            .. and I said,
            ... <Q did I scare you kids Q>?

                                                   (SBCSAE 07: 549–553)

Figure 6.6 displays the rate of unexpressed subjects according to the realization of the previous coreferential subject (as either pronominal or unexpressed) by linking to the preceding clause. The priming effect in both English (on the left) and Spanish (on the right) can be seen at each degree of linking in that the first in each pair of columns – previous unexpressed – is higher than the second – previous pronoun.

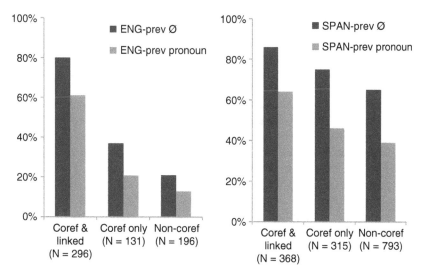

Figure 6.6 Rate of Ø according to priming and linking: English and Spanish
English (SBCSAE): 53/66 vs. 140/230, $p < .01$; 7/19 vs. 23/112, $p = .14$; 6/30
vs. 23/166, $p = .40$.
Spanish (CCCS): 90/220 vs. 95/148; 134/179 vs. 62/136; 288/441 vs.
137/352, $p < 0.0001$ (in all cases, by Fisher's exact test).

Although both languages exhibit coreferential subject priming, the fine
details of this effect are not identical. In English the effect is shorter lived,
dissipating in non-coreferential contexts (Figure 6.6, left panel, third pair of
columns). Thus, while in Spanish, priming and subject continuity moderate
each other (see Chapter 5, Section 5.4.1), in English the two effects are bound
together, such that we get clusters of unexpressed coreferential subjects. This
points to another difference, which is that the priming effect is one-sided in
English – unexpressed subjects are favored by a previous unexpressed, but
pronominal subjects are not favored any more with a previous pronominal
mention than in other environments, as seen in the probability values in
Table 6.1. In English, then, the priming is from unexpressed to unexpressed
only. This is consistent with the general finding that the less frequent variant
primes more; for example, passives prime subsequent passives more than
actives prime actives (Jaeger 2010: 45; Jaeger and Snider 2007). Finally,
English *and*-coordination, which makes up a bigger proportion of the data
than Spanish *y*-coordination does, often counteracts Ø to Ø priming, since the
predominant pattern is a pronominal subject in the first conjunct paired with
an unexpressed subject in the second (Torres Cacoullos and Travis 2014: 30;
Travis and Lindstrom 2016: 115–116).

6.6.4   Lexical Aspect: Dynamic Verbs and Temporal Sequencing

Both languages exhibit an identical effect for dynamic verbs, which favor non-expression. Coded as dynamic are a range of verbs of action (e.g., *put, do, give*), motion *(go, come)*, speech *(say, tell)*, and perception *(see, look)*, and as stative, verbs such as copulas, *have*, and *want*.

The effect of dynamic verbs found in both languages is consistent with the favoring of unexpressed subjects in clauses that are temporally related to the preceding clause (Chapter 5, Section 5.6.2). Temporally related clauses are consecutive main clauses with coreferential subjects that refer to events or situations which are temporally sequential or simultaneous (Travis and Lindstrom 2016: 117). Example (98) illustrates temporal sequentiality (here, in a narrative sequence, cf. Labov and Waletzky 1997 [1967]: 12–13) and example (99) temporal simultaneity. Non-temporally related contexts include those where at least one of the verbs is a stative verb, such as 'have' or 'be', or occurs with habitual aspect, as in (b) in (90) (*he buys hay*) and in (92) (*I build barns*) (unless the events are habitually sequential or simultaneous). Also non-temporally related are cases of a repetition of, or elaboration on, the previous verb, as in (100).

(98)
Jo: *... So I said that's not ... as per our agreement,*
                    he said yes it is,
                    he handed me my check,
                    Ø rolled up his window,
                    and Ø drove off.

                                                            (SBCSAE 53: 289–293)

(99)
Wood: *and he stood opposite me,*
                    and Ø looked at me,

                                                            (SBCSAE 55: 161–162)

(100)
Darlene: *he almost died.*
                    Too.
                    He almost died twice.

                                                            (SBCSAE 52: 1066–1068)

English unexpressed subjects are highly disfavored in the absence of a temporal relationship with the preceding coreferential-subject main clause (Travis and Lindstrom 2016: 114). But in both languages there is a substantially higher rate of non-expression in temporally related than in non-temporally related clauses (for English, 77 percent (172/224) compared with 31 percent (74/238), and, for Spanish, 91 percent (104/114) vs. 68 percent (509/744), considering only coreferential tokens that occur in contexts where temporal relationship is applicable).

This contributes to the favoring of unexpressed subjects by dynamic verbs, given that a far greater proportion of dynamic than non-dynamic (stative and cognition) verbs is associated with temporal sequencing. We saw this in Chapter 5 (Section 5.7) for Spanish, and it is also true for English (where the proportion of temporally related cases is 60 percent, 211/350, for dynamic verbs vs. 12 percent, 13/109 for non-dynamic verbs).

The association between dynamic verbs and temporal sequencing is consonant with the distribution of lexical and grammatical aspect that has been proposed to apply cross-linguistically. Dynamic verbs are more likely to co-occur with perfective aspect, expressing a temporally bounded, or completed, event, whereas stative predicates are more associated with imperfective, or continuing, situations. Imperfectives in turn are associated with "backgrounded" clauses of narratives and changes of subject (Hopper 1979: 215–216). The differential behavior of the aspectual classes of dynamic vs. stative verbs is a candidate for a universal constraint on subject expression cutting across cross-linguistic types.

In sum, we have compared the internal structure of variable subject expression, which is the second step in variationist typology. We can conclude that whereas the variable contexts differ, the probabilistic constraints operative within each are shared across the languages. Linking to the preceding subject (a refined measure of accessibility), priming (of the previous coreferential subject's form) and lexical aspect apply to English as well as Spanish. A difference is that linking between clauses in English is stronger relative to the other constraints in operation. To complete the comparison, we now consider particular constructions, which turn out to be specific to each language.

6.7   Language-specific, Lexically Particular Constructions

In Spanish, cognition verbs strongly disfavor unexpressed subjects, and strongly favor 1sg subject pronoun *yo* 'I'. In Chapter 5 (Section 5.8) we saw evidence for cognition-verb constructions *yo no sé* 'I don't know' and *yo creo* 'I think'. Both qualify as lexically particular constructions having not only distinct subject expression rates but also distinct variation patterns. In English as well, cognition verbs are associated with 1sg subjects, accounting for approximately one-quarter (100/447) of all 1sg tokens, but just one-tenth of 3sg tokens (38/540). But English 1sg cognition verbs do not behave uniformly with respect to subject realization. Their seeming disfavoring of unexpressed subjects (in Table 6.1) is due to *think*, which accounts for over one-third of the 1sg cognition verbs, and has a rate of non-expression of just 8 percent (4/42) (compared with the overall – artificial – rate of 33.3 percent). Further evidence of non-uniform behavior comes from variable subject pronoun stress, with respect to which 1sg cognition-verb expressions display idiosyncratic rates: whereas stress on *I* is favored in *I don't know*, it is not favored in *I think* and is invariably absent in *I mean* and *I guess* (Travis and Torres Cacoullos 2014: 380–381).

Specific to English, a general construction favoring unexpressed subjects is that in which coreferential-subject clauses are conjoined with *and*, which we may depict as [VERB$_i$ *and* Ø VERB$_i$]. Two frequent manifestations are with a verb of motion as the first verb and with a verb of speech as the second verb, as in (101) (Torres Cacoullos and Travis 2014: 31). These two particular constructions together account for approximately one-third (101/344) of all structurally linked (prosodic and/or syntactic) cases and nearly three-quarters (48/68) of all cases of conjuncts in the same IU. Same-IU conjuncts are the most propitious site for unexpressed subjects, notwithstanding the occasional pronominal subject (as seen in (b) in (88) above). While VP coordination does not exist as a discrete category (see Section 6.4), same-IU *and*-constructions anchored in motion or speech verbs are units of maximal linking that are strongly associated with unexpressed subjects.

(101)
[VERB$_i$ *and* Ø VERB$_i$]:
    [MOTION VERB$_i$ *and* Ø VERB$_i$]
    [VERB$_i$ *and* Ø VERB-OF-SPEECH$_i$]

These manifestations of *and*-coordination merit the status of particular constructions by virtue of their frequency and the relatively high rates of unexpressed subjects. The [MOTION VERB$_i$ *and* Ø VERB$_i$] construction has a rate of non-expression over twice the overall average, at 85 percent (50/59). The most frequent motion verbs are *go* and *come*, with other verbs such as *walk* also included. An example with *go* is seen in (102), where the two conjuncts occur in a single IU, and with *come* in (b) in (89), where they occur across IUs in a prosodically linked context (with continuing intonation).

The [VERB$_i$ *and* Ø VERB-OF-SPEECH$_i$] construction has a rate of non-expression of 88 percent (45/51). The most frequent speech verbs are *say* (N = 28) and *tell* (N = 18). This construction is illustrated in (103) across prosodically linked IUs, and in (87), within a single IU. Note that half the tokens of *say* occur in the [VERB$_i$ *and* Ø VERB-OF-SPEECH$_i$] construction, where the subject is nearly categorically unexpressed (26/28). This may give the impression that the verb *say* favors unexpressed subjects (with an overall rate of 55 percent, 28/51). But when we compare with instances outside of this construction, the subject is rarely unexpressed (just 2/23). This suggests, then, that it is the construction, and not *say* itself, that favors non-expression, which underscores that apparent lexical frequency effects may be epiphenomenal of particular constructions, as described in Chapter 5 (Section 5.8).

(102)
Danny: *... So she goes and Ø gets=* .. *the mother.*

(SBCSAE 30: 432)

(103)
Lajuan: *Like he called me last week,*
                 and Ø said he wanted to be with me.

(SBCSAE 44: 1068–1069)

A strong favoring of unexpressed subjects in *y* 'and'-coordinate clauses in the same IU is also evident in the Spanish data – for example, with the verb *coger* 'take, get' as the first verb, illustrated in (104) (a construction also reported for Puerto Rican Spanish; see Cameron 1992: 103). But same-IU 'and' instances are less productive in Spanish, where they account for only 5 percent (12/295) of linked main clauses, whereas in English they account for 20 percent (68/344) of linked clauses.

(104)
Santi: *Tu mamá me coge y Ø me dice un poco de cosas,*
                 'Your mom grabs me and says a bunch of things to me,'

(CCCS 02: 5211)

In sum, lexically particular constructions for subject expression are language-specific and a locus of difference between English and Spanish. Spanish has $[(yo) + \text{COGNITION VERB}_{1SG}]$ constructions, for example, while English displays particular $[\text{VERB}_i \; and \; Ø \; \text{VERB}_i]$ constructions.

6.8   Conclusion

Despite the conspicuous rarity of unexpressed subjects, English displays striking parallels with variation patterns in Spanish, a canonical null-subject language.

These parallels include an effect for coordination. Here, we have confronted the theoretical construct of VP coordination with patterns in speech, and seen that it is not a discrete category. Rather, there is a continuum according to linking to the preceding coreferential-subject clause. There are higher rates of unexpressed subjects with prosodic and syntactic linking, lower rates with either one or the other kind of structural linking between coreferential-subject clauses, and yet lower rates in coreferential contexts lacking structural linking. The same graded effect also applies to Spanish, demonstrating, then, a similarity across the languages in what has been declared a feature specific to

English. Thus, it will be worthwhile to reconceive of accessibility of the subject referent, long put forward as the most important determinant of subject expression, as encompassing not only coreferentiality with the preceding clause subject but also structural – prosodic and syntactic – linking. We further hypothesize that, in addition to accessibility, other candidate cross-language constraints on subject expression will apply independently of classifications of language types. One such tendency is the favoring of non-expression by 3sg human specific over 1sg subjects, as the availability of lexical new mentions results in greater clustering of unexpressed and pronominal subjects for 3sg. Another is coreferential subject priming, whereby speakers favor the form of the previous coreferential subject that they produced. And another is verb aspect, such that dynamic predicates favor unexpressed subjects, an effect that reflects the contribution of a temporal relation to subject expression.

Variationist typology directs us to look at the variable structure internal to each language to elucidate cross-language comparisons. By accounting for the conditioning of variation in the null and non-null-subject languages, we have been able to gain insights into cross-linguistic tendencies. Such insights are unavailable from classifications of language types according to the presence or absence of some feature or even the frequency of the feature, which are not enlightening about interlingual similarities or differences in everyday speech.

Given similarities in the probabilistic constraints in operation and their direction of effect, where are measurable interlingual differences to be found? It is by delving into the fine quantitative patterns that we are able to devise diagnostic tests for convergence. The explorations undertaken here suggest that primary loci of cross-language differences are language-specific restrictions to the variable context, relative magnitude of probabilistic constraints, and lexically particular constructions. First and foremost, the languages are distinguished by their envelopes of variation. In English, unexpressed subjects outside of coordinate clauses are limited to prosodic-initial position, a restriction that is not even a tendency in the same direction in Spanish. Second, linking between clauses is by far the strongest probabilistic constraint, overshadowing all others, in English but not in Spanish. A third site of cross-language difference lies in lexically particular constructions, such as [MOTION VERB$_i$ *and* $\emptyset$ VERB$_i$] and [VERB$_i$ *and* $\emptyset$ VERB-OF-SPEECH$_i$] in English vs. [(*yo*) + COGNITION VERB$_{1SG}$] in Spanish.

Thanks to these diagnostic differences in subject expression, we can now formulate criteria for contact-induced change that overcome the vagaries of overall rates. If English is influencing the Spanish of bilinguals, we should observe that subject pronoun rates are relatively higher or lower according to favoring or disfavoring contextual features.

- Rates will be lower in prosodic-initial position (a tendency toward the prosodic-initial position restriction for unexpressed subjects in English);
- Accessibility as a linking effect will be relatively stronger (due to the greater relative strength in English);
- The favoring of subject pronouns in first-person cognition-verb constructions will be weaker, and y 'and'-coordinate clauses will be extended (under the influence of translation-counterpart lexically particular constructions).

These predictions will serve to diagnose convergence of bilinguals' Spanish toward English in Chapter 8, after we first inquire whether bilinguals' Spanish displays divergence from earlier-stage and monolingual Spanish controls, in Chapter 7.

7   Assessing Change and Continuity

7.1   Accounts of Contact-induced Change

The spontaneous speech of bilingual community members provides an irreplaceable window into grammars in contact. This is the kind of data recorded in the NMSEB corpus, as we saw in Chapters 2, 3, and 4. In Chapters 5 and 6 we characterized and compared Spanish and English subject expression. We are now in a position to address the question of whether change has in fact occurred: is the grammar in contact different from the grammar not in contact?

The most common form of grammatical change attributed to language contact has been described as the development of a minor use pattern into a major use pattern (Heine and Kuteva 2005: 48; Silva-Corvalán 1994: 4). A prominent case study is the increase in frequency of subject pronouns in "null-subject" languages in contact with "non-null-subject" languages, in which subject pronouns are used overwhelmingly. As well as Spanish, other examples are Slavic or Turkish under the influence of English (Backus 2005: 333; Heine and Kuteva 2005: 70). Overextension of subject pronouns has alternatively been explained as a bilingual default processing strategy to manage the demands of multiple constraints. This is to account for increased rates of expression in contact between two null-subject languages, for example, among children speaking Spanish and Italian (Sorace and Serratrice 2009; Sorace, Serratrice, Fillaci, and Baldo 2009). By either account, the prediction is that among Spanish–English bilinguals, Spanish subject pronoun rates will be elevated.

Somewhat paradoxically, the obverse – lower subject pronoun rates – is also a predicted outcome of contact. A lower subject pronoun rate follows from the hypothesis that contact-induced change takes the form of a kind of grammatical simplification, with loss of "pragmatic" constraints on when to use a subject pronoun (Silva-Corvalán 1994: 147). The hypotheses commonly entertained, then, are in conflict when it comes to rates of subject pronouns – expected to be higher, with overextension, or lower, with loss of pragmatic functions. Thus, the outcome of contact-induced change as manifested in overall rates is uncertain.

There seems to be more consensus on predicted alterations in probabilistic constraints on subject expression. It is widely held that, as an indirect other-language effect, bilinguals' use of subject pronouns in a language like Spanish in contact with a language like English becomes less sensitive to conditioning factors. By one account, the surmised absence of equivalent conditioning factors in the non-null-subject language results in their weakening in the null-subject language, as bilinguals have fewer opportunities to practice them (Otheguy and Zentella 2012: 167–168). A similar account, again resting on the premise of the lack of discourse factors in English subject expression, is that the less complex grammar prevails in bilinguals (Sorace 2004: 144). In an alternative explanation, bilingualism intrinsically makes acquisition of discourse conditioning factors more difficult, irrespective of the languages involved (Sorace et al. 2009: 473).

Whatever the rationale, the anticipated outcome is erosion of the functions of subject pronouns in the null-subject language, as instantiated in the conditions on their selection over unexpressed subjects. Most susceptible to contact-induced change are seen to be discourse-pragmatic constraints on when to deploy a subject pronoun and when to leave the subject unexpressed. Especially implicated is the constraint of accessibility according to the recency of the previous subject mention of the referent (Chapter 5, Section 5.3). One idea is that, as an "aspect[ ] of grammar at the syntax-discourse interface," accessibility is "more vulnerable ... than purely syntactic aspects" (Sorace 2004: 143). This is congruent with Heine and Kuteva's proposal that the discourse-pragmatic role of pronouns in presenting new topics may be lost with overextension of their use in contact varieties (2005: 70). Subject continuity has thus become the poster child for loss of discourse-pragmatic constraints in subject pronoun expression.

Despite the prolific literature, the prediction of weakened constraints has only been partially tested. Studies have been limited to one-dimensional comparisons, usually within the same corpus, comparing first- and second-generation or recent and established immigrants, for example. This has been for the good reason that the strength of constraints is not straightforwardly comparable across disparately assembled or non-identically analyzed datasets. In this and the following chapter, we will confront the problem of comparisons across different datasets – relevant whether comparing languages, varieties of the same language, or groups of speakers within the same corpus – by supplementing regression analyses with cross-tabulations and other detailed views of data distributions.

The pivot for the comparisons is subject pronoun expression in bilinguals' Spanish. Section 7.2 specifies the variable context, and reviews critical issues for what to count in spontaneous speech data. Spanish subject expression in the NMSEB corpus is characterized quantitatively in Section 7.3. Comparisons of conditioning factors are then implemented. The first is with an earlier, less bilingual, stage of the same variety to ascertain whether change has occurred (7.4). The second, with non-contact varieties, will reveal whether bilinguals' Spanish diverges from monolingual Spanish (7.5). Comparisons with English varieties, both monolingual and as spoken by the same bilinguals, are the focus of the next chapter.

7.2   Delimiting Subject Expression in Spontaneous Speech Data

The linguistic variable – choice of grammatical means of mentioning an accessible subject – has two variants: the presence of a subject pronoun and the absence of any subject noun phrase, commonly termed an unexpressed or null (∅) subject.

Lexical subjects do not belong to the linguistic variable because they mostly occur with a distant previous mention of the same referent in subject position (Chapter 5, Section 5.9). Also set aside are postverbal subject pronouns, illustrated in (105), because subject pronoun expression and position have different linguistic conditioning. Postverbal placement of the subject pronoun is favored in the presence of preverbal elements in the clause and in the prosodic unit, and with quotative *decir* 'say' (Benevento and Dietrich 2015: 415; Silva-Corvalán 1982: 113).[1]

(105)
Mariana: *puras mujercitas tengo yo.*   'I_POST have all girls.'
                                                (19 School Bus, 40:05–40:07)

The analysis here is circumscribed to first- and third-person singular subjects with human specific referents. By concentrating on 1sg and 3sg we account for the bulk of the subject expression data while bypassing the confounds of contextual distributions particular to plural subjects and of dialect-particular treatments of non-specific *tú* 'you' (Chapter 5, Section 5.9). Non-specific referents (N = 42), such as the unexpressed 'someone else' in (h) in (106) are outside the purview of subject expression because they are virtually never realized as 3sg personal pronouns *él* or *ella* (note that *uno* 'one', N = 43, is not counted as a personal pronoun). Subject relative clauses (N = 110), in which the subject is expressed via a relative pronoun, are also not part of the linguistic variable, for example, *un hombre que trabaja conmigo*, 'a man who works with me' (31, 08:01).

---

[1] The rate of postverbal subject pronouns is 17 percent (280/1,633) in NMSEB. Contra an English-influenced structural convergence hypothesis, this rate is not lower than in monolingual varieties; compare 2 percent (44/2,846) for 1sg and 3sg in the CCCS, 14 percent (64/443) for all persons in Mexico City (Lastra and Butragueño 2015: 41), and 12–17 percent in Peninsular Spanish (Posio 2012: 154).

(106)

a.	Inmaculada:	*no nos caíbanos,*	'we wouldn't fall,
b.		*y nos --*	and we --
c.		*n- --*	w- --
d.		*.. porque a- --*	.. because a- --
e.		*.. con eso jugábanos.*	.. that's what we used to play with.'
f.	Lucy:	*.. mhm.*	'.. mhm.'
g.	Inmaculada:	*que viniera alguien otro,*	'if someone else were to come,
h.		*entonces sí se lastimara.*	then (they) would get hurt.'

(08 Graduación Familiar Pt1, 12:34–12:40)

The linguistic conditioning of pronominal subjects can be discovered only by counting their occurrences against all non-occurrences – that is, unexpressed subjects where a personal pronoun could have been used. The first step, then, is to define the envelope of variation, or variable context – the sum of contexts in which speakers have a choice between variants (cf. Labov 1972b: 72).

All tokens of finite Spanish verbs with pronominal and unexpressed 1sg and 3sg (human specific) subjects were initially extracted. Tokens that fall outside the variable context were then set aside, as were tokens that could not be reliably analyzed.

In identifying non-variable contexts, the question is not a matter of assessing, on a case-by-case basis, whether both variants are theoretically possible, but rather one of giving replicable "broad definitions of clausal and lexical types where variability is low enough to disqualify them from the study" (Otheguy et al. 2007: 776). The non-variable contexts involve *wh*-interrogatives (N = 114), in which subjects are either unexpressed or occur in postverbal position – for example, *a ver qué agarré* 'let's see what (I) got' (12, 15:05), and *qué tengo yo áhi?* 'what do L_{POST} have there?' (12, 42:57). Other types with low, or no, variability are emphatic constructions with *mismo/mero* 'very, same' / *sí* 'yes' (N = 8) and focus constructions (e.g., *la única era ella.* 'The only one was her.' (15, 16:35) (N = 2). These emphatic constructions, though much discussed, are rare in NMSEB, just as in monolingual varieties (Chapter 5, Section 5.1). Conventionalized formulae are also excluded (e.g., *ahí voy* '(I) am coming', N = 5). Formulaic expressions may be variety-specific; thus, for example, *(yo) no sé* '(I) don't know' is variable in NM Spanish, and so included here (see Section 8.4).

Also excluded are cases that cannot be reliably analyzed, as captured by the transcription. These involve potentially unexpressed subjects in contexts of repair (N = 20), for example with the verb in line (b) in (107), where following truncation the speaker partially repeats what she had just said. Excluded, too, are prosodically truncated instances where the speaker cuts off before completing the verb or just after it, and does not produce a subject pronoun, as in line (c) in (108), since there could potentially be a truncated postverbal subject (N = 155). In addition, where we cannot tell whether a candidate subject preceding a subordinating conjunction is functioning as the subject of the subordinate verb, of a following main verb (if there is one), or neither, these are excluded (N = 23), as, for example, in *el Chalo siempre que va a hacer alguna cosa, le duele el espinazo* 'Chalo whenever (he) is going to do something, his backbone hurts' (11, 20:21).

(107)
a. Mónica: *yo no tu- --*   'I wouldn't --
b.   *tuviera miedo de hacerlo,* wouldn't be afraid of doing it,'

(11 El Trabajo, 36:12–36:13)

(108)
a. Rubén: *.. pero yo pensé que=,*   '.. but I thought that,
b.   *...(0.9) que de algún modo,* ...(0.9) that somehow,
c.   *.. era --*   .. (she) was --
d.   *.. parienta,*   .. a relative,'

(29 La Diploma 36:01–36:08)

Nor can we reliably assign pronouns as subjects to verbs that occur in a different IU when they are not prosodically linked – that is, where the IU of the pronoun occurs with either truncation or final intonation (N = 59). Conversely, pronouns separated from the verb by continuing (comma) intonation are counted (N = 43) (Chapter 3, Section 3.6), as are pronouns separated by adverbs such as *nomás* 'only, just', *nunca* 'never', *quizás* 'maybe', *también* 'also', *ya* 'already' (N = 71), since these adverbs also co-occur with unexpressed subjects – for example, *mira que yo ya estoy viejito* 'see I'm already old' (17, 1:03:10); *porque ya Ø estoy retired* 'because (I)'m already retired' (06, 41:27).

Exclusions apply as well to speech insufficiently clear to definitively identify the realization of the subject (N = 41), for example, <X ella X> se llamaba Filomena= '<X she X> was called Filomena' (18, 1:02:32), where material in <X_X> is the transcriber's best guess at unclear speech; instances occurring in word play or as metalinguistic commentary – for example, in joking about the surname Casimiro, homophonous with *casi miro* '(I) nearly see' (N = 14); and expressed subjects in rare configurations (N = 9) – for example, a verb flanked by two pronouns.

The notably small number of contextually ambiguous cases, where the subject cannot be identified, was excluded (N = 25). Even this modest number overstates the incidence of true ambiguity (Chapter 5, Section 5.2). In some cases disambiguation would be inconsequential; for example, in (109), it doesn't matter whether the driver or the car had problems. Other cases arise only because the speaker abandons the utterance, as in (110).

(109)

Mariana:	.. *como que ya no querían .. correr.*	'.. like they didn't want to .. run anymore.'
Gabriel:	*yeah.*	'yeah.'
Mariana:	.. *eso sí.*	'.. that yes.
	.. <u>*tenía*</u> *problemas.*	.. <u>(I/it) had</u> problems.'

(19 School Bus 49:14–49:17)

(110)

Fabiola:	.. *y por qué se vinieron de Santa Clarita?*	'.. and why did you guys return from Santa Clarita?'
Molly:	... *n=- no más <u>Ø estaba</u>,*	'... <u>(I/he) was</u> only,
	.. *I'm glad we did.*	.. *I'm glad we did.'*

(09 La Salvia, 10:38–10:43)

These tokens that fall outside the variable context or that cannot be reliably analyzed sum up to nearly 10 percent of the instances of the variable initially extracted in NMSEB, over 500 tokens. This substantial proportion highlights the importance of methodical transcription and considered extraction to prepare a dataset for analysis.

7.3 Subject Expression in Bilinguals' Spanish

To assess subject pronoun use, we look to factors that condition the choice of a pronominal over an unexpressed subject. The working hypothesis of the variationist method is that "competing variants will occur at greater or lesser rates depending on the features that constitute the context" (Poplack 2001: 405). Thus, conditioning factors are identified via co-occurrence patterns within the variable context. We can predict, for example, that if the subject pronoun is a grammatical device in coding relatively less accessible referents, it should in the aggregate occur at a higher than average rate in non-coreferential contexts. In multivariate analysis, it should be *favored* in this linguistic sub-context.

We make use of logistic regression analysis, which quantifies the effect of multiple conditioning factors acting simultaneously. Table 7.1 presents factors conditioning choice of a pronominal over an unexpressed subject in New Mexican bilinguals' Spanish, the focus in this section, on the left-hand side (on the right is an independent analysis for an earlier variety, the focus of Section 7.4). Variable rule analysis calculates an overall probability ("input") and selects those factor groups that significantly improve the model's fit to the observed distribution of variants (D. Sankoff 1988b; D. Sankoff et al. 2015b; Walker 2010: 31–44).

The number of observations is 5,571 instances of variable subject expression, with an overall pronoun rate of 24 percent and an input of .21. The factor groups (predictors) appear in the left-hand column, with those selected as

Table 7.1 *Factors contributing to occurrence of subject pronouns in bilinguals'*
Spanish (NMSEB) and in earlier variety (earlier NM)

		Bilingual N = 1,353/5,571; Input: .21 (Overall rate: 24%)			Earlier stage 495/1,694; Input: .26 (Overall rate: 29%)		
		Prob	%	N	Prob	%	N
Subject continuity							
Non-coreferential		.57	31%	2642	.55	35%	718
Coreferential		.43	18%	2846	.46	24%	945
	Range	*14*			*9*		
Coreferential subject priming							
Pronominal Spanish		.73	45%	631	.71	47%	260
Outside priming environment*		.60	32%	1965	.60	34%	525
Pronominal English		.43	20%	541	–	–	–
Unexpressed Spanish		.35	13%	2134	.35	16%	699
	Range	*38*			*36*		
Verb class							
Cognition		.72	51%	693	.71	56%	197
Stative		.57	29%	1163	.52	29%	429
Dynamic		.44	18%	3685	.45	24%	1063
	Range	*28*			*26*		
Person							
1sg		.54	29%	3296	.56	35%	1009
3sg		.45	18%	2275	.41	21%	685
	Range	*9*			*15*		
Tense-aspect**							
Imperfective		.51	29%	3424	[51]	33%	1041
Perfective		.46	18%	1314	[.48]	22%	537
	Range	*5*					
Presence of English***							
Absent		[.51]	25%	2690			
Multi-word English		[.48]	22%	1099			
Single-word English		[.49]	22%	954			

* Outside priming environment: previous mentions as full NP or relative pronoun; previous
mentions at a distance of 10 clauses or more; previous postverbal subjects; previous interlocutor
tokens; previous or target in quoted speech (see Chapter 10, Section 10.1). Previous pronominal
English in earlier variety N = 2.

** Perfective excludes *decir* 'say' quotative N = 400 in NMSEB (23% of all Preterit, rate of
expression 3.2%; see Chapter 8, Section 8.4.2).

*** Square brackets indicate non-significant factor groups. English presence not included in
analysis of earlier variety.

significant in bold. These are Subject continuity, Coreferential subject priming, Verb class, Person, and Tense-aspect; not selected is the presence of English elements, the topic of Chapter 9. For each of these explanatory variables, also listed are the factors (predictor levels), which are constituted by features of the linguistic context. The probability values given in the first column of numbers represent the *direction of effect*: factors with higher values (closer to 1) favor the pronominal variant more than factors with lower values (closer to 0), which, conversely, favor the unexpressed variant. The percentage in the second column is the rate with which the subject is expressed with each factor, or in each linguistic sub-context, and the third column gives the number of tokens – pronominal and unexpressed – occurring in each sub-context.

For subject continuity, the first factor group presented here, the prediction about accessibility is borne out: pronominal subjects are favored in non-coreferential contexts, i.e., where the previous mention is farther away than the preceding clause subject, with a probability value of .57. For example, the subject of interest single-underlined in (111), *ella* 'she', is in a non-coreferential context, the preceding clause subject being 'he'. Subject pronouns are also favored when the previous mention by the speaker is pronominal, as illustrated in (111) in a non-coreferential context and (112) in a coreferential context. According to this coreferential subject priming effect, the same referent in the target (underlined) and prime (dotted underline) has the same form (*ella-ella* 'she-she', *yo-yo* 'I-I'). Another pertinent contextual feature is the semantic and aspectual class of the verb itself. Subject pronouns are favored with cognition verbs in the first-person singular, particularly *yo creo* 'I think'. Contrarily, subject pronouns are disfavored with dynamic predicates and perfective aspect. Notice that although the target subject in (112) is coreferential with that of the immediately preceding clause, a context which disfavors subject pronouns all else being equal, other factors act to favor the pronominal variant, here previous pronominal mention, a cognition verb, and 1sg person-number.

(111)
Rocío:	... *ella trabajó por este hombre rico,*	'... she worked for this rich man,
	... *por cuarenta y seis años.*	... for forty six years.
	...*(1.3) hasta que se murió.*	...(1.3) until he died.
	...*(2.6) y um,*	...(2.6) and um,
	.. *ella hablaba solamente español.*	.. she spoke only Spanish.'
		(05 Las Tortillas, 50:13–50:26)

(112)
Francisco:	... *yo oía más antes de las brujas esas y todo,*	'... I used to hear before about the witches and all that,
	yo no creía hasta hasta entonces.	I didn't believe until until then.'
		(18 Las Minas, 1:11:27–1:11:32)

Remember that, within a gamut of stances toward language contact, a common prognosis is that conditioning factors should in some sense be weaker in bilinguals' varieties. An indication of the relative strength of a factor group vis-à-vis the others included in the analysis is the Range of the highest and lowest values. In Table 7.1, Coreferential subject priming and Verb class appear strongest (with Ranges of 38 and 28 respectively), followed by Subject continuity and Person, while Tense-Aspect has the weakest effect.

In the following sections we will inspect the linguistic conditioning in multiple ways, and conduct a series of comparisons, searching for signs of divergence from non-contact Spanish.

7.4   Comparison with an Earlier Variety

A shortcoming of many studies concluding in favor of change is the monolingual baseline they adopt. All too often contact-induced change is construed as deviation from an idealized standard, as intuited by the researcher or as deemed by other university-educated judges, often graduate students in linguistics. However, yet to be supported is "the hope that the introspective judgments of linguists are reliable, reproducible, or general in their application to the speech community" (Labov 1975: 88; Spencer 1973). Not informative either are monolingual controls constituted by affluent, well-educated individuals currently living in the original homeland of the bilinguals' parents, on which many a pronouncement of "incomplete acquisition" has rested, as noted by Otheguy in his critique of the construct (2016: 307–308). For second- or third-generation immigrants, the only appropriate benchmark is speech representing the first generation (Otheguy and Zentella 2012; Silva-Corvalán 1994; cf. Poplack and Levey 2010). For the northern New Mexico bilingual community, we can ascertain the actuality of change by comparison with an earlier stage of the local variety.

The time depth of linguistic studies of northern New Mexico goes back to the early twentieth century (e.g., Espinosa 1911). In the 1990s, NMCOSS was assembled as a large-scale survey of 357 informants for a linguistic atlas of Spanish in New Mexico and Southern Colorado (Bills and Vigil 2008, see Chapter 1, Table 1.1). NMCOSS enables real time-comparisons because it contains stretches of spontaneous speech recorded by community members, amenable to systematic quantitative analysis. Older NMCOSS speakers in whose recordings there are only established borrowings and no multi-word English code-switches provide a benchmark of an earlier – less bilingual – variety of Spanish against which to compare bilingual speakers today. We draw on a sample of 11 such speakers from northern NM, born between 1897 and 1918.[2] These represent the parent generation to the NMSEB bilinguals.

The following excerpts illustrate how this benchmark dataset represents an earlier stage of the same variety. In (113) the speaker, who was born in 1903, recalls how she would help the midwife, in a time when childbirth took place in the home, with women from the community assisting.[3] In (114) we see retention of the root *truj-* of the verb *traer* 'bring, take'; this example also illustrates the local variant *los* of the first-person plural clitic object pronoun, in variation with standard *nos* (Bills and Vigil 2008: 145).

(113)

Adelita:	*tráigamen una bandeja,*	'bring me a tray,
	con poquitita agua nomás.	with just a little water.
	aquí voy a echar el ace- --	here I'm going to put some oi- --
	nomás echaba poquita agua,	I would just put a little water,
	ves,	you see,
((8 intervening lines))		
	y luego arreglaba al muchito,	and then she would arrange the child,
	y le cortaba el ombligo.	and would cut the umbilical cord.'

(NMCOSS 236-1A2, 515–529; born 1903)

(114)

Norma:	*Y ellos trujeron a sus hijos.*	'And they took their children.
	Y áhi,	And there,
	querían traerlos a nosotros también.	they wanted to take us too.
	pero mi amá no quiso.	but my mom refused.
	po=rque se le hacía fiero que nos	because to her it was terrible that they
	trujiéranos.	would take us.'

(NMCOSS, 10-8A, 15–19, born 1904)

7.4.1 Fickleness of Rates, Stability of Conditioning

First, let us compare overall rate of use in NMSEB and this earlier variety represented by older, less bilingual, NMCOSS speakers, and how that compares with other varieties. Figure 7.1 illustrates.

The first two columns give the rate for contemporary bilinguals in New Mexico and for the earlier variety. Contrary to the prediction of increased rates in the contact variety, the Bilingual NM group, at 24 percent, does not display

---

[2] Thanks to Garland Bills and Neddy Vigil for access to NMCOSS recordings to create a comparison sub-corpus. The eleven older, Spanish-dominant speakers are NMCOSS numbers 4, 10, 20, 76, 219, 236, 246, 272, 310, 313, and 316. In our transcriptions, we have used pseudonyms for the participants and the interviewers.

[3] Example (113) illustrates enclitic plural *-n* in *tráigamen* 'you-PL bring me' (rather than standard plural marking directly on the verb, *tráiganme*), registered across the Spanish-speaking world (Kany 1951: 112).

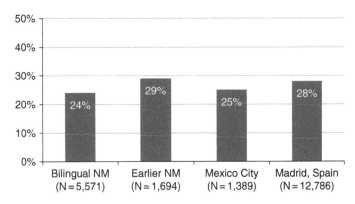

Figure 7.1 Subject pronoun rates across contact and non-contact varieties
Mexico City from Lastra and Butragueño (2015: 43); Madrid from Enríquez
(1984: 348).
Bilingual NM (1,310/5,571) vs. Earlier NM (495/1,694), $\chi2$ = 22.35, p <
0.0001; Earlier NM vs. Madrid (3,596/12,786), $\chi2$ = 0.83, p = .36. Bilingual
NM vs. Mexico City (354/1,389), $\chi2$ = 2.27, p = .13.

a higher rate than the earlier NM group, at 29 percent. In fact, though by just
5 percentage points, the bilingual rate is lower, and statistically significantly so
(by Pearson's Chi-squared test with Yates' continuity correction, p < .0001).

While countering the predicted overextension of subject pronouns, the
lower rate may be consistent with a hypothesis of grammatical simplification.
Before hastening to offer an interpretation for a "lower" rate, however, we
compare the NM rates with rates in non-contact varieties, the third and fourth
columns in Figure 7.1. Notice that the Bilingual NM group shows a near-
identical rate to that reported for Mexico City, while the earlier NM group is
nearly identical to Madrid, Spain. In fact, despite statistical significance,
the overall rates provide no evidence for any linguistically significant differences, since the ordering of varieties – Bilingual NM < Mexico City < Madrid
< Earlier NM – would not be coherent by any hypothesis of change, contact-
induced or otherwise. If by the criterion of overall rate Spain is more innovative than Mexico, then, for instance, why would earlier NM be more
innovative than Bilingual NM (or than Spain, for that matter)?

Beyond the problem of contradictory predictions for rate changes under contact, overall rates prove to be a risky yardstick, as we also saw in Chapter 6.
Overall subject pronoun rate is an equivocal measure of contact-induced change,
on three counts. First, it is susceptible to extra-grammatical factors (genre,
data collection, conversation topic). Second, as indicated again by the comparison in Figure 7.1, statistical significance is insufficient as a gauge of
linguistic significance. Given notable fluctuation due to extra-grammatical

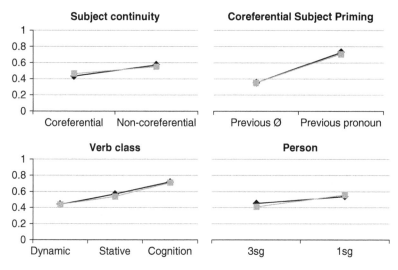

Figure 7.2 Probabilities of subject pronouns in bilinguals' Spanish (NMSEB) and earlier stage (earlier NM)
(from Table 7.1; bilingual: diamonds, earlier stage: squares)

factors, a threshold for a linguistically significant difference cannot be set. A third shortcoming of overall rate as a yardstick of linguistic change is that it cannot speak to directionality, much less mechanisms. For example, as we have seen, the hypothesis of contact-induced change is compatible with opposite predictions as concerns overall rate (Silva-Corvalán 1994: 147).

Fortunately, we can rely on configurations of conditioning factors to assess grammars in contact. We return to Table 7.1, which juxtaposes the results of parallel analyses of subject expression in bilinguals' Spanish (left-hand side) and earlier-stage Spanish (right hand side). The same factors were analyzed, except for the presence of code-switching and English pronominal primes, since there were virtually none in the earlier-stage dataset. The factor groups selected as significant in both datasets were identical, as was the direction of effect.

Zooming in, the set of line graphs in Figure 7.2 directly compares this linguistic conditioning, showing probability values along the vertical axes. As displayed graphically here, the values are near-identical for each of these factor groups. The alignment in direction of effect refutes a scenario of linguistic change. Such perfect alignment is rather testament to grammatical continuity.[4]

---

[4] To compare bilinguals' vs. earlier-stage Spanish we opt for separate logistic regression analyses of each dataset in order to readily display (dis)similarities in direction of effect. A single linear regression model that includes dataset as a fixed effect and interaction term yields the parallels

7.4.2   The Confound of Data Distributions

In the introduction to this chapter we noted that the standard prediction for convergence is that effects of conditioning factors will be weaker. To the contrary, if anything, here subject continuity seems weaker in the earlier-stage than in the bilingual data: whereas in the bilingual data analysis subject continuity is ranked above grammatical person, in the earlier stage analysis subject continuity has a lower range than person, as seen in Table 7.1.

Apparent differences in effect strength, however, may be due to contextual distributions of the data. First, consider subject continuity. In Table 7.1, for the sake of comparability with traditional subject expression studies, subject continuity is configured by aggregating all non-coreferential contexts – that is, where the immediately preceding clause subject has a different referent. Yet distance from the previous mention matters, as we discussed in Chapter 5 (Section 5.3). Here lies the explanation for the apparent difference in effect strength: whereas in NMSEB approximately 20 percent of target subjects have a previous mention at a distance of more than 5 clauses, in the NMCOSS data approximately 10 percent do (Figure 7.3). Contextual distribution differences follow from data collection procedures: NMCOSS was collected to elicit linguistic atlas items, with relatively short stretches of conversation, so that same-referent mentions are more clustered.

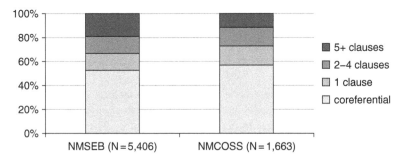

Figure 7.3 Distribution of subjects according to distance from previous mention in two datasets
Disaggregation of non-coreferential contexts, Table 7.1.

explicitly revealed by juxtaposing the separate variable rule analyses in Table 7.1: while dataset is significant (as the higher overall rate in the earlier-stage data would lead us to expect), there are no interactions between dataset and the other predictors, except with Person, the relatively greater strength of which turns out to be due to the greater clustering of same-referent subjects in the earlier-stage dataset (Figure 7.3).

This same genre-driven clustering contributes to Person appearing stronger in the earlier stage than in the bilingual analysis. We saw in Chapter 5 (Section 5.9) that distance impacts 1sg earlier than 3sg, for which the rise in pronoun rate kicks in later. The smaller proportion of tokens with a previous mention at a distance of five or more clauses means that 3sg subjects occur even less in contexts that favor pronominal subjects in NMCOSS than in NMSEB.

7.4.3   Tense-aspect and Verb Class

Another apparent difference is that tense-aspect does not reach significance in the analysis of the earlier stage data but does contribute to bilinguals' choice of the pronominal variant, albeit as a relatively weak effect (having the lowest range of probability values; see Table 7.1). Considering ambiguity in verbal morphology, two interpretations can be entertained. Lack of a significant effect would be consistent with the hypothesis that tense-aspect constraints are lost in bilingual contexts, under the view that bilingualism involves more reliance on contextual cues to disambiguate the subject referent (Silva-Corvalán 1994: 154). A significant effect, on the other hand, could mean that tense-aspect constraints are gained, with bilingualism seen to allow for grammatical complexification (Shin 2014).

Nevertheless, here we run the risk of over-interpreting the difference, since the number of observations for the earlier stage is less than one-third of that for the bilingual dataset, and it is well known that significance is hardly observable with smaller token counts. In addition, we know that tense-aspect effects are inconsistent across studies of non-contact varieties. Most importantly, the direction of effect is the same, with subject pronoun rates lowest in the Preterit (Chapter 5, Section 5.6).

Positive evidence for continuity rather than change comes from the interaction of tense-aspect with verb class (Chapter 5, Section 5.7). In both datasets, the Present, Preterit, and Imperfect together account for most of the data (92 percent NMSEB, 93 percent NMCOSS), as is also the case in non-contact varieties. Verbs were classified as dynamic (e.g., 'do', 'go', 'say') or stative ('have', 'be'), with cognition verbs ('know', 'think') grouped separately. Figure 7.4 shows rates of subject pronouns by verb class and tense-aspect in the two datasets, as well as the data distributions, or the number of instances of each tense-aspect within each verb class.

Tense-aspect does not have a consistent effect on subject expression across verb classes. It is only for dynamic verbs that the predicted order is obtained, with the subject pronoun rate in the Imperfect greater than or equal to that in the Present, which is in turn greater than that in the Preterit. For stative verbs, tense-aspect makes minimal difference in subject pronoun rate. And cognition verbs are concentrated in the Present, so any tense distinction is moot. In fact, the overrepresentation in the Present of cognition verbs, which are most favorable to subject pronouns, helps account for this tense having the highest pronoun rate. Also contributing to the Present having a contextual distribution propitious to pronominal subjects is the overrepresentation of 1sg, again thanks to cognition verbs. These cross-tabulations underscore the limited scope of tense-aspect effects, disproportionate to the interest they have attracted. In sum, the same interplay of tense and verb class influences subject pronoun use in both the bilingual and the earlier variety.

Consider now the distribution of stative predicates across tense-aspect categories. Use of an inherently stative predicate with perfective (Preterit) morphology is illustrated with *tuve* 'I had' in (115), where Ivette talks of having a car as a temporally bounded discrete event reported "for its own sake" (Bybee, Perkins, and Pagliuca 1994: 54; Comrie 1976: 5).

(115)

Ivette:	... okay *tuve el,*	'... okay I <u>had</u> the,
	.. *el white one.*	.. the *white one.*'
Rafael:	...*(1.0) m[hm].*	'...(1.0) m[hm].'
Ivette:	*[and],*	'*[and],*
	el Chevrolet,	the Chevrolet,
	y luego <u>tuve</u>,	and then I <u>had</u>,
	... *the one I can't remember.*	... *the one I can't remember.*'

(06 El Túnico, 57:13–57:20)

Yet statives appear preferentially with imperfective (Imperfect) morphology (comparing the number of observations, shown within parentheses in Figure 7.4), as is common in languages that have a perfective vs. imperfective distinction (Hopper 1979: 215–216). Language contact is proposed to amplify this skewing, with a neutralization of the aspectual distinction resulting in overuse of the Imperfect with stative verbs (Silva-Corvalán 1994: 44). The ratio of Imperfect to Preterit in statives is indeed higher in the bilingual than in the earlier variety. However, rather than neutralization of the aspectual distinction, partly responsible is a fortuitous overrepresentation of Preterit *tener hijos* 'gave birth' (lit. 'had children') in the earlier stage data, where it constitutes 15 percent (24/157) of tokens of *tener* 'have'; in NMSEB, this topic comes up much more rarely, and so the expression occurs only 4 times (of 334 tokens of *tener* 'have').

In this section we compared bilinguals' Spanish with an earlier, less bilingual, stage of the same variety. The five percentage point difference in overall rate of subject pronouns is dismissible as proof of change. Rather, patterns of subject pronoun use are shaped in the same way, as seen in the fine detail of tendencies for subject expression brought to light by multivariate analysis, cross-tabulation of conditioning factors, and consideration of data distributions.

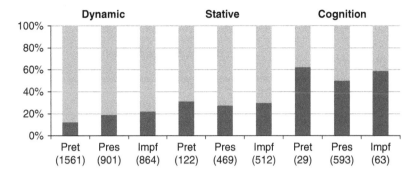

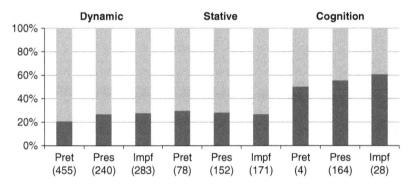

Figure 7.4 Verb class and tense: Rate of subject pronouns and data distributions in bilinguals' Spanish (top) and earlier stage (bottom)

7.5 Comparison with Monolingual Spanish

The evidence so far is that bilingualism does not entail grammatical change. However, comparison with an earlier stage will mask change if the earlier variety was already influenced by contact. The second set of comparisons, then, is with bona fide non-contact varieties.

The subject expression rate in NM Spanish is within the spectrum for monolingual norms, which is patently broad, ranging from 20 percent to 50 percent for 1sg, and from 10 percent to 40 percent for 3sg (Silva-Corvalán and Enrique-Arias 2017: 184). Given the pitfalls of overall rate comparisons that we have seen, where NM Spanish is positioned within this broad spectrum is uninformative. Crucially, it tells us nothing about *how bilinguals use* subject pronouns – do they adhere to Spanish criteria, or has their use become more English-like?

As with the comparison with the earlier variety, we can compare the direction of effect of the probabilistic constraints, which is where use is most palpably characterized. These are shared across varieties. Figure 7.5 depicts widely

	Bilinguals
Subject continuity (accessibility)	Non-coreferential > Coreferential ✓
	- Increased distance from previous mention raises pronoun rate - Interacts with priming: stronger in the absence of pronominal primes
Coreferential subject priming	Previous pronoun > Previous unexpressed ✓
	- Interacts with subject continuity: stronger in coreferential contexts - Weaker for cognition verbs
Verb class (semantic and aspectual)	Cognition > Stative > Dynamic ✓

	- Cognition-verb construction is specific to 1sg,
	  overwhelmingly Present tense
	- Lexically particular constructions idiosyncratically favor or
	  disfavor
	- Dynamic verbs are associated with temporal sequencing

Tense-aspect	Imperfective > Perfective ✓
	- Most instances are Present, Preterit, or Imperfect - Preterit consistently disfavors - Interacts with subject continuity and verb class
Person	1sg > 3sg ✓
	- Person differences largely follow from contextual distributions - 1sg occurs more often with previous mention at greater distance than 3sg (unexpressed and pronominal subjects)
Clause type	Main & Subordinate > Coordinate ✓
	- Clause type effects largely follow from prosodic and syntactic linking between coreferential-subject clauses
Genre	Conversation > Narrative ✓

	- Genre differences in overall rate largely follow from data
	  distributions: more coreferential instances in narrative than in
	  conversation

Figure 7.5 Factors conditioning subject pronoun expression
- direction of effect
- contextual distributions and interactions of the factors

See Chapter 5; see also Silva-Corvalán and Enrique-Arias (2017: 172–187) and Carvalho, Orozco, and Shin (2015: xiv–xv).

reported factors in the vast body of literature on Spanish subject expression, highlighting their direction of effect and observed tendencies for contextual distributions and interactions. There is not a single variety of Spanish – including contact varieties claimed by the rates criterion to have undergone change – in which subject pronouns are less favored in, say, non-coreferential than in coreferential contexts, or with cognition rather than with other kinds of verbs. NM bilinguals' Spanish is no exception, as is evident from the analyses here.

Where contact-induced change in Spanish subject expression has been asserted on the basis of an elevated overall rate, the accompanying claim has not been that direction of effect is reversed, but rather that the probabilistic constraints are weakened. A problem with magnitude of effect is that, unlike the direction of effects, it is not consistent across studies of either contact or non-contact varieties. Effect strength for subject expression, for example, clearly varies by grammatical person; for instance, verb class is stronger for 1sg where cognition verbs are overrepresented.

More generally, magnitude of effect is a less certain criterion for comparisons because it depends on the number and configuration of the other factor groups analyzed. The strength of a predictor can also be impacted by data distributions. We saw in Section 7.4.2 an example with subject continuity, the strength of which was slightly weaker in one of the datasets because of concentrations of subjects with previous mentions at shorter distances. For these reasons, measures of relative strength such as the range of the most and least favorable factors (levels) cannot be directly compared across separate logistic regression analyses as absolute values. If the predictor variables are configured identically in two or more analyses, we can more confidently compare their *relative* ranking within each analysis. As we saw above, by the relative ranking according to range, subject continuity is not weaker in bilinguals than in an earlier stage (Table 7.1).

Since effect strength cannot be directly compared across different studies, we utilize here cross-tabulations to gauge magnitude of effect for comparison with monolingual Spanish. From the few studies of subject expression that have delved into interactions between pairs of predictors, there appears to be substantial uniformity across varieties. Thus, subject continuity intersects with priming, morphological ambiguity, and genre in the same way in monolingual varieties of Spanish. Erosion of the subject continuity effect in bilinguals' Spanish should manifest itself in the modification of these interactions. Contrarily, maintenance of the same fine interactions will be evidence against its weakening and for stability rather than change.

7.5.1   Subject Continuity and Priming

Pronominal subjects prompt pronominal subjects, especially when the pronominal prime has the same referent as the target subject, which we have called *Coreferential subject priming*. We will say that a target has a pronominal prime when the previous subject is a pronoun; in coreferential subject priming, the prime is the previous subject mention of the same referent; alternatively, in adjacent-clause subject priming, the prime is the subject of the immediately preceding clause (Cameron 1994). Coreferential subject priming is illustrated in (116), in a coreferential context, and in (117) in a non-coreferential context, in excerpts of bilinguals' Spanish (see also (111) and (112) above).

(116)

Enrique: *él venía pa'cá,*   'he would come here,
          .. a preguntarme= .. cosas del   .. to ask me .. things about the
          Army,   Army,
          porque después él se fue al servicio,   because afterwards he went into the
                                                      service,'
                                                      (23 El Pacific, 16:39–16:44)

(117)

Víctor: *.. y yo le iba a preguntar a mi hermana,* '.. and I was going to ask my sister,
         ... pero se habían ido.   ... but they had left.'
Rubén: *o[=h],*   'o[h],'
Víctor: *[yo no] pensé que se habían ido,*   '[I] didn't think they had left,'
                                                      (29 La Diploma, 26:21–26:26)

In monolingual varieties, subject continuity moderates priming (and is moderated by priming): priming is stronger in coreferential than in non-coreferential contexts (Cameron 1994: 39–40). Does the same interaction obtain in bilinguals' Spanish?

Insightful here are Cameron's (1994) cross-dialect comparisons. Drawing on these, Figure 7.6 displays the subject pronoun rate in the presence of a preceding pronoun in coreferential and non-coreferential contexts, in three datasets: San Juan and Madrid (the monolingual benchmarks) and Bilingual NM (the contact variety). Relevant here are not the values per se (which differ across varieties), but the values relative to each other, depicted in the relative heights of the paired columns. First, in each pair of columns the one to the right (with a pronominal prime) is higher than the one to the left, confirming the priming effect. Second, the difference between the heights of paired columns is greater under the condition of a coreferential context than under non-coreferential contexts, confirming the interaction (Cameron and Flores-Ferrán 2004: 49). The greater difference in rate of expression between preceding Ø and preceding pronoun in Bilingual NM is simply because the measure applied here is coreferential subject priming, which is stronger than adjacent-clause subject priming, the measure applied in the other datasets in Figure 7.6 (Travis and Torres Cacoullos 2012: 731). In sum,

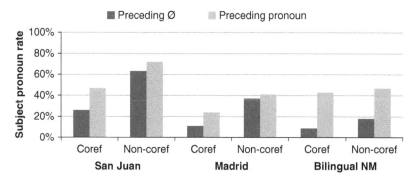

Figure 7.6 Subject continuity interaction with priming, contact variety compared with non-contact varieties
San Juan (N = 1,312) and Madrid (N = 1,068) is adjacent-clause subject priming, all singular persons (from Cameron 1994: 39–40); Bilingual NM (1sg & and 3sg) is coreferential subject priming.
NMSEB subject pronoun rates with previous Ø vs. pronoun are, in coreferential contexts: 9%, 120/1,334 vs. 43%, 160/372; in non-coreferential contexts 18%, 146/800 vs. 47%, 123/259.

the same interaction between subject continuity and priming holds in the three datasets.

7.5.2 Subject Continuity and Morphological Ambiguity

A second interaction we can use to gauge whether subject continuity has eroded as a factor in bilinguals' Spanish subject expression is with morphological ambiguity. For this purpose, pertinent is the distinction among tenses according to whether there is syncretism in person morphology. The Imperfect, which has the same forms for 1sg and 3sg, is expected to favor subject pronouns more than the Present, which has different person suffixes. This effect tends to be "nullified" in the presence of coreferentiality but obtains when there is a switch in reference (Cameron 1993: 317; Ramos 2016: 118). If subject continuity has weakened in the contact variety, it should no longer moderate the effect of syncretism.

Figure 7.7 displays the rate of subject pronouns according to Present vs. Imperfect morphology in the verb, in coreferential and non-coreferential contexts for the same three datasets seen in Figure 7.6. For all three varieties, column heights in the pairs are closer under coreferentiality (in Madrid and Bilingual NM, they are virtually the same) and differ more notably in non-coreferential contexts. That is, an effect for tense is more apparent in non-coreferential than in coreferential contexts. Thus, once again, an interaction of subject continuity – in this case, with tense – is the same in the three datasets.

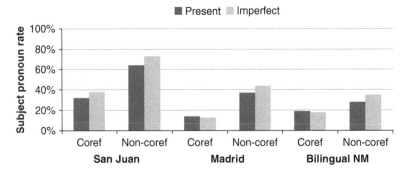

Figure 7.7 Subject continuity interaction with morphological ambiguity, contact variety compared with non-contact varieties
In San Juan (N = 1,270) and Madrid (N = 1,228) counted with Present are Future and Perfect forms and with Imperfect are Conditional and Subjunctive; excluding *ser* 'be', all singular persons (from Cameron 1993: 317–319). Bilingual NM (1sg and 3sg), excluding cognition verbs, subject pronoun rates with Present vs. Imperfect are, in coreferential contexts: 19%, 145/778 vs. 18%, 144/789; in non-coreferential contexts 28%, 159/575 vs. 35%, 202/577.

The literature has highlighted the Imperfect in dwelling on the ambiguity-resolving role ascribed to pronominal subjects (Chapter 5, Section 5.2). However, the favoring effect of the Imperfect in non-coreferential contexts (where ambiguity may be most likely to arise) applies to only a modest fraction of the data: in NMSEB, approximately 10 percent (577 tokens of subjects that are with the Imperfect in non-coreferential contexts out of the total of 5,571), and in San Juan and Madrid, 16 percent and 7 percent, respectively (based on Cameron 1993: Tables 6 and 9).

7.5.3   Subject Continuity and Genre

Our third comparison to assess the anticipated weakening of subject continuity in the contact variety takes us to the question of genre. As with social factors (Chapter 2, Section 2.5) the stylistic or expressive import of subject pronoun expression is the site of inconclusive or inconsistent claims. What we know is that overall rate fluctuates according to situational considerations such as genre, register, and style (Silva-Corvalán and Enrique-Arias 2017: 181). However, differences according to situational context fade when we consider the linguistic conditioning, since they follow to a great extent from contextual distribution differences. For example, Travis (2007: 113) found that a lower rate of subject expression in narratives than in conversations could be

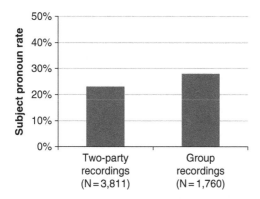

Figure 7.8 Rate of subject pronouns according to recording situation in the
contact variety ($\chi2$ = 14.194, $p < .001$)
20 participants recorded alone with interviewer (two-party); 20 in group
recordings.

accounted for by a higher degree of subject continuity in the narrative – more
monologic – data than in the conversational – more dialogic – data, which in
turn had more shifting of topics (cf. Dumont 2016: 149; Travis and Lindstrom
2016: 112).

If subject continuity is weakened in the contact variety, we may expect genre
differences to have dissipated. As a surrogate for genre, we compare sociolinguistic interviews with one participant – two-party recordings – with those
with two or more participants – group recordings. The group recordings have
denser dialogic interaction between speakers. Figure 7.8 shows that the subject
pronoun rate in bilinguals' Spanish is higher in the group recordings, and thus
that the malleability of rate according to situation is maintained in bilinguals'
Spanish. By the criterion of sensitivity to the situational dimension, then, there
is no evidence for weakening of subject continuity.

The situational difference in subject pronoun rate is fed by a greater incidence of favorable environments in the group recordings. First, there is
a tendency toward less subject continuity (52 percent of the tokens in the
group recordings are in non-coreferential contexts, as compared with 46 percent
in the two-party recordings). Second, in the group recordings there are twice as
many instances in turn-initial position, underlined in (118), than in the two-
party recordings (37 percent vs. 14 percent). Turn-initial position, or occurrence in the first prosodic unit following a contribution by the interlocutor
(Ford and Fox 1996: 152), is another favorable context for subject pronouns
that has been considered in some studies (e.g., Bentivoglio 1987: 38–40; Travis
and Torres Cacoullos 2012: 736–737).

(118)

Fabiola:	... o él agarra órdenes?	'... or does he take orders?'
Molly:	.. mhm.	'.. mhm.'
Fabiola:	... oh yo creí que estaba allá atrás en la cocina.	'... oh I thought that he was back there in the kitchen.'
Molly:	.. no= él=,	'.. no he,
	... las --	... the --
	.. lleva los platos a --	.. (he) takes the dishes to --
	.. a=l,	.. to,'
Fabiola:	.. so él está haciendo tips entonces?	'.. so he is making tips then?'

(09 La Salvia, 03:22–03:32)

Third, in the group recordings there is a higher proportion of cognition verbs, which are approximately twice as frequent (18 percent of the group data vs. 10 percent for two-party recordings). At the same time, the favoring effect of cognition verbs is greater in the group than the two-party recordings (cognition-verb subject pronoun rates are 65 percent, 189/293 vs. 41 percent, 165/400). The difference between group and two-party recordings in rate and distributions of subject pronouns – the maintenance of situational sensitivity – is evidence against loss of discourse factors or erosion of pragmatic functions of subject pronouns.

In this section, we compared the contact variety with established facts about non-contact varieties of Spanish. Not surprisingly, no differences in direction of effects on subject expression surfaced. As to the projected weakening of subject continuity (either as indirect influence from English or as the fallout of bilingualism per se), we took advantage of known interactions with priming, morphological ambiguity, and genre. These remain unaltered in bilinguals' Spanish and thus fail to provide evidence for any diminishing of probabilistic constraints.

7.6   Conclusion

A commonly entertained contact hypothesis is that rates of expression will generally be higher, with overextension of subject pronouns. An equally plausible hypothesis puts forward just the opposite – that rates will generally be lower, with erosion of the functions of subject pronouns. Overall rate, then, even if we had clear thresholds for "higher" and "lower," is necessarily indecisive. By this pair of hypotheses, only an unchanged rate could refute contact-induced change. But overall rates of use are undeniably fickle and thus equivocal, and increased, decreased, or even stable rates cannot be taken as evidence for, or against, convergence.

A more compelling hypothesis has been diminished strength of conditioning factors. For bilinguals' Spanish, accessibility effects are widely touted as vulnerable to contact-induced change. The hypothesis of weakened constraints has been motivated on the grounds that they may be eroded if similar conditioning is absent from, or notably weaker in, the contact language. A convincing test for convergence, then, obliges us to explore the intricacies of linguistic conditioning, through multivariate analysis together with scrutinization of the data by way of cross-tabulations and accounting of contextual distributions (Labov 1969: 735, 742–747; 2004: 10–11; D. Sankoff 1988a). Here, two sets of comparisons with the NMSEB data were conducted: with an earlier stage variety spoken in New Mexico, and with monolingual varieties.

These comparisons provided positive evidence for continuity rather than change. Comparison with the earlier stage variety revealed the same direction of effects. Apparent differences in the magnitude of the effect for subject continuity and person were accounted for by differences in the contextual distributions, specifically the greater clustering of subjects in the earlier, linguistic atlas data, which collected shorter stretches of speech.

In drawing comparisons, we must be wary of claims of differences in strength of effect. A strengthening or weakening of effects cannot be reliably seen in direct comparisons of magnitude of effect across different studies, because it is susceptible to the configuration of the analysis and the distribution of the data to which the analysis is applied. Thus, in order to test for weakening (or strengthening) of constraints, a series of cross-tabulations with subject continuity was conducted. Again, no evidence of (contact-induced) change was found: in bilinguals' Spanish, just as in monolingual varieties, subject continuity impacts priming, tense, and genre effects.

Whereas the prediction of weakened conditioning factors may find support where one language is used substantially less than the other, perhaps in immigrant communities on rapid route to language shift, it need not apply to long-term bilingualism, and it is not upheld in the speakers represented in NMSEB. Loss of constraints, then, is not a necessary fallout of bilingualism.

But before completely dismissing the proposition that bilingualism begets convergence, we must account for both languages. This includes the varieties of the bilingual community, in particular as used by the same speakers. The next set of comparisons, then, involves English, both as a monolingual benchmark and as spoken by the bilinguals themselves.

8   The Most Intimate Contact: The Bilinguals' Two Languages

8.1   Predictions for Convergence

Comparison with the *other* language is essential to knowing if there are changes in the contact variety that go in the *direction* of that language. In the previous chapter we compared bilinguals' Spanish with earlier and monolingual Spanish varieties. In this chapter, comparisons bring English into the picture. By comparing with a monolingual English benchmark as well as a Spanish benchmark, we can ask: has bilinguals' Spanish altered toward English in some way? And by comparing with bilinguals' own English we can address the empirical question at the heart of a hypothesis of contact-induced change: do the varieties spoken by the bilinguals demonstrate convergence?

In the celebrated foundational work for the study of multilingualism, *Languages in Contact*, Weinreich (1953/1968: 2) declared that in order to assess the linguistic outcomes of contact, "Great or small, the differences and similarities between the languages in contact must be exhaustively stated." Until now, such a statement had been missing in the long study of subject expression in Spanish–English contact. It was assumed that English lacks the conditioning factors operative in Spanish, being a non-null-subject language or one with a conspicuously low rate of unexpressed subjects.

However, when we compare the linguistic conditioning of subject expression in English and Spanish, we discover parallel probabilistic effects within the variable contexts, as we saw in the preceding chapter. At the same time, we pinpointed measurable cross-language differences, summarized in Figure 8.1.

From the diagnostic differences, we derive two sets of predictions for language contact, which can be tested by juxtaposing the monolingual benchmarks and the contact varieties. These are stated in Figure 8.2. In this chapter we will see whether either is true. In a departure from the long line of Spanish–English contact studies, in addition to monolingual Spanish we will compare bilinguals' Spanish with an appropriate benchmark of monolingual English speech. This in turn allows us to pose the second set of predictions for the first time – the stringent test of convergence – by adding bilinguals'

---

1. Restriction of prosodic position: Unexpressed subjects in English are restricted to occurrence at the beginning of the Intonation Unit (IU) except in coordinate clauses; not so in Spanish, where unexpressed subjects are more frequent in non-IU-initial position.

2. Strength of structural linking: Beyond coreferentiality with the preceding subject, unexpressed subjects are constrained by structural linking to the preceding clause, via a coordinating conjunction or intonation, more in English than in Spanish.

3. Language-particular constructions: Expressions anchored in particular words or classes of words idiosyncratically favor or disfavor subject pronouns: in English, *and*-coordinate constructions, in Spanish, cognition-verb and quotative constructions.

Figure 8.1 Cross-language diagnostic differences brought out by analysis of English speech data (from Chapters 5 and 6)

- If bilinguals' Spanish has converged with English, then, as compared with monolingual Spanish, it will display
  1. at least some sensitivity to the prosodic-initial restriction;
  2. a stronger effect of structural linking;
  3. and translation-counterpart lexically-particular constructions.
- If bilinguals' Spanish and English have converged with each other, then they will be less different on these measures than the monolingual benchmarks are.

Figure 8.2 Two sets of predictions for convergence to be tested by comparing contact and non-contact varieties of both Spanish and English

English to the picture. Thus, the convergence predictions are ultimately tested by juxtaposing Spanish and English *as spoken by the same bilinguals*.

Remember that the corpus, like the speakers, is truly bilingual, with an even number of clauses in the two languages (Chapter 4, Section 4.4). First of all, we might ask whether the English of NMSEB bilinguals has been influenced by their Spanish. All unexpressed subjects with human specific referents of 1sg and 3sg finite verbs in English were identified (N = 98). The rate of *un*expressed subjects is approximately 1 percent (38/4,500) for 1sg and 2 percent (60/2,600) for 3sg (where the denominators are unexpressed and pronominal subjects). If there had been what Thomason and Kaufman (1988: 38ff) call shift-induced "substratum interference," we would expect more unexpressed subjects than in non-contact English. The NMSEB English rates, however, are not higher than the corresponding figures of 2 percent and 5 percent for the monolingual

SBCSAE corpus (Chapter 6, Section 6.6.2). Nevertheless, by now the reader will rightly be wondering about the linguistic conditioning.

We draw from four comparison datasets constructed in parallel from corpora of spontaneous speech transcribed in the same way: bilinguals' Spanish and bilinguals' English, both from NMSEB, and monolingual Spanish and monolingual English, as represented in the CCCS and the SBCSAE (see Chapter 1, Table 1.1). We consider in turn the language-specific variable contexts (Section 8.2), relative magnitude of effects (8.3), and language particular constructions (8.4).

8.2   The Test of a Diagnostic Difference in the Variable Context

To gauge cross-language grammatical (dis)similarity we use cross-language similarities and diagnostic differences, outside and within the variable context. We will look at rates of subject pronouns in coordinate clauses and, for all other tokens, according to position in the prosodic unit, in the four comparison datasets. Coordinate clauses are ones conjoined via a coordinating conjunction to a coreferential-subject main clause that most often is adjacent, as illustrated in line (c) in (119). Coordinating conjunctions are *and/y*, *but/pero*, and *or/o*, and these in combinations with an adverb, usually *and then*. Prosodic-initial instances are those in which the subject pronoun or the verb alone occur in absolute initial position in the IU, or are preceded at most by non-speech material such as *uh*, *um*, laughter, or pausing, but no other words. In (119), line (a) illustrates non-initial and line (b) initial position for bilinguals' Spanish. In (120), for bilinguals' English, line (b) shows an unexpressed subject in IU-initial position. (In non-initial position pronouns occur invariably, thus the pronoun in line (a), here in an interrogative, falls outside the variable context; see Chapter 6, Section 6.5.)

(119)
a. Susan: ... *como Ø te dije,*   '... like (I) told you,
b.   ... *Ø nació en eighteen sixty nine,* ... (he) was born in 1869,
c.   ... *y Ø murió= .. en um --*   ... and (he) died in um --
d.   ... *nineteen forty eight.*   ... 1948.'

                                                              (01 El Abuelo, 29:42–29:48)

(120)
a. Aurora: *where was I?*
b.   .. *Ø got lost.*

                                                      (15 Las Cosas Viejas, 35:21–32:45)

Coordinate clauses constitute a site of cross-language similarity, as can be seen in Figure 8.3. In both monolingual Spanish and English, the lowest rate of subject pronouns – conversely, the highest rate of unexpressed subjects – is in coordinate clauses, in the first column of each set. The bilingual varieties – Spanish and

English, in the middle set of columns – share this expected pattern. Across the board, coordinate clauses have a subject pronoun rate that is at least half the average.

Position in the prosodic unit, on the other hand, is a patent diagnostic difference. Outside coordinate clauses, English verbs in non-IU-initial position invariably have an expressed subject. This is the prosodic-initial restriction to the variable context. In contrast, Spanish verbs in non-IU-initial position not only appear with unexpressed subjects, but do so with an even higher rate than verbs in IU-initial position.[1] On this diagnostic difference, each of the bilingual varieties shows the respective pattern: in bilinguals' Spanish, the IU-initial subject pronoun rate is greater than in non-IU-initial position; in their English, it is lower. (In English there are no non-IU-initial unexpressed subjects outside coordinate clauses; the samples are constituted by two pronominal for each unexpressed subject; Chapter 6, Section 6.5.1.)

If bilinguals' Spanish were adjusted toward English, there should have been a reversal of the relationship to match the English pattern, a flattening out of the difference, or at least a reduced difference between rates according to prosodic

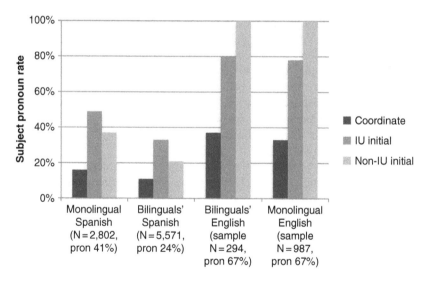

Figure 8.3 Cross-language similarities and diagnostic differences:
Coordinate clauses and prosodic position

---

[1] Spanish prosodic position calculations exclude verbs with unexpressed subjects preceded only by an adverb in the IU (*ahí* 'there', *ahora* 'now', *no más* 'only', *ya* 'already', for example, *ya vino pa' Gallup*, '(he) already came to Gallup' [24, 35:27]), since pronominal subjects appear both before and after these adverbs.

position. Not even the last option obtains. In fact, bilinguals maximally maintain distinct patterns of subject expression according to prosodic position in each of their two languages.

8.3   The Test of Magnitude of a Shared Constraint: Accessibility as Linking

Of the constraints in Spanish and other null-subject languages projected to be undermined by contact, the poster child is projected weakening of subject continuity, on the assumption that it does not condition subject expression in English. However, this assumption can no longer be sustained (Chapter 6). Within the variable context, accessibility is in fact the dominant probabilistic constraint for English. The quandary is that we are left with competing predictions for contact-induced change: the familiar position that accessibility effects will be weaker and the equally plausible view that they will be stronger under English influence. The solution is to submit data to identical multivariate analyses as a diagnostic for grammatical similarity (cf. Poplack and Tagliamonte 2001: 101). Our strategy will be to juxtapose accessibility effects in the four comparison datasets. Do bilinguals' Spanish and English respectively line up with monolingual Spanish and English, or do they line up with each other?

Let us consider linking to the preceding clause subject (Chapter 6, Section 6.6.1). Linking refines accessibility by considering coreferentiality vis-à-vis the preceding clause subject, or semantic linking, together with structural linking – syntactic linking by means of a conjunction and/or prosodic linking though intonation. Syntactically linked to a preceding clause are coordinate clauses and subordinate clauses. Prosodically linked to a preceding clause are clauses in the same IU or following continuing intonation (transcribed with a comma).

Table 8.1 shows probabilities of pronominal subjects according to this composite – semantic and structural – accessibility measure for the four comparison datasets. The first row gives values for non-coreferential contexts, the second for coreferential contexts lacking a structural link, and the third for structurally linked coreferential contexts. Linking is a more discriminating measure of accessibility than subject continuity configured as the binary opposition of coreferential vs. non-coreferential contexts. As we can see both in Table 8.1 and, pictorially, in Figure 8.4, linking is a shared probabilistic constraint across all four datasets, with identical direction of effect.

As to magnitude of effect, the greater strength of linking in English than in Spanish emerges from the difference in the range of probability values in the monolingual columns, on the left- and rightmost sides of the table. Monolingual English has a relatively large range, double that of the other factor groups included in this analysis. (The range is 53, where the most favoring

Table 8.1 *Pronominal subject probabilities according to linking with preceding subject: Bilinguals' Spanish and English, monolingual Spanish and English (four independent analyses)*

Accessibility	Spanish-monolingual 41%, 1,143/2,802 Input: .40		Spanish-bilingual 24%, 1,353/5,571 Input: .21		English-bilingual 67%, 196/294 Input: .71		English-monolingual 67%, 658/987 Input: .71	
	Prob	N	Prob	N	Prob	N	Prob	N
Non-coref	.57	767/1588	.58	829/2642	.78	82/91	.73	352/403
Coref only	.49	261/700	.48	270/1238	.50	52/73	.58	173/226
Coref and linked	.31	98/458	.37	178/1384	.29	62/130	.20	122/344

Other factor groups in the analyses are: Priming, Verb class, Tense-Aspect, and (for Spanish) Person, and (for bilinguals' Spanish) Presence of English. Full results: see Appendix 2 (English, predictors of unexpressed subjects).

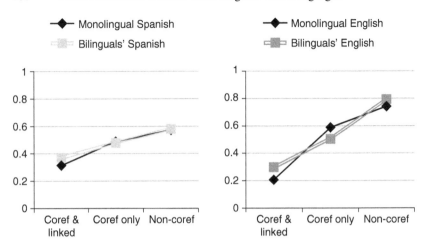

Figure 8.4 Pronominal subject probabilities according to linking with preceding subject: Bilinguals' Spanish and English, monolingual Spanish and English (four independent analyses, from Table 8.1)

factor "Non-coreferential" has a probability weight of .73 and the least favoring factor, "Coreferential and linked," one of .20). In contrast, the range (of 26) in monolingual Spanish is not greater than the ranges of the other major predictors (Table 6.1, Chapter 6).

Where do the bilingual varieties – in the middle pairs of columns – stand? In bilinguals' English the range for linking (of 49) is again double that of the predictor with the next highest range. This is not the case in bilinguals' Spanish, where the range for linking (of 21) is not the largest in the analysis (Appendix 2). We have no evidence, then, of a strengthening of accessibility configured as linking in bilinguals' Spanish. From the preceding chapter, we also have no evidence for a weakening of accessibility configured as subject continuity.[2] Once more, the contact varieties line up with their separate non-contact variety rather than with each other.

We zero in now on coordinate clauses with *and/y*. The conjunction *and/y* realizes maximal syntactic linking between clauses in both languages, as we

---

[2] The analysis of NMSEB Spanish with Accessibility as Linking (Table 8.1) in lieu of as Subject continuity (Table 7.1) has near-identical results, except that Linking is relatively stronger than Subject continuity, as it is in analyses of the monolingual CCCS data. There is a difference in data distributions (Table 8.1) with the CCCS (which records talk among close family and friends) where there are proportionally fewer cases of structural linking because there are proportionally more interlocutor previous mentions (N = 300). These, by definition, are not structurally linked to the target, but can count as coreferential (as in examples (71) and (72), Section 5.3.3.4). Note that quoted speech is excluded from Linking.

saw in our discussion of coordination in Chapter 6 (Section 6.4). As a site of cross-language similarity, a stronger general favoring effect of coordinate over other clause types in bilingual varieties would not be readily informative as to convergence, because it could be as much attributable to contact as to internal change. However, differences between English and Spanish crystallize when we pay attention to prosodic linking, which is realized via occurrence in the same IU or adjacent IUs connected with a continuing intonation contour.

One difference lies in effect strength. Prosodically connected English *and* impacts subject expression more than its Spanish counterpart *y* does. Figure 8.5 shows rates of pronominal subjects according to the presence of *and/y* and prosodic connection in the two monolingual baselines and the bilingual varieties. Comparing the dotted monolingual lines, we see gradation in both. Nevertheless, the slope between prosodically and non-prosodically connected *and/y*-clauses (connecting the first two points on the line) is greater for English than for Spanish, with double the rate increase in pronominal subjects (approximately a 200 percent increase in English vs. 100 percent in Spanish).

Turning to the bilingual NMSEB data, in the solid lines, in parallel fashion the rate increase is approximately double in English compared with Spanish. As in monolingual English, in bilinguals' English an unexpressed subject is markedly more likely if the coreferential-subject clauses conjoined with *and* are prosodically connected – in the same IU or in IUs connected via a continuing intonation

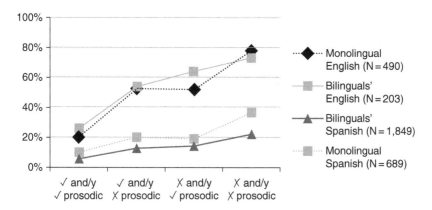

Figure 8.5 Rate of subject pronouns according to maximal syntactic linking and prosodic connection
Between coreferential-subject main clauses, syntactic link via conjunction *and/y;* prosodic link via occurrence in same IU or in IUs connected with continuing intonation. Monolingual Spanish and English previously shown in Chapter 6, Figure 6.2 and Figure 6.3. Bilinguals' data distributions across the four linking configurations: Spanish N = 228, 262, 383, 976; English N = 53, 28, 44, 78.

contour, marked with a comma (121) – than if they are prosodically separated, for example, by final intonation marked with a period (122).

(121)
Benita: *I went running,*
            and took a sh=ower,
            and got ready.

                                                        (31 Speed Limit, 57:12–57:15)

(122)
Betty: *he made it like a=,*
            ... a bench.
            ... around it.
            and he put the=,
            ...(3.5) the grill,
            ... out there.

                                                        (13 La Acequia, 32:04–32:13)

Another difference is distributional. In bilinguals' English, unexpressed subjects in prosodically connected *and*-clauses constitute 40 percent (39/98) of all tokens of unexpressed subjects. In contrast, in bilinguals' Spanish, prosodically connected *y*-clauses make up just 5 percent (214/4,218) of the unexpressed subjects. In the monolingual benchmarks, the corresponding proportions are parallel (43 percent, 141/329, in the SBCSAE vs. 4 percent, 63/1,659, in the CCCS data). The bilingual varieties are more similar to their monolingual counterparts than to each other, once again.

8.4   The Test of Language-particular Constructions

One hypothesized route to grammatical change is other-language lexical incorporations (e.g., Backus 2005: 309). The preceding discussion of prosodically connected *and* expressions brings us to a third test of convergence. Lexically particular constructions are conventionalized syntactic patterns anchored in specific words or semantic groupings of words. If language-particular constructions in each of the languages in contact parallel those found in non-contact varieties, and are distinct from those in the other contact language, then this is an indication that bilinguals are maintaining distinct grammars. We take up here the constructions discussed in previous chapters (Chapter 5, Section 5.8 and Chapter 6, Section 6.7).

8.4.1   And-*constructions in Bilinguals' English*

The behavior of the [VERB$_i$ *and* Ø VERB$_i$] construction is strikingly similar in the monolingual benchmark and bilinguals' English. The same particularly frequent manifestations are evident, namely with a verb of motion as the first verb, as in

(123), and a verb of speech as the second verb, as in (124). These specific constructions occur with similar frequency in the two datasets, accounting for approximately one-third of all structurally linked (prosodic and/or syntactic) cases (101/344 in the SBCSAE and 31/130 in NMSEB). And they account for most of the instances where two conjuncts occur in the same IU, approximately three-quarters of which are found with these two specific constructions (48/68 in SBCSAE and 14/18 in NMSEB). Thus, the New Mexican bilingual speakers have retained the [VERB$_i$ *and* Ø VERB$_i$] construction in their English with all the lexical particularities and details of prosodic structure.

(123)
Sandra: *I went and Ø got the angel from the box,*

(03 Dos Comadres, 14:52–14:52)

(124)
Eduardo: ... *the lady comes back at me and Ø says,*
            ... *you understand Spanish?*

(17 Climate Change, 48:56–49:02)

No such construction is evident in bilinguals' Spanish. Indeed, unexpressed subjects where two *y*-coordinated conjuncts occur in the same IU are as minor in NMSEB as they are in the monolingual baseline. In Spanish, they account for approximately 5 percent of all unexpressed subjects in coordinate or prosodically linked main clauses (50/829 in NMSEB and 12/237 in CCCS). Compare with same-IU [VERB$_i$ *and* Ø VERB$_i$], which accounts for over 25 percent in English (18/68 in NMSEB and 68/222 in SBCSAE).

8.4.2   Cognition-verb and Quotative Constructions in Bilinguals' Spanish

We also find lexically particular constructions in bilinguals' Spanish that are shared with monolingual varieties, and which are absent in English. One is that associated with cognition verbs, which tend to favor an expressed 1sg subject. Cognition-verb constructions supply another fruitful avenue to assess the loss of discourse-pragmatic constraints imputed to language contact.

As we saw in Chapter 7, Table 7.1, the general favoring effect with cognition verbs in bilinguals' Spanish is not weaker than in an earlier-stage benchmark of New Mexican Spanish. Two particular cognition-verb constructions are *(yo) creo* 'I think' and *(yo) no sé* 'I don't know', both of which have been widely reported across the Spanish-speaking world. Another is the Mexican Spanish *se me hace* 'it seems to me' (see (133)), which is used with similar frequency to *(yo) creo* (N = 130) in NMSEB, though, with a non-human subject, it doesn't enter the subject expression data.

The form *(yo) creo* '(I) think' – that is, the positive polarity present tense indicative form – accounts for 92 percent (153/166) of all tokens of the verb *creer* 'to believe, think', with a pronoun rate of 90 percent (138/153). It tends to be used in non-coreferential contexts more than average (82 percent vs. 47 percent for other verbs), but with an equally high *yo* rate in coreferential contexts (Chapter 5, Section 5.8). Furthermore, the *yo* rate is similarly high whether it occurs with a complement clause, as in (125), or without, as in the parenthetical use in (126). In contrast, English *I think* is not distinguished by higher than average rates of *I*. Nor does *I think* have a high rate of stress on the pronoun (which may be functionally equivalent to Spanish pronoun expression, e.g., Payne 1997: 43); rather, *I* tends to be unstressed in *I think* (Travis and Torres Cacoullos 2014: 364).

(125)
Fabiola: ... *Yo creo que trabaja mejor la salvia,*   '... I think that aloe vera works better,'
(09 La Salvia, 19:50–19:52)

(126)
Marco: *el ~Ray nació en uh,*   'Ray was born in um,
         .. Colorado yo creo.   .. Colorado I think.'
(24 La Floresta, 35:16–35:18)

The most frequent manifestation of the verb *saber* 'know' is in the negative polarity present tense indicative form *no sé* '(I) don't know', which accounts for 63 percent (208/326) of all tokens of this verb in NMSEB. *No sé* also favors *yo*, with a rate of 45 percent (94/208) (compared with 29 percent overall for 1sg; Table 7.1). Like *(yo) creo* '(I) think', *(yo) no sé* 'I don't know', occurs both with and without a complement clause, as in (127) and (128). However, subject pronoun *yo* is more frequent when there is a complement (53 percent, 52/110 vs. 37 percent, 39/98). This distinction is consistent with a pattern reported for Spanish in Madrid and Puerto Rico (Posio 2015: 64; Rivas and Brown 2009: 639). If there were a weakening of discourse-pragmatic constraints, we might expect subject expression in *no sé* '(I) don't know' to have lost sensitivity to these contextual features; yet it has not.

(127)
Diana: ... *Yo no sé en dónde andarán ahora*   '... I don't know where the pictures
         los retratos,   would be now,'
(24 La Floresta, 44:35–44:37)

(128)
Mariana: *pues seguro que el programa no*   'well the program probably doesn't
           tenía dinero.   have any money.
           Ø no sé.   (I) don't know.'
(19 School Bus, 49:47–49:50)

Another verb that stands out is *decir* 'say', reported to be among the most frequent verbs in subject expression data. NMSEB is no different in this respect: *decir* is the most frequent verb to occur, accounting for 16 percent

(893/5,571) of all tokens, and occurring over twice as often as the next most frequent verbs (*saber* 'know', N = 326, and *tener* 'have', N = 324). *Decir* does not show the grammatical person skewing that cognition verbs do, being the most frequent verb for both 1sg and 3sg. It does, however, show skewing in terms of tense, with over 55 percent (501/893) occurring in the Preterit – twice the proportion in the data overall.

Quotative use makes up the vast majority of these *decir* 'say' Preterit forms (80 percent, 400/501) and a full 23 percent of all Preterit tokens (400/1,714). The rate of expression for the Preterit quotative, seen in (129), is the lowest of any context, at just 3 percent (13/400). This compares with the higher rate of 19 percent (49/261) for non-quotative uses of *decir*. A further difference is that the Preterit quotative construction is not sensitive to coreferentiality, while other uses of *decir* are.

(129)

Sandra:	... *mira mamá,*	'... look mom,
	Ø le dije,	(I) said,
	lo que te le está pasando a tu mantel.	what is happening to your tablecloth.
	... *qué?*	... what?
	Ø me dijo.	(she) said.'

(03 Dos Comadres, 49:53–49:57)

Thus, we identify a particular construction strongly disfavoring pronominal subjects. As with the cognition-verb constructions, this quotative construction is not unique to New Mexico. For example, in Colombian (CCCS) data, quotative *decir* 'say' disfavors subject pronouns and Preterit *decir* forms are also most frequently used as quotatives (three-quarters of the time: 79/127).

A further distinguishing feature of *decir* 'say' is the high rate of postverbal subjects in bilinguals' Spanish, as in monolingual varieties (cf. Benevento and Dietrich 2015: 414). When occurring with a pronoun, *decir* favors postverbal position in New Mexico particularly in quotative uses, as in (130) (the rate of 1sg and 3sg postverbal subject pronouns is 65 percent, 60/92 for all quotative uses; 50 percent, 80/161, for all *decir*; and 17 percent, 272/1,625 overall, in NMSEB).

(130)

Fabiola:	*es lo que le dije yo=.*	'that is what I$_{-POST}$ said to him.
	... *no tengas mucho apuro le dije yo.*	... don't trouble yourself I$_{-POST}$ said to him.'

(09 La Salvia, 48:30–48:33)

In sum, bilinguals' Spanish and English display different lexically particular constructions. The fact that NM bilinguals do not resort to translation counterparts in structuring subject expression patterns is evidence that they keep their two languages apart. In a usage-based view, the relatively high frequency of particular constructions makes them entrenched, and therefore resistant to change via analogy to some other pattern, be that internal to the language or originating in the contact language (Bybee 1985; Phillips 2001; Torres Cacoullos and Ferreira 2000). However even the more schematic Spanish quotative and the English *and*-constructions are maintained as language-particular constructions. On every single comparison, in this section we have seen that bilinguals' Spanish aligns with monolingual Spanish and their English with monolingual English.

8.5   Conclusion

A glaring lacuna in assessing subject pronoun use in bilinguals' Spanish has been the lack of comparisons with English. The conjecture of reduced sensitivity to probabilistic constraints, especially accessibility, rests precariously on their assumed absence in the non-null-subject language. Contrary to this assumption, thanks to the comparisons with Spanish *and* English benchmarks undertaken here, we now know that, as a probabilistic constraint within the variable context, accessibility manifested as clause linking is actually stronger in English. Thus, following the logic of convergence, we might predict strengthening rather than weakening! Instead, unambivalent criteria for contact-induced change derive from diagnostic differences – sites of different co-occurrence patterns between English and Spanish: the variable context restriction of prosodic-initial position, strength of semantic and structural linking relative to other factors simultaneously in operation, and lexically particular constructions.

Most wanting in claims of convergence has been comparison of the grammars truly in contact – those of the bilingual speakers themselves. Juxtaposition of Spanish and English as used by the same speakers, here in the same conversations, provides the most rigorous test of convergence. The prosodic-initial position restriction in English, an incontrovertible diagnostic difference between monolingual Spanish and English, should have shown up as a locus of change in bilinguals' Spanish in the direction of the English pattern. No such alteration has taken place. For accessibility, measured as structural linking, again, there was no indication of any alteration toward the stronger version at work in English. And finally, language-specific constructions – different ones – are retained in the bilinguals' Spanish and English.

Moreover, there can remain no suspicion of hidden convergence, in the form of bilinguals' English being influenced by their Spanish (e.g., according to a scenario of imperfect learning or substratum interference). Not only do we see no movement of Spanish toward English grammar, we also find no evidence of change in English toward Spanish patterning, either in the rate of unexpressed subjects or in the variable context and conditioning of subject expression.

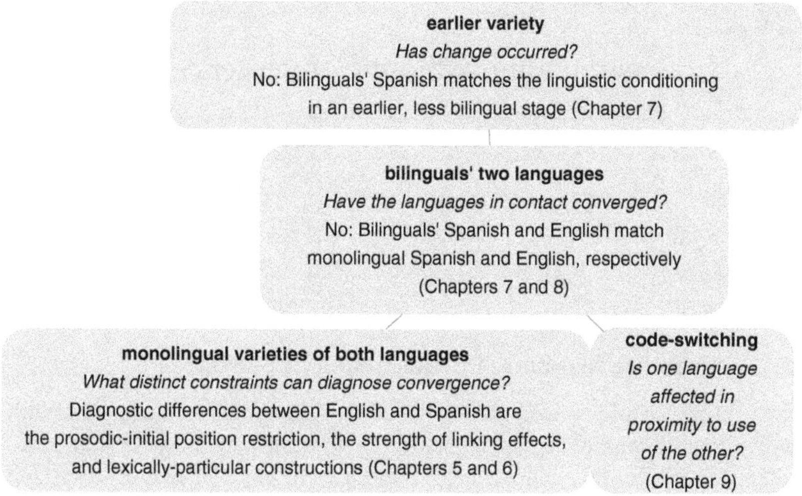

earlier variety
Has change occurred?
No: Bilinguals' Spanish matches the linguistic conditioning
in an earlier, less bilingual stage (Chapter 7)

bilinguals' two languages
Have the languages in contact converged?
No: Bilinguals' Spanish and English match
monolingual Spanish and English, respectively
(Chapters 7 and 8)

monolingual varieties of both languages
What distinct constraints can diagnose convergence?
Diagnostic differences between English and Spanish are
the prosodic-initial position restriction, the strength of linking effects,
and lexically-particular constructions (Chapters 5 and 6)

code-switching
*Is one language
affected in
proximity to use
of the other?*
(Chapter 9)

Figure 8.6 Comparisons of language variation patterns, refuting convergence

The comparisons involving the *other* language provide resounding evidence
that both of the bilinguals' languages adhere to the same model as their
respective monolingual varieties. Thus, we are able to refute convergence –
the grammars of Spanish and English in this bilingual community are kept
separate.

The comparisons so far are summarized in Figure 8.6. There remains the
bottom right rectangle – the view that code-switching intrinsically produces
convergence. The lack of evidence for convergence in these highly bilingual
data indirectly refutes this view. In Chapter 9 we conduct a direct test.

9 Code-switching without Convergence

9.1 Cognitive Accounts of Contact-induced Change

Proposed explanations of contact-induced change should be consonant with known mechanisms of language change. A leading hypothesis is that code-switching (CS), loosely defined as the use of two or more languages in a single discourse event, is an impetus of structural convergence (e.g., Gumperz and Wilson 1971). The reasoning is that, when switching, bilinguals favor structures that are common to the languages, toward "cross-language compromise" (Thomason and Kaufman 1988: 154). However, the mechanisms – the why and how CS begets convergence – remain nebulous (as noted by Winford 2005).

The widely entertained idea is that the use of two languages is somehow cognitively costly. Convergence has been viewed as a consequence of bilinguals (unconsciously) adjusting how they use the structures of one language to better match patterns of the other. Such modulation may follow from strategies of bilingual optimization (Muysken 2013) or syncretization (Matras and Sakel 2007: 832) for "easing of tensions" (Erker and Otheguy 2016: 144) or "lightening the cognitive load of having to remember and use two different linguistic systems" (Silva-Corvalán 1994: 6).

Decisive psycholinguistic evidence for a bilingual cognitive load is still elusive, however. In lab-based studies, competition across two languages appears costly for speed and accuracy in vocabulary-related tasks, such as lexical decision experiments, but may be beneficial to the development of cognitive processes for controlling behavior such as directing attention and inhibiting previously perceived information (for a review of evidence and accounts of the cognitive consequences of bilingualism, see Kroll, Dussias, Bice, and Perrotti 2015). As to blanket processing costs of CS itself, the jury is still out. For example, switches between Spanish progressive auxiliary *estar* 'to be' and an English gerund did not take longer to read than all-Spanish periphrases (e.g., *están cleaning* vs. *están limpiando* 'they are cleaning') in an eye-tracking study when subjects were given a comprehension task, though a cost appeared when they performed an acceptability judgment task (Guzzardo

Tamargo 2012; Guzzardo Tamargo et al. 2016). Besides different costs according to experimental task, psycholinguists now recognize that different communities and different interactional contexts of bilinguals "induce different habits of language control" (Green and Wei 2014: 503).

Ongoing lack of consensus on what exactly CS is, what constrains it, and what impact it has on grammar, is in no small part due to the problem of good data. Arguments in historical or contact linguistics have largely relied on example sentences, with little indication as to whether these are isolated occurrences or represent robust tendencies in some bilingual community. Where quantitative tests are conducted, datasets commonly have been constructed from just a handful of participants or, for larger samples, from participant pools of university students, often second-language learners. Conspicuously scarce has been the evidence of bilingual usage norms in well-defined communities, laid bare by systematic quantitative analysis of spontaneous speech. It is just such analyses that are enabled by the NMSEB corpus (Chapters 2 and 3).

In the preceding chapters we saw that the contact site and bilingual speakers represented in NMSEB have the characteristics that should, according to much bilingualism literature, be propitious to convergence. We compared the bilingual varieties with earlier-stage and monolingual benchmarks, as well as with each other. In this chapter we add a final set of comparisons, bilinguals' behavior in the immediate environment of a switch between their languages: the presence vs. absence of CS in the proximate discourse (Section 9.2). We begin with the impact that proximate use of English has on rates of Spanish subject expression (9.3). Finding these unaltered, we turn to the linguistic conditioning of pronominal subjects (9.4), spotlighting the effect of referent accessibility, which, as discussed in Chapter 7, is widely predicted to be particularly susceptible to contact-induced change (9.5).

9.1.1   An Excursus on Code-switching Cost: Switching at the Complement Clause

If CS entails a processing cost, then this should have consequences for natural language use. Processing costs would ultimately have to be substantiated in spontaneous CS patterns. By patterns of CS we mean the propensity to switch at particular syntactic or prosodic boundaries rather than others: of the places where bilinguals *can* switch, where they *prefer* to do so (Poplack 1993: 277). CS patterns remain to be discovered, since CS theories have been preoccupied with formulating categorical constraints. Nevertheless, knowing where CS is eschewed is a starting point.

According to the Equivalence Constraint, bilinguals tend to avoid CS at points of word order conflicts between the two languages. Less than 1 percent

(11/1,835) of Spanish–English code-switches in the East Harlem, New York Puerto Rican community occurred at points where the word orders were different (Poplack 1980b). A more precise definition, then, is that CS is the concatenation of alternating-language strings (D. Sankoff 1998; D. Sankoff and Poplack 1981).

Since CS boundaries are constrained by word string equivalence, bilingual CS strategies can be understood as dealing with types of juncture rather than with a general processing cost. Evidence would come from junctures of *variable equivalence*, where the word strings of the two languages are equivalent only sometimes (Torres Cacoullos and Poplack 2016). An example is the boundary of main and complement clauses: whereas in Spanish the complementizer *que* is present always, in English the complementizer *that* is present variably. This sometimes-applying difference between the languages means that, for CS at the main and complement clause boundary, there arises the problem of variable equivalence. How is it resolved?

One bilingual strategy is prosodic separation of the two languages at junctures of variable equivalence. In NMSEB, complement clauses are produced in the same IU as the main verb approximately two-thirds of the time in bilinguals' Spanish-only and English-only speech (312/484 and 366/467, respectively). Similar rates of prosodic integration of complement and main clauses are found in monolingual benchmarks of Spanish and English (see Chapter 3, Section 3.6). In contrast, in the same bilinguals' speech, when CS occurs at the boundary between main and complement clause, as in (131) and (132), the clauses are prosodically integrated less than half the time (25/63). The preference is to produce them in different IUs, as in (131) (Steuck and Torres Cacoullos 2016).[1] Most telling is that, when CS occurs elsewhere – within the main or complement clause but not at the boundary between them, as in (133) – the rate of prosodic integration of the two clauses (28/44) is no lower than in bilinguals' Spanish-only and English-only speech or the monolingual benchmarks. Thus, prosodic separation here cannot be due to a general cost of CS per se, but instead is due to a problem of equivalence.

(131)
Pedro: ...*(1.0)* |*creo que*|,   '...(1.0) I think that,
        |*he='s been dead for a while*|.   *he's been dead for a while.*'
                                                      (07 Basketball Teams, 32:44–32:45)

(132)
Aurora: ... |*but I think*| |*que estaba en el rincón*|,   '... *but I think* that it was in the corner,'
                                                      (15 Las Cosas Viejas, 05:02–05:03)

---

[1] Favored at the CS boundary is the quantitatively more readily available variant, Spanish complementizer *que*, regardless of main or complement clause language.

(133)

Dora: ... | *se me hace que era* | *four years ago.* | '... I think that it was *four years ago.*'

(14 Best of Both Worlds, 30:10–30:11)

9.2   A Synchronic Test: Proximity of Code-switching

While CS has featured prominently as a mechanism of contact-induced change, it may arise for a variety of reasons having to do with particular situational parameters. Multi-word other-language strings alternate copiously and unpredictably in some bilingual communities and serve rhetorical functions in others. Northern New Mexico is an exceptionally valuable contact site because CS in this community is what has been called "intrasituational" (Poplack 2015: 918) or "internally generated" (Gullberg, Indefrey, and Muysken 2009: 34). With this kind of CS, use of alternating-language strings is a discourse mode or device: once the situation is seen as appropriate, its occurrence cannot be predicted at the local level any more than we can predict, say, telling a joke (Poplack 1993: 276; D. Sankoff 1998: 39).

Locally unpredictable CS is captured in NMSEB. As we saw in Chapter 4 (Section 4.4), speakers make no mention of any particular topics motivating their choice of one or the other language, and give no indication of distinct affect or rhetorical functions for the two. Neither language is the matrix into which the other is inserted: there is an even number of clauses in English and Spanish (based on the language of the verb) (Figure 4.3). Figure 9.1 now shows the distribution of clauses in each language according to grammatical person. The similarity between Spanish and English evident here would not justify positing distinct rhetorical functions served by each language.

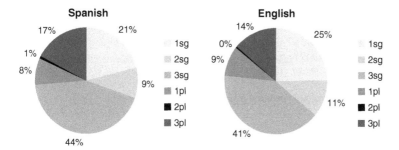

Figure 9.1 Lack of rhetorical functions of code-switching: Distribution of clauses by grammatical person in bilinguals' Spanish and English (Spanish N = 17,689; English N = 18,322)

We have seen that NM bilinguals who regularly code-switch do not differ in their patterns of Spanish subject expression from speakers of non-contact Spanish; they do differ from non-contact English speakers and, most remarkably, from their very selves in their own patterns of English subject expression (Chapters 7 and 8). This does not support the hypothesis that CS is a catalyst for convergence. Nor does it directly contradict it, however. Although time depth of a contact situation allows evaluation of any long-term consequences of that contact, because CS is a synchronic phenomenon, real-time tests of its much-surmised role in convergence must be devised. For this, we need some measure of the proximity of CS to the candidate converging structure.

We introduce here a direct synchronic test of the effect of CS which relies on comparisons of subject pronouns in the presence vs. absence of maximally proximate CS. First, we must define both "code-switching" and "maximally proximate."

9.2.1 Types of Language Mixing: Distinguishing Multi-word Code-switching

Typologies of language mixing are still contentious, but the distinction between multi-word strings and single-word items has proven important. In Muysken's classification, for example, insertion applies to unitary chunks, as distinct from alternation (2015: 254). We distinguish multi-word CS from single-word, or lone, other-language items. This means that English-origin words that are not established loanwords appearing in monolingual dictionaries are classed separately from CS (used here is the Royal Spanish Academy dictionary, www.rae.es). Example (134) illustrates, with lone items in lines (a), (b), and (c) (*eleventh* and the compound *night school*), and CS in (d) (*different credits*), indicated in italics in the English translation on the right.

(134)

LONE	a.	.. ahora Ø va en el *eleventh* y=,	'.. now (he) is in eleventh and,
LONE	b.	.. Ø está yendo al *night school*.	.. (he) is going to night school.
LONE	c.	... porque en el *night school*,	... because in night school,
CS	d.	Ø quiere agarrar *different credits* y=,	(he) wants to take *different credits* and,
PROPER	e.	... yo quiero que vaya al *CNM*,	... I want him to go to CNM,'

(11 El Trabajo, 14:26–14:33)

Much of the controversy surrounding the plethora of conflicting CS theories stems from the treatment of single-word other-language items, most of which are nouns. It is common practice to automatically count these lone items in CS datasets, in many of which they end up constituting the majority of "CS" data.[2] Yet nouns that originate in one language but are embedded in another tend overwhelmingly to assume the linguistic features of loanwords, which in turn reflect those of the recipient language (Poplack 2017). This means that they are borrowed, if only for the nonce (e.g., Poplack and Dion 2012; Poplack and Meechan 1998). Most decisive is that borrowing and CS obey different constraints:

the linguistic properties of CS – of whatever length – have been consistently shown in quantitative studies to contrast diametrically with those of borrowings: both the internal constituency and positioning in the clause of borrowed words come from the recipient language, while the internal constituency of CS is that of the language of origin, but its placement in the sentence tends to respect the word order requirements of both languages in the mix. (Poplack 2015: 923)

In the northern NM community, lone nouns tend to be borrowed (Torres Cacoullos and Aaron 2003) (see Chapter 3, Section 3.1 on kinship terms). Pending analysis of the status of lone English words other than nouns in the northern NM community, as a conservative move we limit CS to multi-word instances.

Proper nouns, such as *CNM* (Central New Mexico Community College, in line (e) in (134)), are also counted separately. This includes the names of places (*Albuquerque*), celebrities or famous characters (*Superman*), institutions (*La Cueva* high school) or businesses (*J.C. Penney*). Proper nouns are among the elements of the linguistic context, like cognates such as *doctor*, proposed to act as CS triggers: "words at the intersection of two language systems ... may cause speakers to lose their linguistic bearings and continue the sentence in the other language" (Clyne 1991: 193). As measured in speech rate, the production of switches at proper nouns as opposed to common nouns may be facilitated (Fricke, Kroll, and Dussias 2016: 117). Nevertheless, pending tests of triggered CS in NMSEB, our reason for setting aside proper nouns is that they may be ambiguous or neutral as to language.

Accordingly, *indisputable instances of CS are multi-word sequences.* Internally, each string abides by the grammatical principles of its respective language. Bilinguals' application of independent, language-particular, grammatical principles was seen in the preceding chapter, where we verified that the differences between Spanish and English subject expression are maintained in the most intimate contact, as bilinguals speak their own varieties. Externally, CS involves alternation rather than a global directionality from one language to the other, seen in the locally unpredictable character of switches from English to Spanish, and Spanish to English.

---

[2] For example, the proposal that a motivation for CS is to encode high information content (Myslín and Levy 2015) would apply only to lone (single-word) items.

9.2.2   Defining "Proximate" Code-switching

Potential effects of CS have been tested by comparing speakers according to their propensity to code-switch (Poplack, Zentz, and Dion 2012a: 207). Alternatively, for speakers who regularly engage in CS, we can make comparisons according to the recency of CS, measured in seconds (Balukas and Koops 2015: 430) or prosodic units (Torres Cacoullos and Travis 2011: 255). To test the convergence-via-CS hypothesis for a morphosyntactic variable such as Spanish subject expression, we adopt a clausal measure of proximity of CS. We focus on maximally proximate CS, where speakers should be at the height of "bilingual mode" and activation of both languages should be at its peak (Grosjean 1998: 136).

Maximally *proximate CS* is operationalized here as the speaker's use of multi-word sequences of the other language in the same or preceding clause as the target verb. This includes the stretch of discourse from the start of the immediately preceding clause to the end of the target clause. Thus, the unexpressed subject in line (a) in (135), with multi-word English in the preceding clause, as well as that in line (d) in (134), with multi-word English following the target verb in the same clause, are both coded as having proximate CS, while the pronoun *yo* 'I' in line (b) in (135) occurs in a Spanish-only environment.

(135)

CS PRESENT	a.	*...(1.0) I don't have that ... energy* *ya para hacer aquí en la* *casa como Ø tenía más antes.*	'*...(1.0) I don't have that ... energy* anymore to do things here at home like (I) had before.
CS ABSENT	b.	*... porque yo venía* *del trabajo,*	... because I would come back from work,
	c.	*...(1.5) and she would have the* *water you know,*	*...(1.5) and she would have the* *water you know,*
	d.	*... ya soaking for the mud* *for .. the adobes?*	... already soaking for the mud *for .. the adobes?* '

(04 Piedras y Gallinas, 48:44–48:57)

The immediately preceding clause is any finite verb, in a main or subordinate clause. Not considered clausal were discourse markers, such as Spanish *mira* 'see' and English *I don't know*, and other deverbal expressions, such as *hace tres años* 'it's been three years/three years ago' (see Chapter 5, Section 5.3.3.1). The end of the target clause is defined as the point at which nothing further is "projected" (Hopper and Thompson 2008). This is straightforward where multi-word Spanish and English occur in the same IU, as in (136). Much more commonly, multi-word Spanish and English occur in different IUs, for example in (137). Here, included are only cases where the first IU projects subsequent material both syntactically (e.g., a verb that projects a direct object) and prosodically (with continuing intonation, Chapter 3, Section 3.4), as in (137).

(136)
Dolores: .. *y Ø se pone* those shiny pa=nts.   '.. and (he) puts on *those shiny pants.*'
                                                                    (22 Farolitos, 52:55–52:58)

(137)
Betty: *y él quería=,*   'and he wanted,
               one story=,   one story,
               for me to read one story,   for me to read one story,'
Carrie: *[mhm].*   '[mhm].'
Betty: *[and you] girls wanted another one.* '*[and you] girls wanted another one.*'
                                                                    (13 La Acequia, 15:20–15:23)

For the most stringent comparison of presence vs. absence of CS, we exclude multi-word English strings and English-origin lone items produced by interlocutors.[3] Thus, in the following analyses, *CS presence* means multi-word English by the same speaker who produced the target verb and *CS absence* is incontrovertibly a Spanish-only environment: no multi- or single-word English and no proper nouns by the speaker, nor any English elements by the interlocutor.

9.3   Proximate Use of English and Subject Pronoun Rates in Spanish

NMSEB is, to the best of our knowledge, a unique corpus in featuring roughly even proportions of multi-word CS and lone other-language items. Figure 9.2 shows the distribution of instances of variable Spanish subject expression according to the presence of English elements in the same clause as the target verb or in the immediately preceding clause. Approximately one-half occur where there is no English in the immediate vicinity, one-fifth in the presence of proximate CS, another fifth in the presence of a lone English-origin item, and 5 percent in the context of a proper noun. This data distribution permits a direct test of the effect of the recent or imminent use of English on the Spanish of these bilingual speakers.

Figure 9.3 now shows bilinguals' Spanish subject pronoun rates according to the presence of English elements. If CS propels contact-induced change in the long term, we may expect that, synchronically, in real time, it should affect the rates of bilinguals' Spanish subject pronouns. Minimally, these should be affected at least by the proximate presence of English multi-word strings, as

---

[3] Also excluded for the comparison of presence vs. absence of English are Spanish subject expression tokens in the presence of words listed in Spanish dictionaries that may be loanwords in this community, e.g., *banco* 'bank', *colegio* 'college', *presente* 'present' (N = 55), and unclear speech (N = 82).

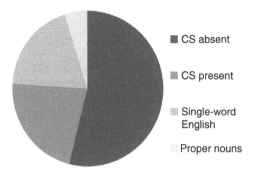

Figure 9.2 Distribution of bilinguals' Spanish subjects according to proximate presence of English
N = 4,988: CS absent (N = 2,690); CS present (N = 1,100); Single-word English (N = 954); Proper nouns (N = 244).

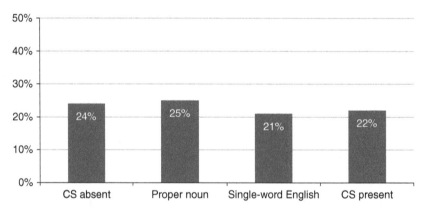

Figure 9.3 Bilinguals' Spanish subject pronoun rate according to proximate presence of English
CS absent (666/2,690) vs. Proper noun (62/244), $\chi2 = 0.02, p = .88$; vs. Single-word English (213/954), $\chi2 = 2.14, p = .14$; vs. CS present (242/1,100), $\chi2 = 3.06, p = .08$.

in line (a) in (135). The prediction is not upheld: the subject pronoun rate is virtually the same in the presence and absence of proximate CS. Nor is the subject pronoun rate significantly different in the presence of lone English-origin items, or of proper nouns.[4]

---

[4] Subject pronoun rates in the context of interlocutor-produced multi- and single-word English are 29 percent (66/176) and 38 percent (79/270), respectively.

9.4   Comparison of Presence and Absence of Code-switching

Beneath the flat rate, there may nevertheless be differences in the linguistic conditioning – the factors shaping the variation between pronominal and unexpressed subjects. Table 9.1 presents four separate logistic regression analyses: monolingual Spanish and English benchmarks, at the extreme left and right, and bilinguals' Spanish in the absence and presence of proximate CS, in the middle. The benchmark datasets are from corpora of conversational Spanish (CCCS) and English (SBCSAE) (see Chapter 1, Table 1.1). The bilinguals' Spanish data is the same as for Table 7.1 in Chapter 7, here divided according to the presence of CS.

If CS promotes change we should see a difference in the conditioning of Spanish subject pronouns in the presence of proximate CS to or from English. The overall probability ("input") of a pronominal subject in the absence and presence of CS is virtually identical, consistent with the flat rate seen in Figure 9.3 (and the non-significance of presence of English in the undivided dataset; see Table 7.1).

For accessibility effects (top half of Table 9.1), the first three datasets are similar, and they differ from the fourth. The comparisons of bilinguals' Spanish with the monolingual benchmarks contradict convergence, in that there is greater parallelism with Spanish than with English independently of the presence of CS. We return to this in Section 9.5.

Priming (bottom half of Table 9.1) also operates the exact same way independently of the presence of CS. To probe the role of CS in priming effects, monolingual benchmarks are not pertinent because by definition monolingual Spanish lacks English primes and monolingual English lacks Spanish primes. Rather, we compare CS presence and absence with each other (middle columns). We see that the order of primes from most to least favorable of pronominal expression (the direction of effect) is the same in both CS presence and absence.[5] The impact of CS on the scope of priming is the topic of the following chapter.

Verb class (note to Table 9.1) is significant and with the same direction of effect in the presence and absence of CS (though, as we will see, pronoun-to-pronoun priming across languages dissipates with cognition verbs; Chapter 10, Section 10.4.1). Finally, the Person effect is identical, while the significance of Tense in the presence of CS cannot be interpreted as CS promoting an ambiguity-resolving function for subject pronouns, since it is due not to a higher rate in the syncretic Imperfect but to a lower rate in the Preterit (see Chapter 5, Section 5.6.1).[6]

---

[5] In the Table 9.1 analyses, English primes are excluded from the priming independent variable in the absence of CS because with no CS, by definition the entire preceding clause must be in Spanish only and therefore, in a coreferential context, the preceding subject is never in English. (There are no instances where the subject pronoun and verb are in different languages.)

[6] Rates for Present–Imperfect–Preterit, CS absent: 21–25–20 percent; CS present: 23–24–12 percent.

Table 9.1 *Pronominal subject probabilities according to linking with preceding subject and priming: Bilinguals' Spanish with code-switching present and absent, monolingual Spanish and English (four independent analyses)*

	Spanish-monolingual 41%, 1,143/2,802 Input: .40		Spanish-bilingual CS absent 25%, 666/2,690 Input: .21		Spanish-bilingual CS present 22%, 242/1,100 Input: .19		English-monolingual 67%, 658/987 Input: .71	
	Prob	N	Prob	N	Prob	N	Prob	N
Accessibility								
Non-coref	.57	767/1588	.58	394/1248	.60	157/543	.73	352/403
Coref only	.49	261/700	.51	125/532	.44	44/252	.58	173/226
Coref and linked	.31	98/458	.37	104/756	.35	29/237	.21	122/344
Priming								
Pronominal Spanish	.62	342/637	.74	163/353	.75	31/67	NA	NA
Outside priming env.	.53	512/1138	.58	301/939	.61	105/331	.55	274/343
Pronominal English	NA	NA	–	20/87	.48	69/372	.51	322/508
Unexpressed	.37	228/841	.36	152/1179	.33	29/271	.34	50/116

For *Spanish-bilingual, CS absent/present*: Accessibility (as shown), Priming (as shown), Verb class (Cognition .74/.67, Stative .59/.63, Dynamic .43/.42), Person (1sg .55/.54, 3sg .43/.44), Tense (Imperfective [.50]/.54 Perfective [.51]/.40). Monolingual varieties: see Table 6.1, Chapter 6.

9.5   Proximate Code-switching and Accessibility Effects

The effect of referent accessibility on choice of a pronominal over an unexpressed subject has been seen as most "vulnerable" to alteration in bilingual speech (Sorace 2004: 143). For Spanish in contact with English, the effect may be weakened, since the limited variability in English means that bilinguals have reduced opportunities to apply it. Or it may be strengthened because, within the restricted envelope of variation in English, accessibility overshadows other probabilistic constraints.

How does accessibility fare under proximate CS? Remember that linking as a composite accessibility measure combines semantic and structural criteria. Beyond coreferentiality with the preceding subject, unexpressed subjects are constrained by structural linking to the preceding clause via a coordinating conjunction or via intonation. While the effect applies to both languages, it is stronger in English, where it predominates over other conditioning factors. In Chapters 7 and 8, we compared bilinguals' Spanish with monolingual benchmarks and failed to find evidence for either a weakening of accessibility configured as subject continuity (predicated on the hypothesis that contact causes erosion of discourse constraints) or a strengthening of accessibility configured as linking (predicated on the strength of this effect in English). We concluded that bilinguals' Spanish is neither dissimilar to non-contact Spanish nor similar to non-contact English. This finding, though, is for the aggregate and may be masking an effect for proximate CS in that portion of the dataset to which it applies.

In order to expose any effects of CS proper, we spotlight accessibility results in the presence of proximate CS. Bear in mind that in the presence of CS, coreferential contexts may involve either a preceding Spanish, or a preceding English, subject mention. For example, in (138), the target verb in line (d) is coreferential with English *he* in line (a). If there is any contact-induced change in the linking (accessibility) effect on bilinguals' Spanish subject pronouns, this will have to be visible in the presence of proximate CS, where accessibility may involve a previous mention of the subject referent in the form of an English pronoun.

(138)
a.	Eduardo:	*he lets me,*	'*he lets me,*
b.		*rattle off,*	*rattle off,*
c.		*... un bonche en mexicano,*	... a whole bunch of Spanish,
d.		*.. y luego Ø me dice,*	.. and then (he) says to me,
e.		*<Q what did you say tata Q>?*	*<Q what did you say tata Q>?*'
			('grandfather')
			(27 Climate Change, 24:35–24:41)

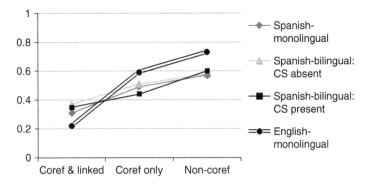

Figure 9.4 Pronominal subject probabilities according to linking with preceding subject: Bilinguals' Spanish with code-switching present and absent, monolingual Spanish and English (four independent analyses; from Table 9.1)

The effect of linking to the preceding clause seen above in Table 9.1 is depicted pictorially in Figure 9.4. In the presence of CS to and from English, bilinguals' Spanish is more similar to monolingual Spanish than to monolingual English. There is not even a sliding toward English: results in CS presence are no less similar to monolingual Spanish – and no less dissimilar from monolingual English – than results in CS absence are.

9.6   Conclusion

The hypothesis that CS is an impetus of structural convergence must, perforce, be tested synchronically. A direct test of the hypothesis is enabled by the NMSEB corpus because it records not only single-word incorporations, but an abundance of incontrovertible instances of CS – that is, multi-word other-language sequences. If bilinguals' recent use of one language affects choice of linguistic variants in the other, CS to and from English should impact patterns of subject pronoun expression in Spanish. Here we established a sharp test according to the maximally proximate presence of CS – within the same or previous clause as the instance of variable subject expression, produced by the same speaker.

Application of this novel test reveals that proximity of English does not impact the overall rate of Spanish subject pronouns. The rate remains flat, unaltered in the absence or presence of English, be that single-word (lone) English items, proper nouns, or multi-word CS to and from English.

Furthermore, the probabilistic constraints under CS are as in monolingual Spanish, with no signs of convergence with English. The answer to the question of a necessary relationship between CS and convergence is an unequivocal "No."

This lack of alteration in the linguistic conditioning includes the effect of accessibility (linking with preceding subject). This is a remarkable result, since accessibility would be weakened according to the general hypothesis of erosion of discourse-pragmatic constraints in language contact or, conversely, would be strengthened in congruence with the greater magnitude of the effect in English. We find neither. What repercussions, then, might CS have?

10   Code-switching and Priming

A long-standing issue in bilingualism research is the interaction between bilingual speakers' linguistic systems. For lexical items, "pervasive parallel activation" is suggested by the facilitated processing of words having similar meaning and form ("cognates," such as English *difference* and Spanish *diferencia*), even in word recognition tasks that require use of only one of the two languages (Kroll et al. 2015: 380–381). For morpho-syntax, the extent to which two grammars overlap in mental representation may be addressed by *cross-language structural priming*. In cross-language structural priming, use of a variant in one language favors subsequent choice of the analogous variant in the other language. An example is with the dative alternation, as in *The lawyer sent his client the contract* vs. *The lawyer sent the contract to his client*, primed both from German to English and from English to German (Loebell and Bock 2003). Such priming has been inter-preted as evidence that bilinguals have a "shared syntax" whereby coincid-ing grammatical structures "are represented once" (Hartsuiker, Pickering, and Veltkamp 2004: 409).

Re-use of parallel structures across languages is "a potential explanatory mechanism for ... language contact phenomena" (Gries and Kootstra 2017: 237). In particular, cross-language structural priming, in which speakers rein-vest in a previously produced or processed structure in either language, would be a mechanism by which code-switching (CS) promotes convergence. The idea is that CS "function[s] to model syntactic patterns which are then subsequently imitated in the base language" (Backus 2005: 334). In this chapter we explore, in bilingual discourse, *coreferential subject priming*, the favoring of a pronominal subject when the previous mention was also realized with a pronoun, which, in the presence of CS, may be a Spanish or an English pronoun. We use priming to evaluate the impact of CS on grammar and to assess the associations between bilinguals' grammars.

We begin by reviewing the relevance of priming to subject expression (Section 10.1). We will see that coreferential subject priming is modulated by CS (10.2). The effect of CS is to produce shifts in contextual distributions: with proximate CS, cross-language priming of English pronoun to Spanish pronoun is enabled, with an accompanying shift in the relative frequency of the different realizations of previous coreferential subjects (10.3). We close with a consideration of priming as a measure of the strength of associations between constructions (10.4), and then, more broadly, of associations across languages (10.5).

10.1 Priming in Spontaneous Speech

Speakers' choices are not independent of their prior choices. One of the earliest priming studies was that of Sankoff and Laberge (1978), in which they demonstrated that "syntagmatic proximity of two occurrences of a variable" affects their realization, for example *nous* vs. *on* for the first-person plural in the Montreal French pronominal system. Weiner and Labov (1983) showed that if there was an agentless passive in the recent discourse, speakers were more likely to use another such passive than an active clause with a general (non-specific) subject pronoun (e.g., *Lower Merion's allowed to smoke in the halls* vs. *they allow Lower Merion to smoke in the halls*). Such structural priming has been explored for several alternations in community-based studies, for example, of subject-verb agreement in Brazilian Portuguese (Scherre and Naro 1991), as well as in large-scale corpus studies, for example, particle placement (*picked up the nuts* vs. *picked the nuts up*) (Gries 2005) and comparisons (*the trickier problem* vs. the *more tricky problem*) (Szmrecsanyi 2005). It is safe to say that priming pervades variation, though its import depends on the linguistic variable and co-occurring environmental features.

In coreferential subject priming, the *prime* is the previous mention, in subject position, of the same referent as the *target* (Chapter 5, Section 5.4). Tokens without a pronominal or unexpressed previous mention are considered to occur outside the priming environment. This is the case for tokens for which the previous mention was a full noun phrase or a relative pronoun (as for the token in line (k) in (139)). Note that not all previous pronominal or unexpressed coreferential subjects count as primes. Thus, also set aside are tokens for which:

- the previous mention was at a distance of greater than ten clauses (N = 662), due to the dissipation of priming effects with increasing distance between target and prime (Travis 2007: 121; Travis et al. 2017: 289–290);
- the previous mention was a postverbal subject, pending investigation of how position (preverbal vs. postverbal) may affect priming of realization (expressed vs. unexpressed);
- the previous mention was produced by the interlocutor, due to the weaker effect of "comprehension-to-production" priming (Gries 2005: 374);

- either the target or the previous mention occurred in quoted speech, as for the second token in line (l) in (139) (unless both occurred as part of the same quoted speech), as it is unknown whether the shift between quoted and non-quoted speech may interrupt priming.

Excluding tokens outside the priming environment (N = 1,965), we are left with two general priming categories: a previous pronoun and a previous unexpressed subject.

Per coreferential subject priming, a previous pronoun favors a subsequent pronoun, and a previous unexpressed subject favors a subsequent unexpressed subject. The previous mention may be the immediately preceding subject or may occur further back in the discourse. For example, in (139), the first token in line (l) *Ø dije* '(I) said' has an unexpressed previous mention in the immediately preceding clause, while for *yo era* 'I was' in line (i), there is a pronominal prime at a distance of two intervening clauses in line (b). There is also a pronominal prime for *yo era* 'I was' in line (b), and here, notice that the previous mention is the English pronoun *I*, an instance of cross-language priming.

(139)

a.	Ivette:	*I wanted to go to the night clubs y=,*	'*I wanted to go the night clubs* and,
b.		*.. yo era la única,*	.. I was the only one,
c.		*de todas las que íbamos,*	of all of us who went,
d.		*... you know,*	... you know,
e.		*que nos juntábamos en los weekends,*	who would get together on the weekends,
f.		*to go dancing,*	to go dancing,
g.		*or [whatever].*	or [whatever].'
h.	Rafael:	*[mhm].*	'[mhm].'
i.	Ivette:	*yo era la única que no sabía arrear.*	'I was the only one who didn't know how to drive.
j.		*...(0.7) y luego cuando,*	...(0.7) and then when,
k.		*... Ø quería arrear,*	... (I) wanted to drive,
l.		*Ø dije pues yo no quiero nomás arrear allá=.*	(I) said well I don't want to just drive there.'

(06 El Túnico, 51:54–52:09)

10.2   Cross-language Priming

One consequence of CS is that cross-language structural priming is enabled. Priming across languages has received attention in lab-based studies, which have reported such an effect across several language pairs and with different structure types; less is known about how cross-language priming works in actual speech (for a review, see Gries and Kootstra 2017). Remember that proximate CS as operationalized here is the use of multi-word English in the same or preceding clause (Chapter 9, Section 9.2). If the English word sequence occurs in the preceding clause, and includes a coreferential subject, then there is a possibility of cross-language coreferential subject priming; *I* to *yo* (as in lines (a)–(b) in (139)), or *she/he* to *ella/él* (as in (140)).

(140)

| a. | Javier: | *she had a fluffy cat,* | '*she had a fluffy cat,* |
| b. | | *y ella lo tenía aquí,* | and she had it here,' |

(17 La Comadreja, 11:16–11:18)

First, let us verify cross-language coreferential subject priming. We saw in Chapter 5 (Section 5.4) that priming holds for speakers independently of their rate of pronominal expression. To dispel any doubt that the priming is only apparent in the aggregate because primes and targets are drawn from the same individuals, some of whom may have particularly high, or particularly low, rates overall, we show here a generalized linear mixed effects (GLMM) regression analysis that included speaker as a random effect. A random effect takes into account the fact that each participant varies in their overall rate of pronominal expression. Table 10.1 gives a model summary, predicting the occurrence of subject pronouns given Priming, Accessibility, and Verb Class.[1] Both cross- and within-language priming are evident: a previous English pronoun and a previous Spanish pronoun significantly increase the likelihood of a pronominal subject as compared with a previous unexpressed subject, seen in the positive coefficients in the first column. (The effects already

Table 10.1 *Generalized linear (mixed) model predicting a pronominal subject*

		β	β (SE)	Z value	p value
(Intercept)		−1.08	0.17	−6.33	< .001
Priming:	Ø vs. English pronoun	0.45	0.14	3.14	< .01
Priming:	Ø vs. Spanish pronoun	1.46	0.11	13.04	< .001
Accessibility:	Coreferential vs. non-coreferential	0.52	0.10	5.22	< .001
Verb class:	Cognition vs. other	−1.29	0.13	−9.89	< .001

Overall pronoun rate: 20 percent (647/3,286). Random effect: Speaker (Variance = 0.29, SD = 0.54; the minimum data points for any speaker (N = 40) was 6).
Excluded from the model were tokens outside the priming environment (N = 1,965), tokens for which the form for the previous realization could not be coded (e.g., due to unclear speech, N = 294); where previous realization was an English unexpressed subject (N = 6); and where verb class was uncodable (N = 20).

---

[1] The GLMM was run with a logistic link function using glmer() from the *R* (R Core Team 2015) package (Bates, Maechler, Bolker, and Walker 2015).

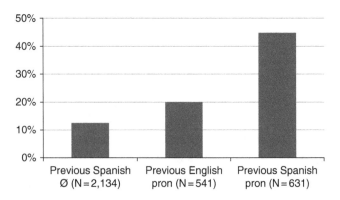

Figure 10.1 Rate of Spanish subject pronouns by realization of the previous mention
(0–9 intervening clauses; N = 3,306)

seen in Table 7.1 for Subject continuity and Verb class are also significant in this model.)

Figure 10.1 shows the subject pronoun rate according to the realization of the previous coreferential subject as a Spanish unexpressed subject, a Spanish pronoun, or an English pronoun; the rarity of previous English unexpressed subjects (N = 6) necessitates their exclusion in these spontaneous speech data. The rate is indeed boosted with a previous English pronominal subject, being one-and-a-half times greater than with a Spanish unexpressed subject (increasing from 12 percent to 20 percent). At the same time, English pronoun to Spanish pronoun priming is notably weaker than Spanish to Spanish priming, under which the rate is nearly four times as great as with a previous unexpressed subject (increasing from 12 percent to 45 percent).

The greater strength of within- than cross-language priming is highlighted by the interaction with accessibility. A generalization across Spanish varieties is that both priming and accessibility are weaker when the other is acting to favor subject pronouns – subject continuity is weakened under pronoun-to-pronoun priming, priming is weakened in non-coreferential contexts (Chapter 7, Section 7.5.1).

Figure 10.2 shows the subject pronoun rate according to the realization of the previous mention in coreferential and non-coreferential contexts. First, an accessibility effect is confirmed for all three priming conditions, as the non-coreferential line is always above the coreferential line. Thus, an accessibility effect is maintained across English and Spanish clauses: the subject pronoun rate is consistently higher in non-coreferential as opposed to coreferential contexts. The accessibility effect holds equally when the immediately preceding clause subject is an English pronoun as when it is an unexpressed

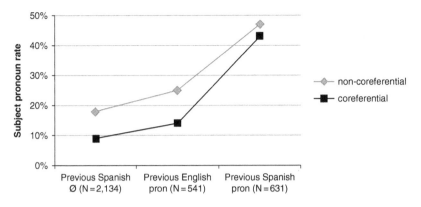

Figure 10.2 Rate of Spanish subject pronouns by realization of the previous mention and accessibility
(0–9 intervening clauses; N = 3,306)

Spanish subject (previous Spanish Ø, 9 percent coref vs. 18 percent non-coref; Previous English pronoun, 14 percent vs. 25 percent).

Second, a priming effect is confirmed regardless of accessibility – both lines rise, as the subject pronoun rate is higher with an English pronoun prime than with a previous Spanish Ø and is higher still with a Spanish pronoun prime. Nevertheless, within-Spanish priming is stronger, seen in the narrower gap between the two lines with a previous Spanish pronoun (43 percent vs. 47 percent). The accessibility effect is clearly weakened with a Spanish pronominal prime.

The maintenance of the workings of priming under CS is plain to see in Figure 10.3, which compares pronoun rates according to prime form and proximate CS (see Table 9.1 in the preceding chapter). The highest rate of pronouns is found in the context of a previous Spanish pronominal subject prime, the lowest rate with a Spanish unexpressed, and an intermediate rate with an English pronoun – in both the absence and presence of CS, with near-identical rates. Consequently, the priming effect is not weaker, remaining intact in the presence of proximate CS. Since the effect of priming, and the interaction between priming and accessibility (Figure 10.2), are retained in the presence of CS, the question still stands: just what *are* the repercussions of CS?

10.3   Contextual Distribution Shifts Under Code-switching

The impact that CS has is on contextual distributions. Figure 10.4 gives the distribution of Spanish subjects according to the realization of the previous mention in the absence (bar on the left) and presence of CS (on the right).

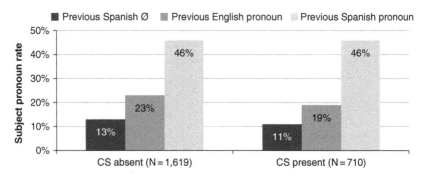

Figure 10.3 Rate of Spanish subject pronouns by realization of the previous mention in presence vs. absence of code-switching (0–9 intervening clauses; N = 2,329)[2]

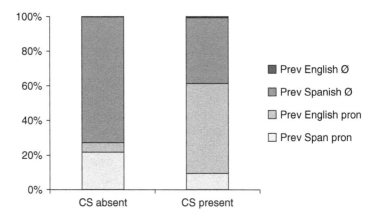

Figure 10.4 Contextual distribution of primes: Previous coreferential subject realization according to code-switching (0–9 intervening clauses, N = 2,335)

In the absence of CS – that is, when the preceding or target clause contains only Spanish – just one-quarter (27 percent) of the data occur with a pronominal prime (Spanish or English, the lighter segments), while when there is multi-word English in the same or preceding clause, close to two-thirds of the data

---

[2] Readers may notice that the numbers of tokens in the cross-tabulations vary. This is due to analysis-specific exclusions. Of 3,306 tokens with a coreferential Spanish or English pronominal or unexpressed subject mention in the previous nine clauses (Figures 10.1 and 10.2), 2,335 occur in the presence or absence of code-switching (Figure 10.4; see Chapter 9, Section 9.2); six have an English Ø as the previous coreferential subject (excluded from Figure 10.3). In considering verb type (Tables 10.1 and 10.2), 20 tokens for which verb type could not be coded are excluded.

(61 percent) occur in the context of a previous pronoun. The proportions are thus inverted: the ratio of instances of the variable whose previous coreferential subject was unexpressed, with respect to tokens whose previous realization was pronominal, is approximately 1:1.5 (39 percent to 61 percent) in the presence of CS, but in its absence approximately 3:1 (73 percent to 27 percent)! This makes sense. Given the rarity of unexpressed subjects in English, when speakers are code-switching, fewer instances of variable Spanish subject expression occur in an environment favorable to unexpressed subjects – that of a previous unexpressed subject – than is the case in the absence of CS. At the same time, there are also fewer opportunities for Spanish pronoun-to-pronoun priming, since about one-half of the time, the previous mention is an English pronoun. The result for the overall rate of subject pronouns is that it stays flat – the same in the presence as in the absence of CS, as we have seen.

We can say that CS "interferes" with the scope of within-language priming, in reducing the opportunities for it to occur. CS does not intrinsically induce grammatical alteration, but rather produces a shift in the frequency of contextual features contributing to variant choice, in particular those relevant to both within-language priming of the same structure and to cross-language priming of a parallel structure. Against a convergence via CS hypothesis, we may call this the *hypothesis of contextual distribution via CS*: a byproduct of CS is a shift in the frequencies of the relevant contexts in which a variable linguistic structure occurs.

Thus, CS may impact the distribution of a linguistic variable across favoring and disfavoring environments. For subject pronoun expression, what we have seen is that proximate CS results in a larger proportion of tokens occurring in the favoring environment of a previous pronoun. Another example is subject pronoun position, which is variable in Spanish, but overwhelmingly preverbal in English. When speakers have recently used English, the distribution of previous coreferential subjects is therefore altered, with fewer postverbal primes. Such CS-instigated shifts in the contextual distributions of a linguistic variable may boost the rate of a variant. For example, while a previous postverbal *yo* 'I' favors post-positioning of the target *yo*, previous preverbal *yo* and preverbal *I* equally disfavor post-positioning (Benevento and Dietrich 2015: 416). Since English *I* is just about always preverbal, its presence will lower the rate of Spanish postverbal *yo*.

The hypothesis of contextual distribution via CS is pertinent beyond cross-language priming effects. Consider, for example, Spanish word-initial /d/, which varies between lenited and stop realizations depending on the preceding phonetic environment, in contrast with the English norm of stop realization. Among NM bilinguals the rate of lenition in Spanish is lower in cognate words such as *doctor* than in non-cognates such as *dolor* 'pain'. Brown (2015) finds that the greater a /d/-initial word's prior exposure to contexts promoting reduction, the greater the likelihood of the reduced variant in the target instance of the word (an effect she terms Frequency in a Favorable Context). More generally, in sound change, the effect of an alternating phonetic environment can be cumulative: words used frequently in a phonetic environment that favors a newer variant undergo change earlier than other words (Bybee 2002). The effect of cognate status on /d/ realization in bilinguals' Spanish follows from such a cumulative usage effect: when Brown factors in speakers' English as well as Spanish, cognate /d/ words are exposed less often than non-cognate words to contexts propitious to reduction, considering that they are associated with the non-reduced English forms (2015: 401). For bilinguals who regularly engage in CS, the distribution of conditioning environments can be impacted by usage patterns in both languages.

Another case where language contact has affected contextual distributions is found in the spread of the English past tense suffix, which is the productive pattern (e.g., -ed has been replacing vowel changes for some verbs, as with *leaped* instead of *leapt*). A determinant of productivity is type frequency, here the range of types (different verbs) that occur with -ed. During the Norman Conquest the number of borrowings from French grew. Past tense -ed was applied to the newly borrowed verbs, resulting in a sharp increase in type frequency, which in turn increased the productivity of the suffixing pattern (Bybee 2015: 97–98). So, here the shift in contextual distributions due to contact enabled a rise in type frequency.

In sum, as with priming effects, what we observe are the repercussions of shifted distributions of contextual features, either as a real-time or a cumulative effect. In both cases, it is not CS or use of the other language per se that has an effect, but mechanisms operative in language variation and change more generally (structural priming, phonetic environment, usage effects).

10.4   Priming as a Gauge of Strength of Associations

A widely cited account of cross-language priming posits the interconnected nature of bilinguals' lexical and syntactic representations. Lemmas for translation equivalents as well as parallel syntactic structures are considered to be linked to common conceptual representations and combinatorial nodes. For example, for an English–Dutch bilingual, there is believed to be an association between the English verb *give* and the Dutch *geven*, as well as between the double object and the prepositional object dative constructions available in both languages. Thus, following the sentence *The chef gives a hat to the swimmer*, the connections between the conceptual, lemma, and combinatorial nodes are activated for both English and Dutch, predicting that a speaker will reproduce a prepositional object dative (Schoonbaert, Hartsuiker, and Pickering 2007).

For bilinguals' Spanish subject expression, the maintenance of the accessibility effect across English previous mentions and Spanish targets is consistent with interconnections, or associations, between the two languages. Also consistent with interconnections is the existence of cross-language priming. However, at the same time, the application of different-strength priming effects within Spanish and from English to Spanish is evidence that bilinguals keep their two languages separate.

We might try to explain stronger within- than cross-language priming as the mere fallout from a lexical boost effect. In experimental studies, priming effects are often enhanced by similarity between the prime and target (Pickering and Branigan 1998). Thus, effects are larger when prime and target sentences contain lexical overlap and, across languages, priming is enhanced by translation equivalents. For instance, from Dutch to English, *De kok geeft een hoed aan de zwemmer* 'the chef gives a hat to the swimmer' is more likely to prime the prepositional object dative if the target contains the translation equivalent *give* than if it contains a distinct verb such as *offer*. Translation equivalent priming is weaker than within-language lexical boost priming (e.g., Schoonbaert et al. 2007: 164). The greater strength of within- than cross-language coreferential subject priming that we find here, then, could be hypothesized to be due to the identity of prime-target form (*yo* to *yo* rather than *I* to *yo*, for example).

The confound of identity of form may be bypassed by comparing non-coreferential subject priming in adjacent clauses within Spanish, for example, *él* 'he' to *yo* 'I', as in (141), and from English to Spanish, for example, *I* to *él* 'he', as in (142). Here, where there is no more identity of form in Spanish–Spanish than in English–Spanish prime-target pairs, there remains an asymmetry between within- and cross-language priming (Travis et al. 2017: 292–293). We must conclude, then, that there is a genuine effect of language membership.

(141)
Enrique: *y él se quedó en Durango.*   'and he stayed in Durango.
        ... de modo que,   ... so,
        yo seguí con mi vida,   I went on with my life,'
                                        (23 El Pacific, 24:02–24:08)

(142)
Javier: *.. I couldn't pick the --*   '.. I couldn't pick the --
        .. !fifty pounds.   .. !fifty pounds.
        .. of beans,   .. of beans,
        ... y él quería un saco entero. ... and he wanted a whole sack.'
                                        (17 La Comadreja, 58:49–58:55)

10.4.1   Priming and Particular Constructions

We can use the relative strength of priming to look into the strength of associations between bilinguals' linguistic representations, building on what is known about priming as a window into associations. Priming provides a measure of the internal structure of linguistic expressions and of the relationships between them, as demonstrated in quantitative studies of variation and change. For example, in English ING variation between velar [ŋ] and alveolar [n] nasals (*working ~ workin'*), there is priming only when prime and target are in the same morphological class (*working* is primed by *kicking* but not by *morning*) (Tamminga 2016). An example from the history of Spanish is with 'be' plus a gerund (e.g., *estar hablando* 'be talking'). This is primed by 'be' in combination with a locative ('be inside') or a predicate adjective ('be ill') in earlier Spanish, but no longer in nineteenth-century texts as it grammaticalizes into a construction expressing progressive aspect. The lack of priming of progressive *estar* by other *estar* constructions indicates the cohesion of a new grammatical unit (Torres Cacoullos 2015).

If priming provides a measure of the structure of a linguistic unit and the relationship between units, we expect there to be varying strengths of priming even between instances of the same general structure or class of expressions. Structural priming is indeed more likely not only when prime and target share verb lemmas, but when other features are shared as well (Snider 2009). For subject expression, coreferential subject priming is stronger when the prime and target verbs have the same tense (Travis 2007: 125–127). On the other hand, priming may be *less* likely for sub-classes that are defined by combinations of concrete features (such as the verb's tense, person, or semantic class) and which display idiosyncratic behavior, that is, for particular constructions.

For Spanish subject expression, we can consider cognition verbs, specifically in the first-person-singular and the present tense. These are lexically particular constructions by the measures of token frequency, contextual distributions, and the rate and linguistic conditioning of subject pronouns (Chapter 5, Section 5.8). If priming provides a measure of the relationship between linguistic units, then targets occurring in these constructions should be less susceptible to priming. The prediction is supported, in an interaction between the effects of coreferential subject priming and verb class. Table 10.2 shows the subject pronoun rate by the realization of the previous mention and the class of verb. The priming effect, even within Spanish, is patently weaker for cognition verbs – the pronoun rate with a previous pronoun is 1.5 times greater than with a previous unexpressed mention (increasing from 37 percent to 62 percent); for other verbs, it is four times as great (increasing from 10 percent to 41 percent). Thus, priming effects are modulated by the particular construction in which the target occurs.

Table 10.2 *Rate of Spanish subject pronouns by realization of the previous mention and verb class*

	Previous Span Ø		Previous English pron		Previous Span pron		Overall	
	%	N	%	N	%	N	%	N
Cognition	37%	172	40%	87	62%	112	45%	371
Other verbs	10%	1,951	16%	450	41%	514	16%	2,915

(0–9 intervening clauses, N = 3,286)

The lower susceptibility of cognition verbs to priming reflects at least in part the behavior of collocations such as *yo creo* 'I think'. Because collocations are frequent, they are more likely to be chunked and accessed as single processing units, rather than analyzed as combinations of subject and verb (see Bybee 2010: chapter 3 on chunking and degrees of autonomy). We can take the weaker priming of subject expression with cognition verbs as evidence that the [(*yo*) + COGNITION VERB$_{1SG}$] sequence is less analyzable than other *yo* 'I'-plus-VERB$_{1SG}$ combinations. Weaker priming can also be seen as evidence for a weaker association between the 1sg subject of cognition verbs and other instances of the 1sg subject as a consequence of chunking. Similarly, the lesser effect of non-coreferential subject priming (e.g., *él* 'he' to *yo* 'I') noted above suggests a weaker association between *yo* and other (non-1sg) subjects than between instances of 1sg subjects.

In sum, within the same language and the same structure, there are varying strengths of association between constructions, as evidenced in stronger or weaker priming. Strength of priming depends on features of the discourse context in which the target occurs, as we saw with the reduced effect of coreferential subject priming in interaction with accessibility. Priming effects also depend on local contextual features defining instances of the structure, seen in the modulation of priming with particular constructions.[3]

10.5 Strength of Cross-language Associations

So, the greater the association between constructions, the greater the likelihood of priming. The differential strength of within- and cross-language priming thus serves as a gauge of the associations between the structures of the two

---

[3] Interactions between Priming and Accessibility (Figure 10.2) and between Priming and Verb class (Table 10.2) were tested in separate GLMMs, as for the model reported in Table 10.1, with the addition of an interaction term, in one model Priming x Verb class, and in the other, Priming x Accessibility. In both cases, the interaction was significant.

languages in contact. It suggests a weaker association between Spanish [(pronoun) + verb] and English [(pronoun) + verb] than between two instances that share the same language.

In envisioning cognitive representations of language, we need not be bound to a strict dichotomy between lemmas and combinatorial nodes or between lexicon and abstract syntactic rules. Evidence that structures are anchored in particular words or classes of words is that structural priming is not independent of lexical item and its cumulative contexts of use. For example, for the dative alternation, the frequency with which a particular verb occurs in the prepositional vs. double object dative moderates the priming effect (Gries 2005). This consequence of the overall tendency of the verb in the prime to occur in one or the other construction been termed a "surprisal" effect (Jaeger and Snider 2007).

In a usage-based approach, the content of grammatical representations may be quite rich (Bybee 2010: chapter 2). Constructions register information about contexts of occurrence, linguistic and extralinguistic, or episodic memories. Evidence for co-activation of linguistic and non-linguistic memories comes from studies of sound change. For example, for the /t/ in words like *city*, which has undergone voicing or tapping in New Zealand English, the older variant is more likely when talking of events in the distant than in the recent past (Hay and Foulkes 2016: 322). If speakers track (register and store) the extralinguistic circumstances of their linguistic experiences, we may hypothesize that they also track the language affiliation of utterances. Support for some kind of tracking of language membership is that "words are likely to reoccur in their language of most recent mention" (Myslín and Levy 2015: 375; cf. Gries and Kootstra 2017: 247).

Bilingual associations are not so different from other kinds of associations in linguistic representations – the two languages may be associated but still kept separate. For the subject pronoun variable, we suggest a depiction of cross-language connections as in Figure 10.5, capturing the relative strength of priming across and within languages. Based on the present state of our knowledge, we do not put forward precise claims about degrees of strength, but rather propose associations that are greater (solid line), and lesser (dotted line), as evidenced in priming effects.

10.6   Conclusion

The results reported in this book are only surprising if we start from an assumption that interconnection between the linguistic systems of bilinguals is equivalent to conflation of the linguistic systems. Clearly this need not be true. The cross-language priming observed here indicates cross-language interconnection between Spanish and English subject pronouns. Yet production of

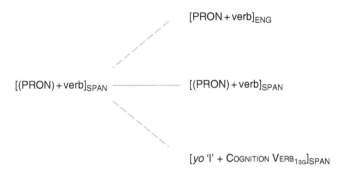

Figure 10.5 Varying strength of associations between parallel structures across and within languages

language structures has been shown to be impervious to other-language influence under what should be the most propitious conditions – that is, with abundant, maximally proximate switching to and from the other language. In the presence of English produced by the same speakers, the rate of Spanish subject pronouns is unaltered. The guiding grammatical principles, as instantiated by probabilistic constraints, also remain intact and, at loci of difference between the two language systems, steadfastly distinct from English (Chapter 9).

We interpret structural priming as a gauge of the associations between constructions of subject pronoun and verb. These exist both within and across languages, but are attenuated in the latter case, as seen in the stronger effect of same-language than other-language coreferential subject primes. The relative strength of within- and cross-language priming becomes visible in spontaneous bilingual speech because it can be assessed in context. Outside the lab, priming does not operate in a vacuum but acts in conjunction with other factors simultaneously operating on speakers' choices, here accessibility and lexically particular constructions. Thanks to community-based speech data, we were able to see whether and how priming interacts with co-occurring linguistic features in configurations as speakers encounter them in everyday language use.

Spontaneous bilingual speech suggests the *contextual distribution-via-code-switching* hypothesis: CS may impinge on the distribution of contexts of occurrence. For Spanish subject expression, rather than CS intrinsically inducing grammatical alteration, what is at work is associated shifts in the frequency of contextual features contributing to variant choice. In particular, a byproduct of CS is a shift in the distribution of primes, or the realization of previous coreferential subjects. Thus, there is an alteration of the scope (opportunities), though not the implementation (direction), of priming. Language

code-switching
Is one language affected in proximity to use of the other?
No: Language-particular conditioning is preserved
Yes: Contextual distributions of structures are shifted

Figure 10.6 Comparisons of language variation patterns, refuting convergence via code-switching: Conditioning vs. contextual distributions – Contextual distribution via code-switching hypothesis

internally, priming operates within Spanish such that pronouns favor subsequent pronouns and unexpressed subjects tend to be followed by unexpressed subjects. Across languages, the effect is that English pronouns favor subsequent Spanish pronouns, but since unexpressed subjects in English are so scarce, there is minimal opportunity for unexpressed-to-unexpressed cross-language priming.

The conclusion is that cross-language associations do not equate with cross-language convergence. As we saw in Chapters 7 and 8, bilinguals apply independent, language-particular, grammatical principles in structuring variable subject expression in their Spanish which are distinct from their English. Here we have seen that bilinguals maintain grammatical independence even when they are code-switching. Figure 10.6 completes the promised series of comparisons.

11   Bilingualism in its Linguistic and Social Context

11.1   Contact without Change

Contact-induced grammatical change is far from a foregone conclusion, nor is it a concomitant of code-switching. Were it so, it would have been detected here, where the community, the data, and the linguistic variable should all conspire to give rise to contact-induced change. The speakers are members of a long-standing community where two languages have been in contact for over 150 years. All speakers regularly *use* both languages, and code-switching is widely engaged in as a community discourse mode, as captured in the spontaneous speech data. The linguistic candidate for convergence has a parallel structure in the two languages allowing for interlingual identifications, but at the same time there are interlingual differences where change, had it occurred, could be observed. Yet change is inexistent.

The hypothesis of convergence is firmly rejected. If there is convergence, then the contact varieties should be less different from each other than the monolingual benchmarks are. Convergence here would be manifested in an extension of Spanish subject pronouns on the model of English; no such extension has occurred. As a rigorous test, an unprecedented four sets of comparisons have been conducted: with an earlier-stage variety, with monolingual benchmarks of both of the languages in contact, between the bilinguals' two language varieties, and in the presence vs. absence of spontaneous code-switching by the same speaker. The linguistic conditioning of subject pronoun expression in New Mexican bilinguals' Spanish is parallel to the conditioning in an earlier stage variety of New Mexican Spanish and in non-contact Spanish; and it is distinct from monolingual English. When we also consider the same bilinguals' English, it is evident that bilinguals' Spanish and English line up with their respective monolingual counterparts and, most remarkably, are different from each other! Structural similarity between Spanish and English has not been achieved on the part of either language. The hypothesis that code-switching promotes convergence must also be rejected, since Spanish-particular patterns hold even in maximal proximity to English. These comparisons – pivoted on diagnostic differences – demonstrate linguistic continuity rather than change, and grammatical separation rather than mixing.

Contact-induced change is absent in these data also for other morphosyntactic variables. Beyond subject expression, independent studies based on the NMSEB corpus show that the patterning of New Mexican bilinguals' Spanish parallels that of non-contact varieties for subject-verb order (Benevento and Dietrich 2015), differential object marking (D. Sankoff, Dion, Brandts, Alvo, Balasch, and Adams 2015: 340–342), and complementizer use (Steuck and Torres Cacoullos 2016). However, influence from English is observed in the sound system. For example, for word-initial /d/ in bilinguals' Spanish, the English-like stop variant [d] occurs at a higher rate in cognate words such as *doctor* (Brown 2015: 400). For voice onset time (VOT) in bilinguals' English, /ptk/-initial words such as *put, teams*, and *coffee* have a shorter than expected VOT (i.e., in the direction of Spanish), and more so following a recent multi-word Spanish code-switch (Balukas and Koops 2015: 432–433).

The asymmetry between grammar and phonology in receptiveness to other-language influence is consistent with the generalization that whereas phonology may be labile, morphosyntax tends to be stable under language and dialect contact (cf. G. Sankoff 2002). Of course, sound systems can also be impervious, as with the maintenance of clan-level variation in lexical tone among the Sui people, an indigenous minority of southwest China with clan exogamy (Stanford 2008). The disparity between morphosyntax and phonology is nevertheless underscored by the relation of African American community patterns to those of surrounding white communities. African American Vernacular English has developed notable uniformity across the United States in morphosyntactic variables, such as deletion of the copula and use of *be* as a marker of habitual aspect, yet in phonology there is regional differentiation and approximation to surrounding patterns (Labov 2014: 2). The integration of loanwords is also instructive. Analyses of bilingual speech involving a variety of diagnostics in diverse language pairs arrive at the same conclusion: nonce, or spontaneous, borrowings assume the morphosyntactic identity of the recipient language independently of achieving phonological adaptation (Poplack 2017).

The question to ask, then, is not why here there has been no grammatical change which, as Poplack and Levey stress, "is not an inevitable, nor possibly even a common, outcome of language contact" (2010: 412). The burden of proof is rather on the contrary proposition, to demonstrate that convergence elsewhere has indeed occurred, and to account for why it did so.

11.2 Contextualizing Contact Situations

Multiple social factors have been implicated in contact-induced change. Commonly cited are the time depth and intensity of the contact, the social status of the speakers of the different languages, and the attitudes of the community toward each language and to language mixing. Hence, there can be no general typology of contact situations from which the linguistic outcomes of contact can be predicted. Attempts to establish general principles of convergence are surely premature, if not "doomed" (Thomason 2000: 311).

A first distinction to make is between situations of stable bilingualism and those of fairly rapid shift to another language (cf. Poplack 1993). The latter is characteristic of many of the immigrant communities on which studies of Spanish in the US have focused. Indications of other-language influence among second-generation immigrants can speak only tentatively to grammatical convergence, in the absence of demonstration of a lasting change in the structures of the minority language. Demonstrating a change in progress simply requires more than a two-generation comparison.

To elucidate the nature of a given change, the data examined must come from a well-defined bilingual speech community (Chapter 2). A case for convergence – or divergence, for that matter – is to be made by juxtaposing the contact varieties *as spoken by the bilinguals themselves*, the acknowledged agents of contact-induced change. With equal proportions of the two languages in contact, unrivalled as far as we know in contact linguistics, the NMSEB corpus (Chapter 3) allows the most stringent test of convergence – comparisons of the same speakers' use of their two languages. Such evidence has been in short supply, especially in assertions of change based on the surmised rules of an idealized monolingual standard.

To argue, additionally, for an instigating role for code-switching, community strategies for different ways of combining two languages must be understood. Norms for borrowing and code-switching differ across contact situations. In the Amazonian Vaupes region, for example, it is reported that languages are kept strictly separate due to a "negative attitude towards language mixing" (Epps 2012: 196). But in New Mexico, as we have seen, both other-language single words and alternating-language word sequences occur regularly. The data for code-switching is also pivotal – participants must be recorded in "unedited performance" (Cedergren and Sankoff 1974: 354). Given the lack of independent corroboration, it is not a safe assumption that spontaneous code-switching would be approximated, let alone replicated, in a laboratory experiment in which subjects are instructed to supply a sentence in one or another language or to produce code-switching in response to prompts. A further unique feature of NMSEB is the recurrent juxtaposition of Spanish and English; it is this abundant code-switching that allowed us to identify its real-time impact.

A second distinction to insist on in evaluating reports of contact-induced change is between principled samples of speakers of known social attributes and collections of assorted individuals. The linguistic behavior of individuals can be interpreted only in the context of the social groups of which they are members (Labov 2010: 7). Studies pooling participants of unknown social affiliations are at best difficult to interpret, even if batteries of tests control for individual bilingual or cognitive abilities. Furthermore, university-educated second language learners, the subject pool for most psycholinguistic studies of bilingualism, have a qualitatively different bilingual experience from those who grow up bilingually. Findings that disregard social information are unlikely to be generalizable to members of bilingual speech communities.

Consequently, we have placed a premium on community norms, and on thoroughly characterizing the speakers providing the data (Chapter 4). Adequate characterization of the bilingual speakers cannot be gleaned solely from general census statistics on the region under study. There is no substitute for social and attitudinal information gathered from the participants themselves and interpreted in light of intimate knowledge of the community. In the NMSEB corpus, such information has been extracted from the sociolinguistic interviews. Thus, the same data source both permits the linguistic analysis and allows us to construct a sociolinguistic profile of the social background and linguistic experience of the participants.

The speech data themselves substantiate the bilingualism of the speakers, and bring to light the limitations of constructs such as language dominance or L1 vs. L2, and dichotomies such as simultaneous vs. sequential, or early vs. late, bilinguals. These constructs continue to be widely employed, and they may indeed be applicable to participants who have learned a second language through formal instruction. But a vital lesson from the present study is that they are incongruous in bilingual communities where using both languages is a way of life. This was patently evident among NMSEB participants, where not only did we find inconsistency in responses to survey questions about self-ratings of English and Spanish (a reflection of linguistic insecurity), but also a lack of a correlation between participant reports of language preference, first language, and self-ratings.

We can use what is known about the social profile of changes in progress (e.g., that women tend to lead change) to buttress a case for or against contact-induced change. Here, as in monolingual varieties of Spanish, social factors found to be relevant for phonological variables in the community did not correlate systematically with subject pronoun rates (Chapter 2). Most pertinent is that subject pronoun rates also did not correlate with individual degrees of contact, whether by extralinguistic measures emerging from optimization of questionnaire responses or the linguistic measure of proportion of English and Spanish clauses produced by the speaker (Chapter 4).

The study of bilingualism, then, must be situated within its social context; as Weinreich put it, "the linguist who makes theories about language influence but neglects to account for the socio-cultural setting of the language contact leaves his study suspended, as it were, in mid air" (1953/1968: 4). Because grammatical change is not predictable from one contact situation to another, the most pressing need in contact linguistics remains accountable studies of sufficiently contextualized contact situations.

11.3 Quantitative Reasoning

To demonstrate convergence, it must be shown that change has occurred, that that change moves the language in the direction of the contact language, and that it is attributable to the contact (and not, for example, to cross-linguistic tendencies). How can each of these tests be met? One of the proposed definitions of contact-induced change is change that would be "less likely to occur" independently of the contact (Thomason 2007: 42). Given that the likelihood of change in a monolingual setting is unknown, this definition has little diagnostic power. Another view is that contact serves to trigger and/or accelerate internal change (Heine and Kuteva 2005; Silva-Corvalán 1994). Again, this criterion is serviceable only to the extent that we know how to measure rates of linguistic change in monolingual settings. Thus, the quantitative reasoning we apply relies on the notion of the linguistic variable.

Solid quantitative evidence requires good data, in both quantity and quality. Claims of convergence have been made in the absence of quantifiable data or on the basis of small numbers of participants, in some cases as few as two. All too often only a fraction (e.g., 15 from 100 participants) of a larger corpus serves for analysis, sometimes because the speaker characteristics do not respond to the research questions, other times because the transcription is not complete. The NMSEB corpus comprises transcriptions of 29 hours (300,000 words) of recorded spontaneous speech, from 40 systematically sampled members of the northern New Mexican community. The transcription adheres to a replicable prosodically based method (cf. Du Bois et al. 1993). Close to 6,000 tokens of variable subject pronoun expression in bilinguals' Spanish have been compared with more than 5,000 drawn from three benchmark speech corpora representing an earlier variety of New Mexican Spanish, monolingual Spanish, and monolingual English (Chapter 1, Table 1.1).

The comparisons take place at various dimensions of quantitative analysis. Figure 11.1 depicts the foundations for utilizing variation to probe contact-induced change.

First is the *variable context*: in what environments are the variants in variation? The variable context itself may be a locus of cross-language dissimilarity, supplying a fundamental test for contact-induced change. For example,

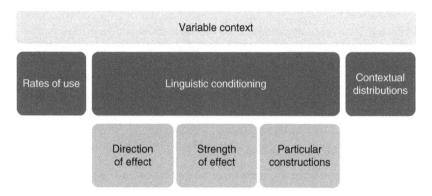

Figure 11.1 Foundations for the study of language contact through the lens of variation

we identified here a diagnostic difference between Spanish and English in the limited envelope of variation in English, due largely to the prosodic-initial restriction on unexpressed subjects, while the trend for prosodic position in Spanish is in the opposite direction (Chapter 6).

Having defined the variable context, meaningful *rates of use* can then be compared: in contexts where both variants could occur, what proportion of the time do they occur? An increase, or drop, in rates of use alone, nevertheless, cannot be considered evidence of convergence, even if statistically significant (Chapter 7).

To interpret any differences or dig below superficial similarities, we look to the *linguistic conditioning* of the variation, privileging three components: direction of effect, strength of effect, and particular constructions. The *direction of effect* – what linguistic contexts favor one variant over another – and *strength of effect* – the magnitude of that favoring – are two further loci of grammatical (dis)similarity. For example, we saw that the direction of effect for accessibility holds across both Spanish and English, consistent with a widely reported cross-linguistic tendency (Chapters 5 and 6). Accessibility still supplies a test of change, however, because structural linking between clauses is a relatively stronger probabilistic constraint in English than in Spanish. Thus, we reasoned that direct English influence should be manifested in the strengthening of this effect in bilinguals' Spanish, and utilized interactions with other constraints to gauge strength of effect, supplementing regression analyses with cross-tabulations (Chapters 7 and 8). And third, though often neglected, also shaping linguistic condition-ing there are language-specific, *lexically particular constructions*. For exam-ple, particular constructions in Spanish with 1sg cognition verbs favor subject pronouns, and in English *and*-coordinated constructions with motion verbs favor unexpressed subjects. The existence and behavior of frequent expressions provide a point of detailed comparisons to test contact-induced change, allowing us to rule out cross-linguistic tendencies or chance.

Even if the direction and strength of effect are identical, as they are in the presence vs. absence of multi-word code-switching (Chapter 9), greater occurrence in a context that favors one or another variant may result in an alteration of overall rate. This is not a change in the grammar, but rather a byproduct of the distribution of contexts of occurrence. A final consideration is thus the distribution of the data, or *contextual distribution* – that is, the frequencies of the relevant contexts in which a variable linguistic structure occurs (Chapter 10). It is in this quantitative dimension that code-switching has an effect, not by intrinsically inducing grammatical alteration, but by concomitantly inducing shifts in the relative frequency of contextual features that contribute to variant choice.

11.4   Code-switching and Grammars in Contact

The data of spontaneous bilingual speech suggest, contra the convergence-via-code-switching hypothesis, the *contextual-distribution-via-code-switching* hypothesis. This states that code-switching may result in a real-time shift in the relevant environments of occurrence of a linguistic variable. Pertinent for Spanish subject pronoun expression turned out to be the frequencies of structural priming contexts. The scope of coreferential subject priming is directly impacted by code-switching, which alters the range of possible primes, now drawn from both languages. This means that the proportion of pronominal primes (the majority variant in English) is increased in the proximate presence of English. Thus, it is not use of the other language per se that has an effect, but mechanisms such as priming, which are operative in language variation and change more generally. The contextual distribution hypothesis may extend to other variable linguistic forms. For example, a redistribution of contexts of occurrence lies behind other-language phonological influence on cognates (Brown 2015). In both cases, at work are consequences of the distribution of contextual features impinging on the variation, either as a cumulative usage effect, in the case of the phonetic environments that cognates are exposed to, or as a real-time effect, for subject priming.

Nevertheless, while priming is operative both within and across languages, it is weaker in the latter case. Cross-language priming has been demonstrated here in the fact that a previous pronominal subject, Spanish *or* English, favors a subsequent pronominal subject in Spanish more than a previous unexpressed subject does. Its weaker character is seen in the greater favoring of a pronominal subject following a Spanish than an English pronominal subject.

This weaker cross-language priming accounts for the conspicuous lack of a code-switching effect on the overall rate of subject pronouns in these data. The contextual distribution shifts toward fewer previous unexpressed subjects (disfavoring a pronominal target), but also toward a redistribution of pronominal primes, with fewer previous Spanish and more English, pronouns (favoring a pronominal target, but less so than Spanish pronouns do).

The relative weakness of cross-language priming bears on the long-standing question of interconnections between bilinguals' linguistic systems. Though parallel structures across languages are associated with each other, they are less strongly associated than are instances of the same structure in the language to which they belong; the two grammars in contact are interconnected, but they are not mixed. Bilinguals can produce the grammars of their languages separately, even as they smoothly alternate between them.

The evidence from priming that the two languages are kept separate undermines the motivation for the hypothesis that code-switching promotes grammatical change. In code-switching, speakers alternate from one language to another, each language retaining the same grammatical patterns as in the absence of code-switching. Grammars are not inexorably rendered permeable through contact in bilingual communities, where speakers can independently apply language-specific grammatical principles.

Appendix 1 Transcription Conventions

All examples given are from the New Mexico Spanish-English Bilingual corpus (NMSEB), unless otherwise indicated. Within brackets is the recording number, name, and time stamp, given in (hour:)minutes:seconds. Examples are reproduced verbatim from the transcripts. The only exceptions, for the purposes of readability, are the removal of some vocal noises (in- and out-breaths (H), (Hx); tongue clicks (TSK); glottal stops (%)) and two instances of marked voice quality (e.g., whispering).

Prosodically based transcription conventions (Du Bois et al. 1993)

Carriage return	new Intonation Unit
.	final intonation contour
,	continuing intonation contour
?	appeal intonation contour
--	truncated intonation contour
..	short pause (0.2 secs)
...	medium pause (0.3–0.6 secs)
...( )	timed pause (0.7 secs or longer)
-	truncated word
=	lengthened syllable
[ ]	overlapped speech (not indicated where only one side of an overlap is given in the first or last line of an example)
[2 2]	consecutive overlapped speech (numbers used to distinguish what is overlapped with what)
(( ))	transcriber's comment
!	booster; speech pronounced with notably high pitch
X	one syllable of unclear speech
<X X>	unclear speech (transcriber's best guess)
@	one syllable of laughter
<@ @>	speech uttered while laughing
<Q Q>	quoted speech uttered with marked voice quality
~	pseudonymized proper noun
Capital initial letter	Higher initial pitch level

Example Translation Conventions

- In examples where Spanish and English are used, the original appears on the left, and the translation on the right, with stretches of speech (two or more words) originally produced in English appearing in italics.
- Truncated words are translated with the most likely translation.
- Not reproduced are lengthening (=) and ~ before pseudonyms.

Appendix 2 Factors Conditioning Subject Expression across Bilingual and Monolingual Varieties

Two independent analyses of factors significant to pronominal vs. unexpressed subjects, monolingual Spanish and bilingual Spanish
(See Chapter 6 for monolingual Spanish; Chapters 7 and 8 for bilingual Spanish)

	Spanish-monolingual 1,143/2,802; Input: .40 (Overall rate: 41%)			Spanish-bilingual 1,353/5,571; Input: .21 (Overall rate: 24%)		
	Prob	%	N	Prob	%	N
Accessibility						
Non-coreferential	.57	48%	1588	.58	31%	2642
Coreferential only	.49	37%	700	.48	22%	1238
Coreferential and linked	.31	21%	458	.37	13%	1384
Range	*26*			*21*		
Priming						
Pronoun	.62	54%	637	.74	45%	631
Other*	.53	45%	1138	.59	32%	1965
Previous English				.43	20%	541
Unexpressed	.37	27%	841	.36	13%	2134
Range	*25*			*38*		
Verb class						
Cognition	.65	65%	335	.72	51%	693
Stative	.59	47%	685	.57	29%	1163
Dynamic	.43	33%	1761	.44	18%	3685
Range	*22*			*28*		
Person						
1sg	.57	50%	1389	.53	29%	3296
3sg	.43	32%	1413	.45	18%	2275
Range	*14*			*8*		
Tense-aspect						
Present/Imperfective		45%	1780	.51	29%	3424
Perfective		34%	667	.47	18%	1314
Range				*4*		
Presence of English						
English absent					25%	2690
Single word					22%	954
Multi-word code switch					22%	1099

* Other = previous mentions as full NP, relative, or postverbal pronoun; previous interlocutor tokens; previous or target in quoted speech; previous mentions at a distance of 10+ clauses.

Two independent analyses of factors significant to unexpressed vs. pronominal subjects,
bilinguals' English and monolingual English
(See Chapter 6 for monolingual English; Chapter 8 for bilingual English)

	English-bilingual 98/294; Input: .29 (Artificial rate: 33.3%)			English-monolingual 329/987; Input: .29 (Artificial rate: 33.3%)		
	Prob	%	N	Prob	%	N
Accessibility						
Non-coreferential	.22	10%	91	.27	13%	403
Coreferential only	.49	29%	73	.42	24%	226
Coreferential and linked	.71	52%	130	.80	65%	344
Range	*49*			*53*		
Priming						
Other*		33%	258	.48	30%	851
Unexpressed		34%	35	.66	57%	116
				18		
Verb class						
Stative, Cognition	.33	16%	68	.42	20%	348
Dynamic	.56	40%	217	.55	41%	627
Range	*23*			*13*		
Tense-aspect						
Present		27%	44		28%	235
Past		35%	241		36%	718

* Other = previous mentions as full NP, relative, or postverbal pronoun; previous interlocutor tokens; previous or target in quoted speech; previous mentions at a distance of 5+ clauses; for English-bilingual: previous Spanish (10 cases of previous unexpressed; none of previous pronominal).

For English, where pronouns predominate, the model is framed in terms of where unexpressed subjects (as the outcome) are favored. The results for pronouns, shown in Chapter 8 to facilitate cross-language comparisons, can be derived by subtracting each of the factor weights from 1 (Walker 2010: 39).

References

Aaron, Jessi Elana. (2015). Lone English-origin nouns in Spanish: The precedence of community norms. *International Journal of Bilingualism* 19(4):459–480.

Aijón Oliva, Miguel Angel, and Serrano, María José. (2010). El hablante en su discurso: Expresión y omisión del sujeto de creo. *Oralia* 13:7–38.

Aikhenvald, Alexandra Y. (2002). *Language contact in Amazonia*. Oxford: Oxford University Press.

Akmajian, Adrian, and Heny, Frank. (1980). *An introduction to the principles of transformational syntax*. Cambridge, MA: The MIT Press.

Alfaraz, Gabriela. (2015). Variation of overt and null-subject pronouns in the Spanish of Santo Domingo. In: A. M. Carvalho, R. Orozco, and N. L. Shin (eds.), *Subject pronoun expression in Spanish: A cross-dialectal perspective*. Georgetown: Georgetown University Press. 3–16.

Altarriba, Jeanette, Kroll, Judith F., Sholl, Alexandra, and Rayner, Keith. (1996). The influence of lexical and conceptual constraints on reading mixed-language sentences: Evidence from eye fixations and naming time. *Memory & Cognition* 24 (4):477–492.

Amaral, Patricia Matos, and Schwenter, Scott A. (2005). Contrast and the (non-) occurrence of subject pronouns. In: D. Eddington (ed.), *Selected proceedings of the 7th Hispanic Linguistics Symposium*. Somerville: Cascadilla Press. 116–127.

Ariel, Mira. (1994). Interpreting anaphoric expressions: A cognitive versus a pragmatic approach. *Journal of Linguistics* 30(1):3–42.

Auer, Peter. (1995). The pragmatics of code-switching: A sequential approach. In: L. Milroy and P. Muysken (eds.), *One speaker, two languages: Cross disciplinary perspectives on code switching*. Cambridge: Cambridge University Press. 115–135.

Ávila Jiménez, Barbara I. (1995). A sociolinguistic analysis of a change in progress: Pronominal overtness in Puerto Rican Spanish. *Cornell Working Papers in Linguistics* 13:25–47.

Backus, Ad. (2005). Codeswitching and language change: One thing leads to another? *International Journal of Bilingualism* 9(3–4):307–340.

Bailey, Guy, and Tillery, Jan. (2004). Some sources of divergent data in sociolinguistics. In: C. Fought (ed.), *Sociolinguistic variation: Critical reflections*. Oxford: Oxford University Press. 11–30.

Balukas, Colleen, and Koops, Christian. (2015). Spanish-English bilingual VOT in spontaneous code-switching. *International Journal of Bilingualism* 19(4):423–443.

215

Bates, Douglas, Maechler, Martin, Bolker, Ben, and Walker, Steve. (2015). Fitting linear mixed-effects models using lme4. *Journal of Statistical Software* 67(1):1–48, DOI:10.18637/jss.v18067.i18601.

Bayley, Robert, Cárdenas, Norma L., Treviño Schouten, Belinda, and Vélez Salas, Carlos Martin. (2012). Spanish dialect contact in San Antonio, Texas: An exploratory study. In: K. Geeslin and M. Díaz-Campos (eds.), *Selected Proceedings of the 14th Hispanic Linguistics Symposium*. Somerville: Cascadilla Proceedings Project. 48–60.

Bayley, Robert, Greer, Kristen, and Holland, Cory. (2013). Lexical frequency and syntactic variation: A test of a linguistic hypothesis. *University of Pennsylvania Working Papers in Linguistics* 19(2):21–30.

Bayley, Robert, and Pease-Alvarez, Lucinda. (1997). Null pronoun variation in Mexican-descent children's narrative discourse. *Language Variation and Change* 9 (3):349–371.

Benevento, Nicole, and Dietrich, Amelia. (2015). I think, therefore *digo yo*: Variable position of the 1sg subject pronoun in New Mexican Spanish-English code-switching. *International Journal of Bilingualism* 19(4):407–422.

Bentivoglio, Paola. (1987). *Los sujetos pronominales de primera persona en el habla de Caracas*. Caracas: Universidad Central de Venezuela.

Bhatt, Akesh M., and Bolonyai, Agnes. (2011). Code-switching and the optimal grammar of bilingual language use. *International Journal of Bilingualism* 14(4):522–546.

Biber, Douglas, Johansson, Stig, Leech, Geoffrey, Finegan, Edward, and Conrad, Susan. (1999). *The Longman grammar of spoken and written English*. London: Longman.

Bills, Garland D., Hernández Chávez, Eduardo, and Hudson, Alan. (1995). The geography of language shift: Distance from the Mexican border and Spanish language claiming in the Southwestern US. *International Journal of the Sociology of Language* 114: 9–27.

Bills, Garland D., and Vigil, Neddy A. (1999a). Ashes to ashes: The historical basis for dialect variation in New Mexican Spanish. *Romance Philology* 53(1):43–66.

Bills, Garland D., and Vigil, Neddy A. (1999b). El cambio lingüístico en el español nuevomexicano: los factores de edad y educación. In: J. A. Samper Padilla and M. Troya Déniz (eds.), *Actas del XI Congreso Internacional de la Asociación de Lingüística y Filología de la América Latina*. Las Palmas de Gran Canaria. 877–885.

Bills, Garland D., and Vigil, Neddy A. (2008). *The Spanish language of New Mexico and southern Colorado: A linguistic atlas*. Albuquerque: University of New Mexico Press.

Bock, J. Kathryn, and Griffin, Zenzi M. (2000). The persistence of structural priming: Transient activation or implicit learning. *Journal of Experimental Psychology: General* 129(2):177–192.

Bock, J. Kathryn, and Warren, Richard K. (1985). Conceptual accessibility and syntactic structure in sentence formulation. *Cognition* 21:47–67.

Bolinger, Dwight. (1976). Meaning and memory. *Forum Linguisticum* 1(1):1–14.

Bowern, Claire. (2010). Fieldwork and the IRB: A snapshot. *Language* 86(4):897–904.

Bresnan, Joan, Dingare, Shipra, and Manning, Christopher D. (2001). Soft constraints mirror hard constraints: Voice and person in English and Lummi. In: M. Butt and

T. Hollaway (eds.), *Proceedings of the LFG01 Conference*. Stanford: CSLI Publications. 13–31.

Brown, Esther L. (2005a). New Mexican Spanish: Insight into the variable reduction of "*la ehe inihial*" (/s-/). *Hispania* 88(4):813–824.

Brown, Esther L. (2005b). Syllable-initial /s/ in Traditional New Mexican Spanish: Linguistic factors favoring reduction *ahina*. *Southwest Journal of Linguistics* 24 (1–2):13–30.

Brown, Esther L. (2015). The role of discourse context frequency in phonological variation: A usage-based approach to bilingual speech production. *International Journal of Bilingualism* 19(4):387–406.

Brown, Esther L., and Raymond, William D. (2012). How discourse context shapes the lexicon: Explaining the distribution of Spanish f- / h- words. *Diachronica* 92 (2):139–161.

Brown, Esther L., and Torres Cacoullos, Rena. (2002). Qué le vamoh aher?: Taking the syllable out of Spanish /s/-reduction. *University of Pennsylvania Working Papers in Linguistics (PWPL), Papers from NWAV 30* 8(3):17–31.

Bullock, Barbara E., and Toribio, Almeida Jacqueline. (2004). Introduction: Convergence as an emergent property in bilingual speech. *Bilingualism: Language and Cognition* 7(2):91–94.

Butt, John, and Benjamin, Carmen. (2004). *A new reference grammar of modern Spanish*, 4th edn. London: Edward Arnold.

Bybee, Joan. (1985). *Morphology: A study of the relation between meaning and form*. Philadelphia: John Benjamins.

Bybee, Joan. (2002). Word frequency and context of use in the lexical diffusion of phonetically conditioned sound change. *Language Variation and Change* 14 (3):261–290.

Bybee, Joan. (2009). Language universals and usage-based theory. In: M. H. Christiansen, C. Collins, and S. Edelman (eds.), *Language universals*. Oxford: Oxford University Press. 17–39.

Bybee, Joan. (2010). *Language, usage and cognition*. Cambridge: Cambridge University Press.

Bybee, Joan. (2015). *Language change*. Cambridge: Cambridge University Press.

Bybee, Joan, Perkins, Revere, and Pagliuca, William. (1994). *The evolution of grammar: Tense, aspect and modality in the languages of the world*. Chicago: University of Chicago Press.

Bybee, Joan, and Torres Cacoullos, Rena. (2009). The role of prefabs in grammaticization: How the particular and the general interact in language change. In: R. L. Corrigan, E. Moravcsik, H. Ouali, and K. Wheatley (eds.), *Formulaic language, Vol. 1: Distribution and historical change*. Amsterdam: John Benjamins. 187–217.

Cameron, Richard. (1992). *Pronominal and null subject variation in Spanish: Constraints, dialects, and functional compensation*. Doctoral dissertation. Philadelphia: University of Pennsylvania.

Cameron, Richard. (1993). Ambiguous agreement, functional compensation, and non-specific *tú* in the Spanish of San Juan, Puerto Rico, and Madrid, Spain. *Language Variation and Change* 5(3):305–334.

Cameron, Richard. (1994). Switch reference, verb class and priming in a variable syntax. *Papers from the Regional Meeting of the Chicago Linguistic Society: Parasession on variation in linguistic theory* 30(2):27–45.

Cameron, Richard. (1995). The scope and limits of switch reference as a constraint on pronominal subject expression. *Hispanic Linguistics* 6–7:1–27.

Cameron, Richard, and Flores-Ferrán, Nydia. (2004). Perseveration of subject expression across regional dialects of Spanish. *Spanish in Context* 1(1):41–65.

Cárdenas, Daniel N. (1975). Mexican Spanish. In: E. Hernández Chávez, A. Cohen, and A. F. Beltramo (eds.), *El lenguaje de los chicanos*. Arlington: Center for Applied Linguistics. 1–5.

Carvalho, Ana M., and Child, Michael. (2011). Subject pronoun expression in a variety of Spanish in contact with Portuguese. In: J. Michnowicz and R. Dodsworth (eds.), *Selected Proceedings of the 5th Workshop on Spanish Sociolinguistics*. Somerville: Cascadilla Proceedings Project. 14–25.

Carvalho, Ana M., Orozco, Rafael, and Shin, Naomi Lapidus. (2015). Introduction. In: A. M. Carvalho, R. Orozco, and N. L. Shin (eds.), *Subject pronoun expression in Spanish: A cross-dialectal perspective*. Georgetown: Georgetown University Press. xiii–xxvi.

Cedergren, Henrietta. (1973). On the nature of variable constraints. In: C.-J. N. Bailey and R. W. Shuy (eds.), *New ways of analyzing variation in English*. Washington DC: Georgetown University Press. 13–22.

Cedergren, Henrietta, and Sankoff, David. (1974). Variable rules: Performance as a statistical reflection of competence. *Language* 50:333–355.

Chafe, Wallace. (1988). Linking intonation units in Spoken English. In: J. Haiman and S. A. Thompson (eds.), *Clause combining in grammar and discourse*. Amsterdam/Philadelphia: John Benjamins. 1–27.

Chafe, Wallace. (1994). *Discourse, consciousness and time: The flow and displacement of conscious experience in speaking and writing*. Chicago: University of Chicago Press.

Chociej, Joanna. (2011). *Polish null subjects: English influence on heritage Polish in Toronto*. Department of Linguistics, University of Toronto. Ms.

Chomsky, Noam. (1981 [1993]). *Lectures on Government and Binding: The Pisa lectures*, 7th edn. Holland: Foris Publications.

Christiansen, Morten H., and Chater, Nick. (2016). The Now-or-Never bottleneck: A fundamental constraint on language. *Behavioral and Brain Sciences* 39: e62; DOI:10.1017/S0140525X1500031X.

Claes, Jeroen. (2011). ¿Constituyen las Antillas y el Caribe continental una sola zona dialectal? Datos de la variable expresión del sujeto pronominal en San Juan de Puerto Rico y Barranquilla, Colombia. *Spanish in Context* 8(2):191–212.

Clark, Herbert H. (1996). *Using language*. Cambridge: Cambridge University Press.

Clyne, Michael. (1991). *Community languages: The Australian experience*. Cambridge: Cambridge University Press.

Comajoan, Llorenc. (2006). Continuity and episodic structure in Spanish subject reference. In: J. C. Clements and J. Yoon (eds.), *Functional approaches to Spanish syntax: Lexical semantics, discourse and transitivity*. New York: Palgrave Macmillan. 53–79.

Company Company, Concepción. (1995). Old forms for new concepts: The recategorization of possessive duplications in Mexican Spanish. In: H. Andersen (ed.), *Historical Linguistics 1993: Selected papers from the 11th International Conference on Historical Linguistics, Los Angeles, 16–20 August 1993.* Amsterdam/Philadelphia: John Benjamins. 77–92.

Company Company, Concepción. (2006). Subjectification of verbs into discourse markers: Semantic-pragmatic change only? In: B. Cornillie and N. Delbecque (eds.), *Topics in subjectification and modalization.* Amsterdam: John Benjamins. 97–121.

Comrie, Benrard. (1976). *Aspect: An introduction to the study of verbal aspect and related problems.* Cambridge: Cambridge University Press.

Corrigan, Roberta L., Moravcsik, Edith A., Ouali, Hamid, and Wheatley, Kathleen. (2009). *Formulaic language.* vol. I: Distribution and historical change. Amsterdam: John Benjamins.

Couper-Kuhlen, Elizabeth, and Ono, Tsuyoshi. (2007). "Incrementing" in conversation: A comparison of practices in English, German and Japanese *Pragmatics* 17 (4):513–552.

Croft, William. (1995). Intonation units and grammatical structure. *Linguistics* 33:839–882.

Croft, William. (2001). *Radical construction grammar: Syntactic theory in typological perspective.* Oxford: Oxford University Press.

Croft, William. (2007). Intonation units and grammatical structure in Wardaman and in cross-linguistic perspective. *Australian Journal of Linguistics* 27(1):1–39.

Cruttenden, Alan. (1986). *Intonation.* Cambridge: Cambridge University Press.

Crystal, David. (1979). Neglected grammatical factors in conversational English. In: S. Greenbaum, G. Leech, and J. Svartvik (eds.), *Studies in English linguistics.* London: Longman. 153–166.

D'Introno, Francesco, and Sosa, Juan M. (1986). La elisión de la /d/ en el español de Caracas: Aspectos sociolingüísticos e implicaciones teóricas. In: R. N. Cedeño, I. Páez Urdaneta, and J. M. Guitart (eds.), *Estudios sobre la fonología del español del Caribe.* Caracas: La Casa de Bello. 135–163.

Dąbrowska, Eva. (2012). Different speakers, different grammars: Individual differences in native language attainment. *Linguistic Approaches to Bilingualism* 2(3):219–253.

Dahl, Östen. (2000). Egophoricity in discourse and syntax. *Functions of Language* 7 (1):37–77.

Davidson, Brad. (1996). "Pragmatic weight" and Spanish subject pronouns: The pragmatic and discourse uses of *tú* and *yo* in spoken Madrid Spanish. *Journal of Pragmatics* 26(4):543–565.

Delancey, Scott. (1981). An interpretation of split ergativity and related patterns. *Language* 57(3):626–657.

Doğruöz, A. Seza, and Backus, Ad. (2007). Postverbal elements in immigrant Turkish: Evidence of change? *International Journal of Bilingualism* 11(2):185–220.

Dryer, Matthew S. (2013). Expression of pronominal subjects. In: M. S. Dryer and M. Haspelmath (eds.), *The world atlas of language structures online.* Leipzig: Max Planck Institute for Evolutionary Anthropology. Available online at http://wals.info /chapter/101.

Du Bois, John W. (1987). The discourse basis of ergativity. *Language* 63(4):805–855.

Du Bois, John W., Chafe, Wallace L., Myer, Charles, Thompson, Sandra A., Englebretson, Robert, and Martey, Nii. (2000–2005). *Santa Barbara corpus of spoken American English, Parts 1–4*. Philadelphia: Linguistic Data Consortium.

Du Bois, John W., Schuetze-Coburn, Stephan, Cumming, Susanna, and Paolino, Danae. (1993). Outline of discourse transcription. In: J. Edwards and M. Lampert (eds.), *Talking data: Transcription and coding in discourse*. Hillsdale: Lawrence Erlbaum Associates. 45–89.

Dumont, Jenny. (2010). Testing the cognitive load hypothesis: Repair rates and usage in a bilingual community. *Studies in Hispanic and Lusophone Linguistics* 3 (2):329–352.

Dumont, Jenny. (2016). *Third person references: Forms and functions in two spoken genres of Spanish*. Amsterdam/Philadelphia: John Benjamins Publishing Company.

England, Nora C. (1992). Doing Mayan linguistics in Guatemala. *Language* 68 (1):29–35.

Englebretson, Robert, and Helasvuo, Marja-Liisa. (2014). Discourse participants in interaction: Cross-linguistic perspectives on subject expression and ellipsis. *Journal of Pragmatics* 63:1–4.

Enríquez, Emilia V. (1984). *El pronombre personal sujeto en la lengua española hablada en Madrid*. Madrid: Consejo Superior de Investigaciones Científicas, Instituto Miguel de Cervantes.

Epps, Patience. (2012). On form and function in language contact: A case study from the Amazonian Vaupés region. In: C. Chamoreau and I. Léglise (eds.), *Dynamics of contact-induced language change*. Berlin/Boston: Mouton de Gruyter. 195–230.

Erker, Daniel, and Guy, Gregory R. (2012). The role of lexical frequency in syntactic variability: Variation subject personal pronoun expression in Spanish. *Language* 88 (3):526–557.

Erker, Daniel, and Otheguy, Ricardo. (2016). Contact and coherence: Dialectal leveling and structural convergence in NYC Spanish. *Lingua* 172–173:131–146.

Erman, Britt, and Warren, Beatrice. (2000). The idiom principle and the open choice principle. *Text* 20:29–62.

Espinosa, Auerlio M. (1911). The Spanish language in New Mexico and Southern Colorado. *Santa Fe Historical Society of New Mexico* 16.

Evans, Nicholas. 2014. The Wellsprings of Linguistic Diversity, www.dynamicsoflanguage.edu.au/the-wellsprings-of-linguistic-diversity/ Australian Research Council funded Laureate Project, 2014–2019, Australian National University

Ewing, Michael C. (2014). Motivations for first and second person subject expression and ellipsis in Javanese conversation. *Journal of Pragmatics* 63:48–62.

Fernández-Gibert, Arturo. (2010). From voice to print: Language and social change in New Mexico, 1880–1912. In: S. Rivera-Mills and D. J. Villa (eds.), *Spanish of the US Southwest: A language in transition*. Madrid: Iberoamericana. 45–62.

Fernández-Soriano, Olga. (1999). El pronombre personal. Formas y distribuciones. Pronombres átonos y tónicos. In: V. Demonte and I. Bosque (eds.), *Gramática descriptiva de la lengua española*. Madrid: Espasa-Calpe. 1209–1273.

Ferreira, Victor S. (2008). Ambiguity, accessibility, and a division of labor for communicative success. *Psychology of Learning and Motivation* 49:209–226.

Fleischman, Suzanne. (1991). Discourse pragmatics and the grammar of Old French: A functional reinterpretation of *si* and the personal pronouns. *Romance Philology* 44 (3):251–283.

Flores-Ferrán, Nydia. (2002). *Subject personal pronouns in Spanish narratives of Puerto Ricans in New York City: A sociolinguistic perspective.* Munich: Lincom Europa.

Flores-Ferrán, Nydia. (2010). ¡Tú no me hables! Pronoun expression in conflict narratives. *International Journal of the Sociology of Language* 203:61–82.

Ford, Cecilia E., and Fox, Barbara A. (1996). Interactional motivations for reference formulation: *He* had. *This* guy had, a beautiful, thirty-two olds. In: B. A. Fox (ed.), *Studies in anaphora.* Amsterdam: John Benjamins. 145–168.

Ford, Cecilia E., Fox, Barbara A., and Thompson, Sandra A. (2002). Constituency and the grammar of turn increments. In: C. E. Ford, B. A. Fox, and S. A. Thompson (eds.), *The language of turn and sequence.* Oxford: Oxford University Press. 14–38.

Ford, Cecilia E., and Thompson, Sandra A. (1996). Interactional units in conversation: Syntactic, intonational, and pragmatic resources for the management of turns. In: E. Ochs, E. A. Schegloff, and S. A. Thompson (eds.), *Interaction and grammar.* Cambridge: Cambridge University Press. 134–184.

Fox, Barbara A. (1987). Anaphora in popular written English narratives. In: R. S. Tomlin (ed.), *Coherence and grounding in discourse.* Amsterdam/ Philadelphia: John Benjamins. 157–174.

Fricke, Melinda, Kroll, Judith F., and Dussias, Paola E. (2016). Phonetic variation in bilingual speech: A lens for studying the production–comprehension link. *Journal of Memory and Language* 89:110–137.

Gara, Tom, and Hercus, Luise. (2005). Oral history: Dr Luise Hercus' work in the Lake Eyre Basin, 1965–2005: Report to the Native Title Section, Crown Solicitor's Office.

García, Mary Ellen, and Tallon, Michael. (2000). *Estar* in Mexican-American Spanish: Phonological or morphological variability? In: A. Roca (ed.), *Research on Spanish in the United States: Linguistic issues and challenges.* Somerville: Cascadilla Press. 348–359.

García-Acevedo, María Rosa. (2000). The forgotten diaspora: Mexican immigration to New Mexico. In: E. Gonzales-Berry and D. R. Maciel (eds.), *The contested homeland: A Chicano history of New Mexico.* Albuquerque: University of New Mexico Press. 215–238.

Gili y Gaya, Samuel. (1964). *Curso superior de sintaxis española,* 9th edn. Barcelona: Bibliograf.

Givón, T. (1979). *On understanding grammar.* New York: Academic Press.

Givón, T. (1983). Topic continuity in discourse: An introduction. In: T. Givón (ed.), *Topic continuity in discourse: A quantitative cross-linguistic study.* Amsterdam: John Benjamins. 1–41.

Givón, T. (1990). *Syntax: A functional-typological introduction.* vol. II. Amsterdam: John Benjamins.

Givón, T. (2001). *Syntax: An introduction.* vol. 2, 2 vols, 2nd edn. Amsterdam: John Benjamins.

Gonzales, María Dolores. (1999). Crossing social and cultural borders: The road to language hybridity. In: L. Galindo and M. D. Gonzales (eds.), *Speaking Chicana: Voice, power and identity*. Tucson: University of Arizona Press. 13–38.

Gonzales-Berry, Erlinda. (2000). Which language will our children speak? The Spanish language and public education policy in New Mexico, 1890–1930. In: E. Gonzales-Berry and D. R. Maciel (eds.), *The contested homeland: A Chicano history of New Mexico*. Albuquerque: University of New Mexico Press. 169–189.

Gonzales-Berry, Erlinda, and Maciel, David R. (eds.). (2000). *The contested homeland: A Chicano history of New Mexico*. Albuquerque: University of New Mexico Press.

Goodwin, Charles. (1980). Restarts, pauses, and the achievement of a state of mutual gaze at turn-beginning. *Sociological Inquiry* 50(3–4):272–302.

Granda, German de. (1972). *Transculturación e interferencia linguistica en el Puerto Rico contemporáneo (1898–1968)*. Río Piedras, Puerto Rico: Editorial Edil.

Green, David W., and Wei, Li. (2014). A control process model of code-switching. *Language, Cognition and Neuroscience* 29:499–511.

Greenough, J.B., Kittredge, G.L., Howard, A.A., and D'ooge, Benj. L. (1903). *Allen and Greenough's new Latin grammar for schools and colleges*. Boston and London: Ginn & Company Publishers.

Gries, Stefan Th. (2005). Syntactic priming: A corpus-based approach. *Journal of Psycholinguistic Research* 34(4):365–399.

Gries, Stefan Th., and Kootstra, Gerrit Jan. (2017). Structural priming within and across languages: A corpus-based perspective. *Bilingualism: Language and Cognition* 20 (2):235–250.

Grosjean, François. (1998). Studying bilinguals: Methodological and conceptual issues. *Bilingualism: Language and Cognition* 1(2):131–149.

Grosjean, François. (2001). The bilingual's language modes. In: J. L. Nicol (ed.), *One mind, two languages: Bilingual language processing*. Massachusetts: Blackwell Publishers. 1–22.

Grosjean, François. (2015). The complementarity principle and its impact on processing, acquisition, and dominance. In: C. Silva-Corvalán and J. Treffers-Daller (eds.), *Language dominance in bilinguals: Issues of measurement and operationalization*. Cambridge: Cambridge University Press. 36–65.

Gudmestad, Aarnes, House, Leanna, and Geeslin, Kimberly. (2013). What a Bayesian analysis can do for SLA: New tools for the sociolinguistic study of subject expression in L2 Spanish. *Language Learning* 63(3):371–399.

Gullberg, Marianne, Indefrey, Peter, and Muysken, Pieter. (2009). Research techniques for the study of code-switching. In: B. E. Bullock and A. J. Toribio (eds.), *The Cambridge handbook on linguistic code-switching*. Cambridge: Cambridge University Press. 21–39.

Gumperz, John J. (1976/1982). Conversational code-switching. In: J. J. Gumperz (ed.), *Discourse Strategies*. Cambridge: Cambridge University Press. 59–99.

Gumperz, John J., and Wilson, Robert. (1971). Convergence and creolization: A case from the Indo-Aryan/Dravidian border in India. In: D. Hymes (ed.), *Pidginization and creolization of languages*. Cambridge: Cambridge University Press. 151–167.

Guy, Gregory R. (1980). Variation in the group and the individual: The case of final stop deletion. In: W. Labov (ed.), *Language in time and space*. New York: Academic Press. 1–36.

Guzzardo Tamargo, Rosa. (2012). *Linking comprehension costs to production patterns during the processing of mixed language*. Doctoral dissertation, Penn State University.

Guzzardo Tamargo, Rosa, Valdés Kroff, Jorge, and Dussias, Paola E. (2016). Examining the relationship between comprehension and production processes in code-switched language. *Journal of Memory and Language* 89: 138–161.

Haegeman, Liliane. (1994). *Introduction to Government and Binding Theory*, 2nd edn. Oxford: Wiley-Blackwell.

Haegeman, Liliane. (2013). The syntax of registers: Diary subject omission and the privilege of the root. *Lingua* 130:88–110.

Haeri, Niloofar. (1989). Overt and non-overt subjects in Persian, *IPrA Papers in Pragmatics* 3(1):155–166. DOI: 10.1075/iprapip.3.1.05hae.

Haiman, John, and Munro, Pamela. (1983). Introduction. *Switch reference and universal grammar: Proceedings of a symposium on switch reference and universal grammar*. Amsterdam: John Benjamins.

Halliday, M. A. K., and Greaves, William S. (2008). *Intonation in the grammar of English*. London: Equinox Publishers.

Halliday, M. A. K., and Hasan, Ruqaiya. (1976). *Cohesion in English*. London: Longman.

Harrell, Frank E. Jr, with contributions from Charles Dupont and many others. (2015), *Hmisc: Harrell Miscellaneous. R package version 3.17–0*. https://cran.r-project.org /web/packages/Hmisc/index.html.

Harris, Martin. (1978). *The evolution of French syntax: A comparative approach*. London/New York: Longman.

Hartsuiker, Robert J., Pickering, Martin J., and Veltkamp, Eline. (2004). Is syntax separate or shared between languages. *Psychological Science* 15(6):409–414.

Harvie, Dawn. (1998). Null subject in English: Wonder if it exists? *Cahiers Linguistiques d' Ottawa* 16:15–25.

Haspelmath, Martin. (2004). Coordinating constructions: An overview. *Typological Studies in Language* 58:3–40.

Hay, Jennifer, and Foulkes, Paul. (2016). The evolution of medial /t/ over real and remembered time. *Language* 92(2):298–330.

Heine, Bernd, and Kuteva, Tania. (2005). *Language contact and grammatical change*. Cambridge: Cambridge University Press.

Heine, Bernd, and Kuteva, Tania. (2011). The areal dimension of grammaticalization. In: B. Heine and H. Narrog (eds.), *Handbook of grammaticalization*. Oxford: Oxford University Press. 291–301.

Helasvuo, Marja-Liisa. (2014). Searching for motivations for grammatical patternings. *Pragmatics* 24(3):453–476.

Hernández, José Esteban. (2009). Measuring rates of word-final nasal velarization: The effect of dialect contact on in-group and out-group exchanges. *Journal of Sociolinguistics* 13(5):583–612.

Hernández, José Esteban. (2011). Measuring rates and constraints of word-final nasal velarization in dialect contact. In: L. A. Ortíz-López (ed.), *Selected Proceedings of the 13th Hispanic Linguistics Symposium*. Somerville: Cascadilla Proceedings Project. 54–69.

Hochberg, Judith G. (1986). Functional compensation for /s/ deletion in Puerto Rican Spanish. *Language* 62(3):609–621.

Hock, Hans Henrich, and Joseph, Brian D. (1996). *Language history, language change, and language relationship*. Berlin: Mouton de Gruyter.

Hoffman, Michol F., and Walker, James A. (2010). Ethnolects and the city: Ethnic orientation and linguistic variation in Toronto English. *Language Variation and Change* 22(1):37–67.

Holmquist, Jonathan. (2012). Frequency rates and constraints on subject personal pronoun expression: Findings from the Puerto Rican highlands. *Language Variation and Change* 24(2):203–220.

Hopper, Paul J. (1979). Aspect and foregrounding in discourse. In: T. Givón (ed.), *Discourse and syntax*. New York: Academic Press. 213–241.

Hopper, Paul J., and Thompson, Sandra A. (2008). Projectability and clause combining in interaction. In: R. Laury (ed.), *Crosslinguistic studies of clause combining: The multifunctionality of conjunctions*. Amsterdam: John Benjamins. 99–123.

Horvath, Barbara, and Sankoff, David. (1987). Delimiting the Sydney speech community. *Language in Society* 16(2):179–204.

Huddleston, Rodney, and Pullum, Geoffrey K. (2002). *The Cambridge grammar of the English language*. Cambridge: Cambridge University Press.

Huerta, Ana. (1978). *Code-switching among Spanish-English bilinguals: A sociolinguistic perspective*. Doctoral dissertation, University of Texas at Austin.

Iwasaki, Shoichi, and Tao, Hongyin. (1993). A comparative study of the structure of the Intonation Unit in English, Japanese, and Mandarin Chinese. *Paper presented at the Annual Meeting of the Linguistic Society of America*, Los Angeles, CA, January 9, 1993.

Izre'el, Shlomo (2005). Intonation Units and the Structure of Spontaneous Spoken Language: A View from Hebrew. In: C. Auran, R. Bertrand, C. Chanet, A. Colas, A. Di Cristo, C. Portes, A. Reynier, and M. Vion (eds.), *Proceedings of the IDP05 International Symposium on Discourse-Prosody Interfaces*. CD ROM. Downloadable at: http://aune.lpl.univ-aix.fr/~prodige/idp05/actes/izreel.pdf.

Jaeger, T. Florian. (2010). Redundancy and reduction: Speakers manage syntactic information density. *Cognitive Psychology* 61(1): 23–62.

Jaeger, T. Florian, and Snider, Neal. (2007). Implicit learning and syntactic persistence: Surprisal and cumulativity. In: L. Wolter and J. Thorson (eds.), *University of Rochester Working Papers in the Language Sciences*, vol. 3 (1): 26–44.

Jaffe, Alexandra, and Walton, Shana. (2000). The voices people read: Orthography and the representation of non-standard speech. *Journal of Sociolinguistics* 4(4):561–587.

Jia, Li, and Bayley, Robert. (2002). Null pronoun variation in Mandarin Chinese. *University of Pennsylvania Working Papers in Linguistics* 8(3):103–116.

Kany, Charles E. (1951). *American-Spanish syntax*, 2nd edn. Chicago: University of Chicago Press.

Kato, Mary Aizawa. (1999). Strong and Weak Pronominals in the Null Subject Parameter. *Probus* 11:1–37.

Kiparsky, Paul. (1982). *Explanation in phonology*. Dordrecht: Foris.

Kootstra, Gerrit Jan, Van Hell, Janet G., and Dijkstra, Ton. (2010). Syntactic alignment and shared word order in code-switched sentence production: Evidence from bilingual monologue and dialogue. *Journal of Memory and Language* 63:210–231.

Kroll, Judith F., Bobb, Susan C., and Wodniecka, Zofia. (2006). Language selectivity is the exception, not the rule: Arguments against a fixed locus of language selection in bilingual speech. *Bilingualism: Language and Cognition* 9:119–135.

Kroll, Judith F., Dussias, Paola E., Bice, Kinsey, and Perrotti, Lauren. (2015). Bilingualism, mind, and brain. *Annual Review of Linguistics* 1:377–394.

Labov, William. (1969). Contraction, deletion, and inherent variability of the English copula. *Language* 45(4):715–762.

Labov, William. (1972a). *Language in the inner city: Studies in the Black English vernacular*. Philadelphia: University of Pennsylvania Press.

Labov, William. (1972b). *Sociolinguistic patterns*. Oxford: Basil Blackwell.

Labov, William. (1972c). Some principles of linguistic methodology. *Language in Society* 1(1):97–120.

Labov, William. (1975). Empirical foundations of linguistic theory. In: R. Austerlitz (ed.), *The Scope of American Linguistics*. Lisse: The Peter de Ridder Press. 77–113.

Labov, William. (1982). Building on empirical foundations. In: W. P. Lehmann and Y. Malkiel (eds.), *Perspectives on Historical Linguistics*. Amsterdam: John Benjamins. 17–92.

Labov, William. (1984). Field methods of the project on linguistic change and variation. In: J. Baugh and J. Sherzer (eds.), *Language in use: Readings in sociolinguistics*. Englewood Cliffs: Prentice Hall. 28–53.

Labov, William. (1989). Exact description of the speech community: Short A in Philadelphia. In: R. Fasold and D. Schiffrin (eds.), *Language change and variation*. Philadelphia: John Benjamins. 1–57.

Labov, William. (1994). *Principles of linguistic change: Internal factors*. vol. 1, 3 vols. Oxford: Basil Blackwell.

Labov, William. (1996). When intuitions fail. *Papers from the Regional Meeting of the Chicago Linguistic Society* 32(2):77–105.

Labov, William. (2001). *Principles of linguistic change: Social factors*. vol. 2, 3 vols. Oxford: Blackwell.

Labov, William. (2004). Quantitative reasoning in linguistics. In: U. Ammon, N. Dittmar, K. J. Mattheier, and P. Trudgill (eds.), *Sociolinguistics/Soziolinguistik: An international handbook of the science of language and society*, vol. 1. Berlin: Mouton de Gruyter. 6–22.

Labov, William. (2007). Transmission and diffusion. *Language* 83(2):344–387.

Labov, William. (2010). *Principles of linguistic change: Cognitive and cultural factors*. vol. 3, 3 vols. Oxford: Blackwell.

Labov, William. (2014). The role of African Americans in Philadelphia sound change. *Language Variation and Change* 26(1):1–19.

Labov, William, and Waletzky, Joshua. (1997 [1967]). Narrative analysis: Oral versions of personal experience. *Journal of Narrative and Life History* 7(1/4):3–38.

Lamiroy, Béatrice, and De Mulder, Walter. (2011). Degrees of grammaticalization across languages. In: H. Narrog and B. Heine (eds.), *The Oxford Handbook of Grammaticalization*. Oxford: Oxford University Press. 302–317.

Lastra, Yolanda, and Butragueño, Pedro Martín. (2015). Subject pronoun expression in oral Mexican Spanish. In: A. M. Carvalho, R. Orozco, and N. L. Shin (eds.), *Subject pronoun expression in Spanish: A cross-dialectal perspective*. Georgetown: Georgetown University Press. 39–57.

Lausberg, Hedda, and Sloetjes, Han. (2009). Coding gestural behavior with the NEUROGES-ELAN system. *Behavior Research Methods, Instruments, and Computers* (Max Planck Institute for Psycholinguistics, The Language Archive, Nijmegen, The Netherlands. http://tla.mpi.nl/tools/tla-tools/elan/). 41(3):841–849.

Lee, Duck-Young, and Yonezawa, Yoko. (2008). The role of the overt expression of first and second person subject in Japanese. *Journal of Pragmatics* 40(4):733–767.

Leroux, Martine, and Jarmasz, Lidia-Gabriela. (2005). A study about nothing: Null subjects as a diagnostic of the convergence between English and French. *University of Pennsylvania Working Papers in Linguistics* 12(2):1–14.

Levinson, Stephen C. (1987). Pragmatics and the grammar of anaphora: A partial pragmatic reduction of binding and control phenomena. *Journal of Linguistics* 23 (2):379–434.

Li, Charles, and Thompson, Sandra A. (1979). Third-person pronouns and zero-anaphora in Chinese discourse. *Syntax and Semantics* 12:311–335.

Lipski, John M. (2008). *Varieties of Spanish in the United States*. Washington, DC: Georgetown University Press.

Loebell, Helga, and Bock, Kathryn. (2003). Structural priming across languages. *Linguistics* 41(5):791–824.

Lope Blanch, Juan M. (1987). El estudio del español hablado en el suroeste de los Estados Unidos. *Anuario de Letras* 25:201–208.

Lozano, Anthony G. (1977). El español chicano y la dialectología. *Aztlán* 7:13–18.

Luján, Marta. (1999). Expresión y omisión del pronombre personal. In: I. Bosque and V. Demonte (eds.), *Gramática descriptiva de la lengua española*, vol. 1. Madrid: Espasa-Calpe. 1275–1315.

Martín Butragueño, Pedro, and Lastra, Yolanda. (2011). *Corpus sociolingüístico de la ciudad de México*. vol. 1: nivel alto. México: El Colegio de México.

Matras, Yaron, and Sakel, Jeanette. (2007). Investigating the mechanisms of pattern replication in language convergence. *Studies in Language* 31(4):829–865.

Matsumoto, Kazuko. (2003). *Intonation units in Japanese conversation: Syntactic, information and functional structures*. Amsterdam: John Benjamins.

Mayol, Laia. (2010). Contrastive pronouns in null subject Romance languages. *Lingua* 120:2497–2514.

McKee, Rachel, Schembri, Adam, McKee, David, and Johnston, Trevor. (2011). Variable "subject" presence in Australian Sign Language and New Zealand Sign Language. *Language Variation and Change* 23(3):375–398.

Meyerhoff, Miriam. (2009). Replication, transfer, and calquing: Using variation as a tool in the study of language contact. *Language Variation and Change* 21 (3):297–317.

Miller, Jim. (1995). Does spoken language have sentences? In: F. R. Palmer (ed.), *Grammar and meaning: Essays in honour of Sir John Lyons*. Cambridge: Cambridge University Press. 116–135.

Mithun, Marianne. (1988). The grammaticization of coordination. In: J. Haiman and S. A. Thompson (eds.), *Clause combining in grammar and discourse*. Amsterdam: John Benjamins. 331–359.

Morales, Amparo. (1986). *Gramáticas en contacto: Análisis sintáctico sobre el español de Puerto Rico*. San Juan: Editorial Playor.

Munro, Pamela. (1980). Studies of switch-reference. *UCLA papers in syntax 8*. Stanford: UCLA.

Muysken, Pieter. (2013). Language contact outcomes as the result of bilingual optimization strategies. *Bilingualism: Language and Cognition* 16(4):709–730.

Muysken, Pieter. (2015). Déjà voodoo or new trails ahead? Re-evaluating the Mixing Typology Model. In: R. Torres Cacoullos, N. Dion, and A. Lapierre (eds.), *Linguistic variation: Confronting fact and theory* New York: Routledge. 242–261.

Muysken, Pieter. (2016). Areal and Universalist Perspectives on Bilingual Compound Verbs. *Languages* 1(1):2, DOI:10.3390/languages1010002.

Myers-Scotton, Carol. (1993). *Duelling languages*. Oxford: Oxford University Press.

Myers-Scotton, Carol. (2002). *Contact linguistics: Bilingual encounters and grammatical outcomes*. Oxford: Oxford University Press.

Myhill, John. (2005). Quantitative methods of discourse analysis. In: R. Köhler, G. Altmann, and R. Piotrowski (eds.), *Quantitive linguistik: Ein internationales handbuch*. Berlin/New York: Walter de Gruyter. 471–497.

Myhill, John, and Xing, Zhiqun. (1996). Towards an operational definition of contrast. *Studies in Language* 20(2):303–360.

Myslín, Mark, and Levy, Roger. (2015). Code-switching and predictability of meaning in discourse. *Language* 91(4):871–905.

Nagy, Naomi, Aghdasi, Nina, Denis, Derek, and Motut, Alexandra. (2011). Null subjects in heritage languages: Contact effects in a cross-linguistic context. *University of Pennsylvania Working Papers in Linguistics* 17(2): http://repository.upenn.edu/cgi/viewcontent.cgi?article=1202&context=pwpl.

Nagy, Naomi, and Meyerhoff, Miriam. (2015). Extending ELAN into variationist sociolinguistics (description and tutorial). *Linguistic Vanguard* ISSN (Online) 2199–174X, DOI: 10.1515/lingvan-2015–0012, October 2015

Napoli, Donna Jo. (1982). Initial material deletion in English. *Glossa* 16:85–111.

Naro, Anthony J. (1981). Morphological constraints on subject deletion. In: D. Sankoff and H. Cedergren (eds.) *Variation Omnibus*: Edmonton: Linguistic Research. 351–357.

Oh, Sun-Young. (2006). English zero anaphora as an interactional resource II. *Discourse Studies* 8(6):817.

Oh, Sun-Young. (2007). Overt reference to speaker and recipient in Korean. *Discourse Studies* 9(4):462–492.

Ono, Tsuyoshi, and Thompson, Sandra A. (1997). Deconstructing "zero anaphora" in Japanese. *Berkeley Linguistics Society* 23:481–491.

Orozco, Rafael. (2015). Pronominal variation in Colombian Costeño Spanish. In: A. M. Carvalho, R. Orozco, and N. L. Shin (eds.), *Subject pronoun expression in Spanish: A cross-dialectal perspective*. Georgetown: Georgetown University Press. 17–37.

Orozco, Rafael, and Guy, Gregory R. (2008). El uso variable de los pronombres sujetos: ¿qué pasa en la costa caribe colombiana? In: M. Westmore and J. A. Thomas (eds.), *Selected proceedings of the 4th workshop on Spanish sociolinguistics*. Somerville: Cascadilla Proceedings Project. 70–80.

Otheguy, Ricardo. (2016). The linguistic competence of second-generation bilinguals: A critique of "incomplete acquisition". In: C. Tortora, M. den Dikken, I. L. Montoya, and T. O'Neill (eds.), *Romance Linguistics 2013: Selected papers from the 43rd Linguistic Symposium on Romance Languages (LSRL), New York, 17–19 April, 2013*. Amsterdam: John Benjamins. 301–319

Otheguy, Ricardo, and Stern, Nancy. (2010). On so-called Spanglish. *International Journal of Bilingualism* 15(1):85–100.

Otheguy, Ricardo, and Zentella, Ana Cecilia. (2012). *Spanish in New York: Language contact, dialect levelling, and structural continuity*. Oxford: Oxford University Press.

Otheguy, Ricardo, Zentella, Ana Cecilia, and Livert, David. (2007). Language and dialect contact in Spanish of New York: Toward the formation of a speech community. *Language* 83(4):770–802.

Owens, Jonathan, Dodsworth, Robin, and Kohn, Mary. (2013). Subject expression and discourse embeddedness in Emirati Arabic. *Language Variation and Change* 25 (2):255–285.

Paredes, Silva, and Vera, Lucia. (1993). Subject omission and functional compensation: Evidence from written Brazilian Portuguese. *Language Variation and Change* 5 (1):35–49.

Parkinson, Dilworth B. (1987). Constraints on the presence/absence of "optional" subject pronouns in Egyptian Arabic. *15th Annual Conference on New Ways of Analyzing Variation*: 348–360.

Payne, Thomas E. (1997). *Describing morphosyntax: A guide to field linguists*. Cambridge: Cambridge University Press.

Penny, Ralph. (2000). *Variation and change in Spanish*. Cambridge: Cambridge University Press.

Phillips, Betty S. (2001). Lexical diffusion, lexical frequency, and lexical analysis. In: J. Bybee and P. Hopper (eds.), *Frequency and the emergence of linguistic structure*. Amsterdam/Philadelphia: John Benjamins. 123–136.

Pickering, Martin J., and Branigan, Holly P. (1998). The representation of verbs: Evidence from syntactic priming in language production. *Journal of Memory and Language* 39(4):633–651.

Pierrehumbert, Janet, and Hirschberg, Julia. (1990). The meaning of intonational contours in the interpretation of discourse. In: P. R. Cohen, J. Morgan, and M. E. Pollack (eds.), *Intentions in communication*. Cambridge: MIT Press. 271–311.

Plaistowe, Jennifer. (2015). Coordinated code-switching? An investigation of language selection in bilingual conversation: Unpublished honours thesis: Australian National University.

Poplack, Shana. (1979). *Function and process in a variable phonology.* Doctoral dissertation, University of Pennsylvania.

Poplack, Shana. (1980a). The notion of the plural in Puerto Rican Spanish: Competing constraints on (s) deletion. In: W. Labov (ed.), *Locating language in time and space.* New York: Academic Press. 55–67.

Poplack, Shana. (1980b). "Sometimes I'll start a sentence in Spanish y termino en español": Toward a typology of code-switching. *Linguistics* 18(7/8):581–618.

Poplack, Shana. (1981). Syntactic structure and social function of code-switching. In: R. P. Durán (ed.), *Latino language and communicative behavior.* Norwood: Ablex Publishing Corporation. 169–184.

Poplack, Shana. (1983). Bilingual competence: Linguistic interference or grammatical integrity? In: E. Olivares (ed.), *Spanish in the US setting: Beyond the Southwest.* Arlington: National Clearinghouse for Bilingual Education. 107–131.

Poplack, Shana. (1989). The care and handling of a mega-corpus: The Ottowa-Hull French project. In: R. Fasold and D. Schiffrin (eds.), *Language change and variation.* Amsterdam: John Benjamins. 411–451.

Poplack, Shana. (1993). Variation theory and language contact: Concepts, methods and data. In: D. R. Preston (ed.), *American dialect research.* Amsterdam: John Benjamins. 251–286.

Poplack, Shana. (1997). The sociolinguistic dynamics of apparent convergence. In: G. R. Guy, C. Feagin, D. Schiffrin, and J. Baugh (eds.), *Towards a social science of language. Papers in honor of William Labov: Social interaction and discourse structures,* vol. 2. Amsterdam: John Benjamins. 285–309.

Poplack, Shana. (1998). Contrasting patterns of code-switching in two communities. In: P. Trudgill and J. Cheshire (eds.), *The sociolinguistics reader: Multilingualism and variation,* vol. 1. London: Arnold Publishers. 44–65.

Poplack, Shana. (2000 [1980]). Sometimes I'll start a sentence in Spanish *y termino en español*: Toward a typology of code-switching. In: L. Wei (ed.), *The bilingualism reader.* London/New York: Routledge. 221–256.

Poplack, Shana. (2001). Variability, frequency, and productivity in the irrealis domain in French. In: J. Bybee and P. J. Hopper (eds.), *Frequency and the emergence of linguistic structure.* Amsterdam/Philadelphia: John Benjamins. 405–428.

Poplack, Shana. (2015). Code Switching (Linguistic). In: J. D. Wright (ed.), *International encyclopedia of the social and behavioral sciences* (2nd edn.). Oxford: Elsevier. 918–925.

Poplack, Shana. (2017). *Borrowing: Loanwords in the speech community and in the grammar.* Oxford: Oxford University Press.

Poplack, Shana, and Dion, Nathalie. (2012). Myths and facts about loanword development. *Language Variation and Change* 24(3):279–315.

Poplack, Shana, and Levey, Stephen. (2010). Contact-induced grammatical change: A cautionary tale. In: P. Auer and J. E. Schmidt (eds.), *Language and space:*

An international handbook of linguistic variation, vol. 1: Theories and methods. Berlin: Mouton de Gruyter. 391–419.

Poplack, Shana, and Meechan, Marjory. (1998). Introduction: How languages fit together in codemixing. *International Journal of Bilingualism* 2(2):127–138.

Poplack, Shana, and Sankoff, David. (1984). Borrowing: The synchrony of integration. *Linguistic Inquiry* 22(1):99–135.

Poplack, Shana, Sankoff, David, and Miller, Christopher. (1988). The social correlates and linguistic processes of lexical borrowing and assimilation. *Linguistics* 26 (1):47–104.

Poplack, Shana, and Tagliamonte, Sali. (2001). *African American English in the diaspora*. Malden: Blackwell Publishers.

Poplack, Shana, Walker, James A., and Malcolmson, Rebecca. (2006). An English "like no other"?: Language contact and change in Quebec. *Canadian Journal of Linguistics/Revue canadienne de Linguistique* 51(2):185–213.

Poplack, Shana, Zentz, Lauren, and Dion, Nathalie. (2012a). Phrase-final prepositions in Quebec French: An empirical study of contact, code-switching and resistance to convergence. *Bilingualism: Language and Cognition* 15(2):203–225.

Poplack, Shana, Zentz, Lauren, and Dion, Nathalie. (2012b). What counts as (contact-induced) change. *Bilingualism: Language and Cognition* 15(2):247–254.

Posio, Pekka. (2012). The functions of postverbal pronominal subjects in spoken Peninsular Spanish and European Portuguese. *Studies in Hispanic and Lusophone Linguistics* 5:149–190.

Posio, Pekka. (2013). The expression of first-person-singular subjects in spoken Peninsular Spanish and European Portuguese: Semantic roles and formulaic sequences. *Folia Linguistica* 47(1):253–291.

Posio, Pekka. (2015). Subject pronoun usage in formulaic sequences: Evidence from Peninsular Spanish. In: A. M. Carvalho, R. Orozco, and N. L. Shin (eds.), *Subject pronoun expression in Spanish: A cross-dialectal perspective*. Washington, DC: Georgetown University Press. 59–78.

Preston, Dennis R. (1982). Ritin' Fowklower daun' Rong: Folklorists' Failures in Phonology. *Journal of American Folklore* 95:304–326.

Preston, Dennis R. (1985). The Li'l Abner Syndrome: Written representations of speech. *American Speech* 60(4):328–336.

Quirk, Randolph, Greenbaum, Sidney, Leech, Geoffrey, and Svartvik, Jan. (1985). *A comprehensive grammar of the English language*. London: Longman.

R Core Team. (2015). *R: A language and environment for statistical computing*. Vienna, Austria: R Foundation for Statistical Computing, http://www.R-project.org

RAE [Real Academia Española], and AALE [Asociación de Academias de la Lengua Española]. (2010). *Nueva gramática de la lengua española. Manual*. Madrid: Espasa.

Ramos, Miguel. (2016). Continuity and change: First person singular subject pronoun expression in earlier Spanish. *Spanish in Context* 13(1):103–127.

Ranson, Diana L. (1991). Person marking in the wake of /s/ deletion in Andalusian Spanish. *Language Variation and Change* 3(2):133–152.

Ranson, Diana L. (1999). Variable subject expression in Old and Middle French prose texts: The role of verbal ambiguity. *Romance Quarterly* 56(1):33–45.

Rickford, John R., and McNair-Knox, Faye. (1994). Addressee- and topic-influenced style shift: A quantitative sociolinguistic study. In: D. Biber and E. Finegan (eds.), *Sociolinguistic perspectives on register.* New York: Oxford University Press. 235–276.

Rivas, Javier, and Brown, Esther L. (2009). *No sé* as a discourse marker in Spanish: A corpus-based approach to a cross-dialectal comparison. In: A. Sánchez and P. Cantos (eds.), *A survey on corpus-based research: Panorama de investigaciones basadas en corpus.* Murcia: AELINCO. 631–645.

Roberts, Ian, and Holmberg, Anders. (2010). Introduction: Parameters in minimalist theory. In: T. Biberauer, A. Holmberg, I. Roberts, and M. Sheehan (eds.), *Parametric variation: Null subjects in minimalist theory.* Cambridge: Cambridge University Press. 1–57.

Roland, Douglas, Elman, Jeffrey L., and Ferreira, Victor S. (2006). Why is that? Structural prediction and ambiguity resolution in a very large corpus of English sentences. *Cognition* 98:245–272.

Ross, Malcolm. (2001). Contact-induced change in Oceanic languages in North-west Melanesia. In: A. Y. Aikhenvald and R. M. W. Dixon (eds.), *Areal diffusion and genetic inheritance: Problems in comparative linguistics.* Oxford: Oxford University Press. 134–166.

Sánchez-Ayala, Ivo. (2001). Prosodic integration in Spanish complement constructions. In: A. Cienki, B. J. Luka, and M. B. Smith (eds.), *Conceptual and discourse factors in linguistic structure.* Stanford: Center for the Study of Language and Information. 201–213.

Sankoff, David. (1988a). Sociolinguistics and syntactic variation. In: F. Newmeyer (ed.), *Linguistics: The Cambridge survey (Vol. 4, Language: The socio-cultural context).* Cambridge: Cambridge University Press. 140–161.

Sankoff, David. (1988b). Variable rules. In: U. Ammon, N. Dittmar, and K. J. Mattheier (eds.), *Sociolinguistics: An international handbook of the science of language and society,* vol. 2. Berlin: Walter de Gruyter. 984–997.

Sankoff, David. (1998). A formal production-based explanation of the facts of code-switching. *Bilingualism: Language and Cognition* 1(1):39–50.

Sankoff, David, Dion, Nathalie, Brandts, Alex, Alvo, Mayer, Balasch, Sonia, and Adams, Jackie. (2015). Comparing variables in different corpora with context-based model-free variant probabilities. In: R. Torres Cacoullos, N. Dion, and A. Lapierre (eds.), *Linguistic variation: Confronting fact and theory.* New York: Routledge. 335–346.

Sankoff, David, and Laberge, Suzanne. (1978). Statistical dependence among successive occurrences of a variable in discourse. In: D. Sankoff (ed.), *Linguistic variation: Models and methods.* New York: Academic Press. 119–126.

Sankoff, David, and Poplack, Shana. (1981). A formal grammar for code-switching. *Papers in Linguistics: International Journal of Human Communication* 14(1):3–45.

Sankoff, David, Poplack, Shana, and Vanniarajan, Swathi. (1990). The case of the nonce loan in Tamil. *Language Variation and Change* 2(1):71–101.

Sankoff, David, Tagliamonte, Sali, and Smith, Eric. (2015). Goldvarb Yosemite: A variable rule application for Macintosh. University of Toronto. http://individual .utoronto.ca/tagliamonte/goldvarb.html.

Sankoff, Gillian. (2002). Linguistic outcomes of language contact. In: J. K. Chambers, P. Trudgill, and N. Schilling-Estes (eds.), *The handbook of language variation and change*. Oxford: Blackwell. 638–668.

Scheibman, Joanne. (2000). *I dunno*: A usage-based account of the phonological reduction of *don't* in American English conversation. *Journal of Pragmatics* 32 (1):105–124.

Scheibman, Joanne. (2001). Local patterns of subjectivity in person and verb type in American English conversation. In: J. Bybee and P. J. Hopper (eds.), *Frequency and the emergence of linguistic structure*. Amsterdam: John Benjamins. 61–89.

Scherre, Maria Marta Pereira, and Naro, Anthony J. (1991). Marking in discourse: "Birds of a feather." *Language Variation and Change* 3(1):23–32.

Schoonbaert, Sofie, Hartsuiker, Robert J., and Pickering, Martin J. (2007). The representation of lexical and syntactic information in bilinguals: Evidence from syntactic priming. *Journal of Memory and Language* 56(2):153–171.

Schwenter, Scott A. (1996). Some reflections on *o sea*: A discourse marker in Spanish. *Journal of Pragmatics* 25:855–874.

Serratrice, Ludovica. (2009). Carving up referential space: A priming account of pronoun use in Italian. In: J. Chandlee, M. Franchini, S. Lord, and G.-M. Rheiner (eds.), *Proceedings of the 33rd Annual Boston University Conference on Language Development*. Somerville: Cascadilla Press. 468–479.

Shenk, Petra S. (2006). The interactional and syntactic importance of prosody in Spanish-English bilingual discourse. *International Journal of Bilingualism* 10 (2):179–205.

Shin, Naomi Lapidus. (2014). Grammatical complexification in Spanish in New York: 3sg pronoun expression and verbal ambiguity. *Language Variation and Change* 26 (3):303–330.

Shin, Naomi Lapidus, and Otheguy, Ricardo. (2013). Social class and gender impacting change in bilingual settings: Spanish subject pronoun use in New York. *Language in Society* 42:429–452.

Sigurðsson, Halldór Ármann, and Maling, Joan. (2010). The Empty Left Edge Condition. In M. Putnam (ed.), *Exploring crash-proof grammars*. Amsterdam: John Benjamins. 59–86.

Silva-Corvalán, Carmen. (1982). Subject expression and placement in Mexican-American Spanish. In: J. Amastae and L. Elías Olivares (eds.), *Spanish in the United States: Sociolinguistic aspects*. New York: Cambridge University Press. 93–120.

Silva-Corvalán, Carmen. (1994). *Language contact and change: Spanish in Los Angeles*. Oxford: Clarendon Press.

Silva-Corvalán, Carmen. (1997). Avances en el estudio de la variación sintáctica: La expresión del sujeto. *Cuadernos del Sur* 27:35–49.

Silva-Corvalán, Carmen, and Enrique-Arias, Andrés. (2017). *Sociolingüística y pragmática del español*, 2nd edn. Washington, DC: Georgetown University Press.

Silva-Corvalán, Carmen, and Treffers-Daller, Jeanine (eds.). (2015). *Language Dominance in bilinguals: Issues of measurement and operationalization*. Cambridge: Cambridge University Press.

Silveira, Agripino S. (2011). *Subject expression in Brazilian Portuguese: Construction and frequency effects*. Doctoral dissertation, University of New Mexico.

Snider, Neal. (2009). Similarity and structural priming. In: N. Taatgen and H. van Rijn (eds.), *Proceedings of the 31st Annual Meeting of the Cognitive Science Society*. 815–820.

Sorace, Antonella. (2004). Native language attrition and developmental instability at the syntax–discourse interface: Data, interpretations and methods. *Bilingualism: Language and Cognition* 7(2):143–145.

Sorace, Antonella, and Serratrice, Ludovica. (2009). Internal and external interfaces in bilingual language development: Beyond structural overlap. *International Journal of Bilingualism* 13(2):195–210.

Sorace, Antonella, Serratrice, Ludovica, Fillaci, Francesca, and Baldo, Michaela. (2009). Discourse conditions on subject pronoun realization: Testing the linguistic intuitions of older bilingual children. *Lingua* 119(3):460–477.

Spencer, Nancy J. (1973). Differences between linguists and nonlinguists in intuitions of grammaticality-acceptability. *Journal of Psycholinguistic Research* 2(2):83–98.

Stanford, James. (2008). A sociotonetic analysis of Sui dialect contact. *Language Variation and Change* 20(3):409–450.

Steuck, Jonathan. (2016). Exploring the syntax-semantics-prosody interface: Complement clauses in conversation. In: A. Cuza, L. Czerwionka, and D. Olson (eds.), *Inquiries in Hispanic linguistics: From theory to empirical evidence*. Amsterdam/Philadelphia: John Benjamins. 73–94.

Steuck, Jonathan, and Torres Cacoullos, Rena. (2016). Code-switching and prosody: English-Spanish bilingual complements. Paper presented at the New Ways of Analyzing Variation (NWAV) 45, Simon Fraser University/University of Victoria, November 3–6, 2016.

Stirling, Leslie. (2006). Switch-Reference. In: K. Brown (ed.), *Encyclopedia of language and linguistics*, vol. 12. Oxford: Elsevier. 316–323.

Szmrecsanyi, Benedikt. (2005). Language users as creatures of habit: A corpus-based analysis of persistence in spoken English. *Corpus Linguistics and Linguistic Theory* 1 (1):113–149.

Tamminga, Meredith. (2016). Persistence in phonological and morphological variation. *Language Variation and Change* 28:335–356.

Tannen, Deborah. (1987). Repetition in conversation: Toward a poetics of talk. *Language* 63(3):574–605.

Thomason, Sarah G. (2000). Linguistic areas and language history. In: D. Gilbers, J. Nerbonne, and J. Schaeken (eds.), *Languages in contact*. Amsterdam: Rodopi. 311–327.

Thomason, Sarah G. (2001). *Language contact: An introduction*. Washington DC: Georgetown University Press.

Thomason, Sarah G. (2007). Language contact and deliberate change. *Journal of Languages and Contact* 1:41–62.

Thomason, Sarah G. (2009). How to establish substratum interference. *Senri Ethnological Studies* 75:319–328.

Thomason, Sarah G., and Kaufman, Terrence. (1988). *Language contact, creolization and genetic linguistics*. Berkeley: University of California Press.

Thompson, Sandra A. (2002). "Object Complements" and conversation: Towards a realistic account. *Studies in Language* 26(1):125–163.

Tieken-Boon van Ostade, Ingrid. (1982). Double negation and eighteenth-century English grammars. *Neophilologus* 66(2):278–285.

Toribio, Almeida Jacqueline. (2000). Setting parametric limits on dialectal variation in Spanish. *Lingua* 110(5):315–341.

Torres Cacoullos, Rena. (2015). Gradual loss of analyzability: Diachronic priming effects. In: A. Adli, G. Kaufmann, and M. García (eds.), *Variation in language: System- and usage-based approaches*. Berlin: de Gruyter. 267–289.

Torres Cacoullos, Rena, and Aaron, Jessi Elana. (2003). Bare English-origin nouns in Spanish: Rates, constraints and discourse functions. *Language Variation and Change* 15(3):289–328.

Torres Cacoullos, Rena, and Berry, Grant M. (2018). Language variation in US Spanish: Social factors. In: K. Potowski (ed.), *Handbook of Spanish as a Minority/Heritage Language*. London/New York: Routledge.

Torres Cacoullos, Rena, and Ferreira, Fernanda. (2000). Lexical frequency and voiced labiodental-bilabial variation in New Mexican Spanish. *Southwest Journal of Linguistics* 19(2):1–17.

Torres Cacoullos, Rena, and Poplack, Shana. (2016). Code-switching in spontaneous bilingual speech, National Science Foundation 1624966.

Torres Cacoullos, Rena, and Travis, Catherine E. (2011). Testing convergence via code-switching: Priming and the structure of variable subject expression *International Journal of Bilingualism* 15(3):241–267.

Torres Cacoullos, Rena, and Travis, Catherine E. (2014). Prosody, priming and particular constructions: The patterning of English first-person singular subject expression in conversation. *Journal of Pragmatics* 63: 19–34.

Torres Cacoullos, Rena, and Travis, Catherine E. (2015). Foundations for the study of subject pronoun expression in Spanish in contact with English: Assessing interlinguistic (dis)similarity via intralinguistic variability. In: A. M. Carvalho, R. Orozco, and N. L. Shin (eds.), *Subject pronoun expression in Spanish: A cross-dialectal perspective*. Georgetown: Georgetown University Press. 83–102.

Torres Cacoullos, Rena, and Travis, Catherine E. (To appear). Variationist typology: Shared probabilistic constraints across (non-)null subject languages. *Linguistics*.

Torres Cacoullos, Rena, and Walker, James A. (2009). On the persistence of grammar in discourse formulas: A variationist study of *that*. *Linguistics* 47(1):1–43.

Torres Cacoullos, Rena, and Walker, James A. (2011). Chapter 18: Collocations in grammaticalization and variation. In: B. Heine and H. Narrog (eds.), *Handbook of grammaticalization*. Oxford: Oxford University Press. 225–238.

Travis, Catherine E. (2005). *Discourse markers in Colombian Spanish: A study in polysemy*. Berlin/New York: Mouton de Gruyter.

Travis, Catherine E. (2007). Genre effects on subject expression in Spanish: Priming in narrative and conversation. *Language Variation and Change* 19(2):101–135.

Travis, Catherine E., and Lindstrom, Amy M. (2016). Different registers, different grammars? Subject expression in English conversation and narrative. *Language Variation and Change* 28(1):103–128.

Travis, Catherine E., and Torres Cacoullos, Rena. (2012). What do subject pronouns do in discourse? Cognitive, mechanical and constructional factors in variation. *Cognitive Linguistics* 23(4):711–748.

Travis, Catherine E., and Torres Cacoullos, Rena. (2013). Making voices count: Corpus compilation in bilingual communities. *Australian Journal of Linguistics* 33 (2):170–194.

Travis, Catherine E., and Torres Cacoullos, Rena. (2014). Stress on *I*: Debunking unitary contrast accounts *Studies in Language* 38(2):360–392.

Travis, Catherine E., and Torres Cacoullos, Rena. (2018). Discovering structure: Person and accessibility. In: N. L. Shin and D. Erker (eds.), *First names – How theoretical primitives shape the search for linguistic structure (Festschrift in honor of Ricardo Otheguy)*. Amsterdam/Philadelphia: John Benjamins.

Travis, Catherine E., Torres Cacoullos, Rena, and Kidd, Evan. (2017). Cross-language priming: A view from bilingual speech *Bilingualism: Language and Cognition* 20(2):283–298.

United States Census Bureau. (2011). 2007–2011 5-Year American Community Survey, http://factfinder2.census.gov.

United States Census Bureau. (2014). 2010–2014 5-Year American Community Survey, http://factfinder2.census.gov.

van der Wel, Robrecht P.R.D., Fleckenstein, Robin M., Jax, Steven A., and Rosenbaum, David A. (2007). Hand path priming in manual obstacle avoidance: Evidence for abstract spatiotemporal forms in human motor control. *Journal of Experimental Psychology: Human Perception and Performance* 33(5):1117–1126.

Walker, James A. (2010). *Variation in Linguistic Systems*. London/New York: Routledge.

Wasserstein, Ronald L., and Lazar, Nicole A. (2016). The ASA's statement on p-Values: Context, process, and purpose. *The American Statistician* 70(2):129–133.

Weiner, E. Judith, and Labov, William. (1983). Constraints on the agentless passive. *Journal of Linguistics* 19(1):29–58.

Weinreich, Uriel. (1953/1968). *Languages in contact: Findings and problems*. The Hague: Mouton.

Weinreich, Uriel, Labov, William, and Herzog, Marvin I. (1968). Empirical foundations for a theory of language change. In: W. P. Lehmann and Y. Malkiel (eds.), *Directions for historical linguistics: A symposium*. Austin: University of Texas Press. 95–188.

Weir, Andrew. (2012). Left-edge deletion in English and subject omission in diaries. *English Language and Linguistics* 16(1):105–129.

Wilson, Damián Vergara, and Dumont, Jenny. (2015). The emergent grammar of bilinguals: The Spanish verb *hacer* 'do' with a bare English infinitive. *International Journal of Bilingualism* 19(4):444–458.

Winford, Donald. (2005). Contact-induced change: classification and processes. *Diachronica* 22(2):373–427.

Index